INTELLECTUAL PROPERTY RIGHTS, TRADE AND BIODIVERSITY

THE IUCN PROJECT ON THE CONVENTION ON BIOLOGICAL DIVERSITY AND THE INTERNATIONAL TRADE REGIME

This publication is part of the IUCN project on the Convention on Biological Diversity and the International Trade Regime, which is supported by the German Federal Ministry for Economic Co-operation (BMZ). The objective of the project, launched in 1997, is to support greater coherence at both the national and international levels between two international regimes vital to the achievement of sustainable development: the trade regime of the World Trade Organization and the Convention on Biological Diversity. The project promotes the development of policy recommendations from three pilot projects to be presented at the national and regional level in legislatures and relevant agencies or regional organisations, and at the international level in the forums of the Convention on Biological Diversity, World Trade Organization, and others.

INTELLECTUAL PROPERTY RIGHTS, TRADE AND BIODIVERSITY

SEEDS AND PLANT VARIETIES

Graham Dutfield

The World Conservation Union

Earthscan Publications Ltd, London

This publication has been made possible in part by funding from the Bundesministerium für wirtschaftliche Zusammenarbeit und Entwicklung (BMZ), the German Federal Ministry for Economic Co-operation.

First published in the UK in hardback in 2000 and in paperback in 2002 by
Earthscan Publications Ltd

A catalogue record for this book is available from the British Library

ISBN: 1 85383 903 5

The designation of geographical entities in this book, and the presentation of the material, do not imply the expression of any opinion whatsoever on the part of IUCN or the German Federal Ministry for Economic Co-operation (BMZ) concerning the legal status of any country, territory, or area, or of its authorities, or concerning the delimitation of its frontiers or boundaries.

The views expressed in this book do not necessarily reflect those of IUCN or the German Federal Ministry for Economic Co-operation (BMZ).

Typesetting by PCS Mapping & DTP, Newcastle upon Tyne
Printed and bound by Creative Print and Design Wales, Ebbw Vale
Cover design by Susanne Harris

For a full list of publications please contact:
Earthscan Publications Ltd
120 Pentonville Road
London, N1 9JN, UK
Tel: +44 (0)171 278 0433
Fax: +44 (0)171 278 1142
Email: earthinfo@earthscan.co.uk
http://www.earthscan.co.uk

22883 Quicksilver Drive, Sterling, VA 20166-2012, USA

This book is printed on elemental chlorine-free paper
Earthscan is an editorially independent subsidiary of Kogan Page Ltd and publishes in association with WWF-UK and the International Institute for Environment and Development

This book is printed on elemental chlorine-free paper

CONTENTS

List of Case Studies, Tables and Boxes

Case Studies

Tables

Boxes

ACRONYMS AND ABBREVIATIONS

ASSINSEL	International Association of Plant Breeders
BMZ	German Federal Ministry for Economic Co-operation
Bt	*Bacillus thuringiensis*
CBD	Convention on Biological Diversity
CGIAR	Consultative Group on International Agricultural Research
CIAT	International Centre for Tropical Agriculture
CIMMYT	International Centre for the Improvement of Maize and Wheat
CIP	International Potato Centre
COP	Conference of the Parties (to the CBD)
CSIR	Council of Scientific and Industrial Research (India)
CTE	Committee on Trade and Environment
DNA	deoxyribonucleic acid
EMR	exclusive marketing right
EPO	European Patent Office
FAO	Food and Agriculture Organization (UN)
FIS	International Seed Trade Federation
GATT	General Agreement on Tariffs and Trade
GMO	genetically modified organism
HYV	high yielding variety
IAI-TPTF	International Alliance of Indigenous-Tribal Peoples of the Tropical Forests
IARC	international agricultural research centre
ICARDA	International Centre for Agricultural Research in the Dry Areas
ICRISAT	International Crop Research Institute for the Semi-Arid Tropics
IITA	International Institute for Tropical Agriculture
ILRI	International Livestock Research Institute
INIBAP	International Network for the Improvement of Bananas and Plantains
IPGRI	International Plant Genetic Resources Institute
IPRs	intellectual property rights

IRRI	International Rice Research Institute
ISB	Information Systems for Biotechnology
IUCN	The World Conservation Union (formerly the International Union for Conservation of Nature and Natural Resources)
LDC	less developed country
NBIAP	National Biological Impact Assessment Program
NGO	non-governmental organization
NIC	newly industrialized country
NRC	National Research Council
OECD	Organisation for Economic Co-operation and Development
PBR	plant breeder's right
PTO	Patent and Trademark Office (US)
R&D	research and development
RAFI	Rural Advancement Foundation International (Canada)
SAARC	South Asian Association for Regional Cooperation
SBSTTA	Subsidiary Body on Scientific, Technical and Technological Advice
SRISTI	Society for Research and Initiatives for Sustainable Technologies and Institutions (India)
TBA	Technical Board of Appeal
T-GURT	trait-specific genetic use restriction technologies
TRIPS	Trade-Related Aspects of Intellectual Property Rights
UN	United Nations
UNCTAD	United Nations Conference on Trade and Development
UPOV	Convention of the International Union for the Protection of New Varieties of Plants
V-GURT	variety-specific genetic use restriction technologies
WARDA	West Africa Rice Development Association
WIPO	World Intellectual Property Organization (UN)
WTO	World Trade Organization
WWF	World Wide Fund For Nature (World Wildlife Fund in the US and Canada)

Foreword

Few issues illustrate the gulf between the trade and environment cultures as starkly as intellectual property rights (IPRs). For the trade world, IPRs are one of the pillars on which the entire trade edifice is built. Without widespread recognition of property rights, without a considerable degree of harmony in how these rights are recognized, and without an assurance that these rights will be respected and – where necessary – enforced, the confidence necessary for international commerce is difficult to muster.

For the environment world, on the other hand, too exclusive a focus on private property rights not only circumscribes the ability to provide recognition, and thereby give value to, communally-held knowledge, or knowledge not easily attributable to an individual or a corporate entity, it also tilts the balance of power in favour of the corporate world, giving it undue influence on the course of human affairs.

To complicate matters further, the Uruguay Round of multilateral trade negotiations, in adopting the Agreement on Trade-Related Aspects of Intellectual Property Rights (the TRIPS agreement) substantially shifted the balance further in the direction of private property protection, adopting as a global norm an approach to intellectual property rights developed on a common law base and adapted to the US and European legal systems. Despite the clear international undertakings contained in such agreements as the Convention on Biological Diversity (CBD), the TRIPS agreement represents a move away from accommodation of essential environmental priorities, making the achievement of internationally-endorsed environmental aims that much more difficult.

Perhaps nowhere is this gulf between trade and environmental objectives so marked as in the field of biodiversity, and within this field nowhere are the issues better illustrated than in the case of seeds and plant varieties. Indeed, seeds and plant varieties represent the vast bulk of biodiversity exchanged commercially or otherwise – in short, it is in this area where the impact of trade rules on environmental aims is felt most sharply.

Graham Dutfield takes us on a comprehensive tour of the issue. Unusually for a text written from an environmental perspective, he manages to keep a fully open mind. Because if it is true that tightened IPR protection can make it more difficult to achieve certain environmental aims, there are a variety of ways in which it can also protect the environment – principally by giving a market value to what previously was considered common property. At the same time, while it is clearly accepted that we must find a way to recognize indigenous and traditional knowledge, find ways of rewarding communally-held knowledge, and avoid private companies registering as their own invention knowledge that is already in the public domain, the obstacles to doing this are formidable, and only some of them are caused by the trading system. It is not as if the environmental world had fully worked-out solutions which are being resisted by the trade world for narrow, corporatist reasons.

Indeed, as Dutfield shows, the reality is far more subtle and complicated than the common caricature would have it. On many of the issues, the jury is still very much out. Tightening of intellectual property protection can be both good and bad for the environment. Where the balance lies is still difficult to say. The fact that the International Union for the Protection of New Varieties of Plants (UPOV) is being promoted as the natural alternative model to the patenting of plant varieties is widely regarded as a serious problem by the environmental community, clearly to the disfavour of small farmers and cultivators in the developing world. Dutfield shows that, while there is substance to this fear, the issue is not as clear-cut as has been imagined, and in many important ways there is no empirical evidence to demonstrate the case conclusively one way or the other.

The issues underlying the role of IPRs in international economic relations are heating up rapidly, and promise to provide some of the most controversial obstacles to making further progress on trade liberalization. The issue of genetically modified organisms (GMOs) has already emerged as a problem of titanic proportions, in which the IPR dimension is central. The impact on biodiversity could be colossal. More generally, the veering of the trade system towards stronger international IPR protection has awakened the sleeping giant of risk assessment versus the precautionary principle, an issue which could end up being the 'Star Wars' between the trade and environmental world.

In this controversial and unstable situation, Dutfield's book will serve as an objective, dispassionate, but very thorough guide to the issues, dangers and opportunities for both the trade and environment communities. The former can find in it an excellent summary of environmental thinking and concerns. The latter can find a sobering assessment of the situation, written from a position of sympathy for environmental aims, but also recognizing the legitimacy of trade objectives, the capacity of the trading system to contribute to environmental aims, and the issues which still need to be resolved before a final common ground can be found.

Mark Halle
Project Director, IUCN project on the Convention on
Biological Diversity and the International Trade Regime

ACKNOWLEDGEMENTS

Considering the critical nature of this study of IPRs, it would be hypocritical to pretend that this document resulted from the creativity or 'sweat of the brow' of just the individual cited as the author. I am grateful to all the participants at the 2nd Meeting of the Advisory Committee of the IUCN project on the Convention on Biological Diversity and the International Trade Regime for their valuable and authoritative comments and suggestions: Mark Halle, Ashish Kothari, David Downes, James Cameron, Richard Tarasofsky, Frank Vorhies, Chikako Takase, Charles Barber, Gustavo Alanis Ortega, Daniel Sabsay and Tina Winqvist. Special acknowledgement must be extended to David Downes (Center for International Environmental Law, Washington), André Heitz (UPOV, Geneva), Susan Bragdon (IPGRI, Rome), Kristina Plenderleith (Oxford), Chikako Takase (CBD Secretariat, Montreal), Ashish Kothari (Kalpavriksh, Pune), Manuel Ruiz (Sociedad Peruana de Derecho Ambiental, Lima), Richard Tarasofsky (Berlin), Lyle Glowka (Bonn), James Cameron, Ruth McKenzie and Jacob Werksman (Foundation for International Environmental Law and Development, London), and Utkarsh Ghate (Indian Institute of Science, Bangalore). All of these individuals took the trouble to rigorously review one or more drafts. André Heitz, David Downes, Wend Wendland (WIPO, Geneva) and Shakeel Bhatti (also WIPO) kindly sent me very useful published materials. Naturally, the opinions expressed and any errors and deficiencies are the author's responsibility and have nothing to do with these individuals or their organizations.

During most of the past six years I have been fully engaged in biodiversity and IPR-related issues. There is no doubt that my thinking on these topics has benefited tremendously from working with such able and knowledgeable collaborators and friends as Darrell Posey and Kristina Plenderleith. They will certainly recognize their ideas within the text.

Much of the writing was done under severe time constraints and I must give recognition to my wife Seokyoon for her unstinting support and encouragement.

Last but not least, it remains for me to thank Mark Halle for commissioning me to write this book, and Tina Winqvist, whose administrative abilities ensured that my involvement in the project was – for me at least – a pleasant experience in every respect.

Graham Dutfield
Oxford, UK
September 1999

1 PLANT GENETIC RESOURCES IN THE GLOBAL ECONOMY

The importance of plant genetic resources for agriculture to human welfare and the world economy is incalculable. According to Stephen Brush (1994), plant genetic resources provide 'the foundation of all food production, [and] the key to feeding unprecedented numbers of people in times of climate and other environmental change', and therefore comprise perhaps the most important category of biological resources.

However, estimating the economic value of crop genetic resources is extremely difficult. An indirect sense of their value may be inferred by estimating the global sales value of products derived from genetic resources. Even then, the estimates can vary widely. The International Seed Trade Federation (FIS) and the International Association of Plant Breeders (ASSINSEL), two international NGOs that represent the seed industry in over 60 countries, calculate that the commercial seed market has a value of US$30 billion/year (FIS and ASSINSEL 1998). On the other hand, Putterman (nd) estimates a global sales figure for agricultural seeds of only US$13 billion. Whichever is a more accurate figure, it is commonly agreed that the value of crop germplasm is increasing. This is due to increasing food demand due to population growth, the limited amount of new land being opened up for food production, and also the increasing adoption of new biotechnologies[1] (Brush 1994), which allow gene transfer between more distantly related organisms. At a time when the Earth may be experiencing an 'extinction spasm' (Myers 1989; Wilson 1992), gene transfer technologies are expanding the pool of genes potentially available for the breeding of new crop varieties (see Prescott-Allen and Prescott-Allen 1983), thereby increasing the value of existing genetic resources.

However, these figures indicate the global market value only of modern crop varieties, not of the other types of crop germplasm as raw materials for these varieties or as cultivars in themselves. These other types include: (i) wild crop progenitors and relatives, (ii) semi-domesticated crop relatives, and (iii) landraces (or folk varieties) of ancestral crop species.[2] Although seeds of landraces may be bought and sold as agricultural products, as raw materials in industrial breeding they have most commonly been made available to industrial breeders at no greater expense than the cost of collecting or transporting them. In the absence of a market, it is very difficult to estimate their economic value as inputs in modern plant breeding. Even so, attempts have been made to calculate the economic value of landraces, including a study on the use and value of landraces for rice breeding in India (Evenson 1996; NRC, in Brush 1994). It was estimated that rice landraces acquired from India and overseas contributed 5.6 per cent, or US$75 million, to India's rice yields. Assuming that landraces contribute equally to other countries where rice is cultivated, the global value added to rice yields by use of landraces can be estimated at US$400 million per year.

But it must be emphasized that calculating the economic value of plant genetic resources as inputs into commercial crop breeding programmes can in no way reflect their importance for the millions of subsistence farmers who depend upon them for their survival. Moreover, the social, cultural and spiritual values of biodiversity cannot possibly be quantified in monetary terms (see Posey 1999).

Most of the seed companies best able to add value to germplasm are located in the North. However, since most of the world's biodiversity-rich countries are developing countries located in the tropics, one might assume that these nations are in a strong position to benefit substantially by trading in crop genetic resources such as landraces. In fact, this is far from the case. With pharmaceuticals, biodiversity-rich countries may be in a slightly stronger position to dictate favourable terms of access to genetic resources.[3] With plant genetic resources for the seed industry, the bargaining positions of individual biodiversity-rich developing countries are generally weak and the benefit-sharing possibilities are less promising. There are six main reasons for this:[4]

1 *Apportioning the benefits fairly may be impossible or unfeasible*
   Unlike a new pharmaceutical product derived or modelled on a single natural compound, a new plant variety is often the product of generations of breeding and cross breeding, which in turn are the result of selection and breeding by farmers in many parts of the world (see Brush 1994, 1996) and of the evolution of non-domesticated varieties. This means that many countries and/or communities may legitimately claim entitlement to a share of benefits.

2 *Countries are interdependent and not even tropical developing countries are self-sufficient*

Whereas importers of genetic resources for pharmaceutical research are likely to be located in the North and the suppliers mostly in the South, there is a greater degree of interdependence between countries for the supply of suitable crop germplasm. Therefore, it may be counterproductive for each country to adopt a stringent access regime, or to favour bilateral agreements. In fact, all countries are *ultimately* dependent upon exotic germplasm and therefore benefit from free access to germplasm collected previously in other countries (Brush 1994) even if many of them may be quite independent in the short-term. Countries are also likely to be dependent on exotic germplasm when they are starting up crop breeding programmes.[5] The interdependence of countries is borne out by figures showing the destination of germplasm samples provided by the International Agricultural Research Centres of the Consultative Group on International Agricultural Research (CGIAR) (Table 1.1).

3 *A great deal of germplasm is held in* ex situ *collections*

A tremendous quantity of wild crop progenitors, semi-domesticated crop relatives, and landraces are stored in *ex situ* collections, such as those at universities, botanic gardens and the CGIAR system (see p105), and it is to the professional plant breeder's advantage to acquire genetic material from these sources. This is not only because the collections are so extensive and are freely available, but also because information (albeit usually quite basic) is usually available about individual accessions. Moreover, CGIAR breeding programmes have already selected some of the material for its desirable characteristics.

4 *Crop breeders tend not to use exotic landraces and wild[6] varieties in their breeding programmes*

Breeders, especially of the most widely-used agricultural crops, do not consider themselves to be dependent on the collection of 'genes from the wild'. Most commonly, they find it more efficient to use modern varieties as resources in their breeding programmes rather than exotic landraces, which may be a useful source of desirable single genes but will not be adapted for local conditions, and also may require considerable work to breed out extraneous genetic material. As a rule they tend to use varieties held in their own collections and those bred in public institutions. Indeed, the likelihood that the main inputs in a breeding programme are other proprietary modern varieties is one of the main reasons for the existence of the so-called 'breeders' exemption' in the UPOV Convention (see pp26, 50). The exemption is one of the key differences between plant variety rights and patent law. Moreover, increased adoption of genetic engineering and

Table 1.1 *Percentage of germplasm samples distributed annually by CGIAR centres, by sector 1992–94*

	Other IARCs	Developing country National Agricultural Research System	Developed country National Agricultural Research System	Private sector
	%	%	%	No
International Centre for Tropical Agriculture (CIAT)				
Phaseolus	0	54	46	0
Manihot	0	59	40	1
Forage legumes	16	51	27	6
Total	7	53	37	3
International Centre for the Improvement of Maize & Wheat (CIMMYT)				
Maize	0	20	72	8
Wheat	0	69	28	3
Total	0	45	49	6
West Africa Rice Development Association (WARDA)				
Total	25	75	0	0
International Centre for Agricultural Research in the Dry Areas (ICARDA)				
Total	5	63	32	0
International Potato Centre (CIP)				
Potato	no data	93	7	no data
Sweet potato	no data	95	5	no data
Total	no data	93	7	no data
International Institute For Tropical Agriculture (IITA)				
Total	13	66	21	0
International Crop Research Institute for the Semi-Arid Tropics (ICRISAT)				
Total	0	91	2	7
International Rice Research Institute (IRRI)				
Total	7	52	39	2
International Livestock Research Institute (ILRI)				
Total	9	64	7	20
International Network for the Improvement of Bananas & Plantains (INIBAP)				
Total	3	64	33	0
Total	**4**	**72**	**21**	**3**

Source: FAO 1996

other biotechnological techniques including transgenics is expected to further reduce dependency on exotic plant germplasm (and local knowledge and skills).[7] However, it is important not to overstate the point. There are exceptions to this tendency not to use exotic germplasm in breeding programmes. For example, such germplasm may be used when particular traits are sought, new breeding programmes are being started, or for long-term genetic-enhancement, and also in the breeding of certain crops (eg potatoes). Also some International Agricultural Research Centres use exotic germplasm in their breeding strategies (Heitz pers comm 1998).

5   *Developing countries lack scientific and technological capacity to capture the benefits from agro-biodiversity*
    While the useful attributes of landraces are well-known to the local communities that breed or cultivate them, only some of these attributes have widespread utility. Large industrial concerns (public and, increasingly, private) that supply a global market are much better placed than local communities to identify such widely useful characteristics and then to appropriate their value through advanced breeding techniques. Many developing countries lack the technological means to capture the full potential economic benefits possible from industrial breeding (and for that matter, from pharmaceutical research). Scientific and technological capacity building are vital for developing countries for this among other reasons.

6   *Temperate countries may lack the species richness of tropical countries yet still be well-endowed in terms of crop genetic diversity*
    The concentration of the world's biodiversity-richness in the tropical zone may not necessarily coincide with the geography of agro-biodiversity-richness, especially in the case of the major food crops. Temperate developed countries that have cultivated certain crops for centuries or longer may be rich in their supply of balanced genetic structures, genes and traits that are desirable for crop breeders, and developing countries may need to import crop germplasm from these countries.

Strong evidence suggests, then, that if a developing country establishes a strong regulatory regime for access to crop germplasm, industrialized world crop breeders would be affected far less than breeders in the South that might wish to exchange germplasm with countries sharing the same agro-climatic conditions. But this does not mean that Northern plant breeder/seed companies have no stake in the *in situ* conservation of genetic resources, nor a moral obligation to assist developing countries. In fact, it is very much in the interests of this industrial sector as a whole to support *in situ* conservation and it is vital that they do so. Even though a survey revealed that only 2.4 per cent of germplasm used in the development of new varieties comes from wild species or landraces maintained *in situ* (see Swanson 1996), these resources are far from being of marginal importance. Securing effective protection from diseases and pests in the long-term is absolutely dependent on inputs of genes and traits that are new to the system in the sense of being undiscovered or known only to indigenous or traditional communities. According to Swanson (ibid):

> *the vast majority of R&D will always be undertaken on those varieties which are already standardised and well-understood within the system. This is not a substitute for new germplasm; it is merely a continuation of a programme of research on germplasm that was input into the system at an earlier point in time.... However, all stocks of information must originally derive from outside the process, and it is essential to input new supplies at the optimal rate necessary in order to sustain the R&D process. ... The stock of existing commercial varieties may be seen as the information base from which bio-industries develop innovations, whereas the sources of new diversity (wild species, induced mutation) may be seen as the sources of increments to the information base.*

Brush (1994) also supports the view that it is in the long-term interests of developed countries and industrial plant breeding institutions to cooperate in supporting *in situ* conservation of crop genetic resources through financial or other means. He identifies four essential benefits that only *in situ* conservation of genetic resources can provide:[8,9]

1 *in situ* conservation preserves evolutionary processes that generate new germplasm under conditions of natural selection.
2 *in situ* conservation will maintain important field laboratories for crop biology and biogeography.
3 It provides a continuing source of co-adapted germplasm for *ex situ* collections.
4 Support for *in situ* conservation would help to satisfy the need for the inclusion and recognition of farmers, encourage wider participation in international efforts, and allow for a more equitable role for nations rich in agro-biodiversity.

NOTES

1 According to the US Office of Technology Assessment (1989), 'biotechnology, broadly defined, includes any technique that uses living organisms (or parts of organisms) to make or modify products, to improve plants or animals, or to develop micro-organisms for specific uses'.

2 It should be noted that there is considerable resistance from the corporate sector to the argument that modern varieties can be lumped together for legal purposes with these other types of germplasm. To do so would render them subject to the sovereignty claims of the countries from where genetic material to produce a variety was originally acquired and thereby severely restrict or eliminate the ability of a corporation to acquire intellectual property right protection. This particular issue has been a major bone of contention in the context of the FAO International Undertaking on Plant Genetic Resources (see p102) and in debates over the status of germplasm held in international genebanks. (Although the CBD affirms national sovereignty rights to *in situ* resources, these rights do not extend to accessions in *ex situ* collections outside the country of origin which were acquired prior to the entry into force of the CBD.)

3 Though overly stringent or bureaucratic regulations may discourage companies from supporting or carrying out bioprospecting.

4 The following section benefited considerably from the advice of André Heitz and Kristina Plenderleith.

5 For example, when Brazil started to breed soybeans, the country imported varieties from the US. Interestingly, the origin of soybean is East Asia, not North America.

6 Distinguishing between wild species and landraces is problematic. According to Posey (1996), 'indigenous peoples and a growing number of scientists find unacceptable the assumption that just because landscapes and species appear to outsiders to be "natural", they are "wild" and therefore unowned.' Posey coins the term 'non-domesticated resources' in place of 'wild resources' for this reason.

7 For a presentation of this position see: ASSINSEL (1998).

8 It should be noted that wider environmental benefits are not considered by Brush. These include ecosystem functioning and stabilizing climate.

9 It should be noted that developments in biotechnology may reduce industry's benefits from *in situ* conservation.

2 INTELLECTUAL PROPERTY RIGHTS IN THE GLOBAL ECONOMY

THE GLOBAL INTELLECTUAL PROPERTY REGIME

The international law of intellectual property consists of:

1   Multilateral treaties, most of which are administered by the World Intellectual Property Organization (WIPO), a specialized agency of the United Nations which has 171 member states.[1] The most well known of these treaties are the *Patent Cooperation Treaty*, the *Paris Convention for the Protection of Industrial Property*, and the *Bern Convention for the Protection of Literary and Artistic Works* (see p95).
2   Regional treaties, such as the European Patent Convention and the European Community Directive on the Legal Protection of Biotechnological Inventions.
3   Bilateral agreements.

By far the most significant IPR treaties in the context of plants, biodiversity and the international trade regime are the *Agreement on Trade-Related Aspects of Intellectual Property Rights* (henceforward The TRIPS Agreement or TRIPS), and the *Convention of the International Union for the Protection of New Varieties of Plants* (The UPOV Convention). The former, which is administered by the World Trade Organization, is so important because it is the first and only international treaty which seeks to establish enforceable universal minimum standards of protection for all the major intellectual property rights. The latter, which is administered by another intergovernmental organization, the International Union for the Protection of New Varieties of Plants (UPOV), is significant because it deals specifically with plant varieties. These two treaties will be considered in greater detail in the next chapter.

Overall we find that the evolution of developed country IPR regimes this century has been characterized by three phenomena:

1   *The broadening of existing rights*
    Examples of the broadening of existing rights include the extension of copyright protection for computer programs as if they are literary works, and the application of patent protection to cover genetically modified organisms and cloned genes.
2   *The creation of new (*sui generis*) rights*
    Examples of *sui generis* systems created this century include plant variety rights, rights to layout-designs of integrated circuits, and performers' rights.
3   *The progressive standardization of the basic features of IPRs*
    For instance, patent regulations increasingly provide 20-year protection terms; require prior art searches and examinations for novelty, inventive step (or non-obviousness) and industrial application; assign rights to the first applicant rather than the first inventor; and provide protection for inventions in all industries and fields of technology.

Even in developed countries these trends are very recent. Most of the examples given date back no further in time than the 1960s, while some of these innovations go back only to the 1980s (eg the patenting of cloned genes). In the developing world, in contrast, there was little interest in 'modernizing' IPR systems at least to anywhere near such an extent. With the coming into force of the TRIPS Agreement in 1995 we can expect that this situation will change rapidly as the minimum standards of IPR protection established in this agreement become universal to the extent that all but a few countries will have to adopt such changes in their national laws within the next few years.

At a superficial level it may be argued that this evolution reflects the development of new technologies, the growth of industrial sectors that use them, and also the increased importance of IPRs to world trade. At a more philosophical level, what appears to be going on is that IPRs in many legal jurisdictions have this century drifted away from instrumentalism and ever closer to proprietarianism (see Drahos 1996). Drahos defines proprietarianism as 'a creed which says that the possessor should take all, that ownership privileges should trump community interests and that the world and its contents are open to ownership'. So, for example, the notion that patent rights should sometimes be limited for the purpose of keeping prices of essential foods and medicines at a level that the poor can afford is increasingly being dispensed with by legislatures, courts and trade ministries. This trend has not been unidirectional. There has in fact always been a tension between the two, resulting in a degree of unpredictability such that legislators, courts and policy makers sometimes revert to instrumentalism. This situation is in large part due to the fact that IPR law relates to and is shaped by other areas of law and policy which it may complement or conflict with, or may even be a component of (see Doern 1999). Examples include such areas as competition, anti-trust/monopolies and mergers, and international trade.

INTELLECTUAL PROPERTY RIGHTS IN INTERNATIONAL TRADE

The role of intellectual property rights (IPRs) in international trade, the global economy and international relations has grown considerably, especially since the 1970s. To understand why, we need to be aware of the recent tremendous advances in two technological fields: electronic information-processing and communications, and biotechnology (Kaplinsky 1989). Both fields have multiple industrial applications, and many large corporations involved in such sectors as computers, telecommunications, healthcare, entertainment, financial services, retailing, chemicals, agriculture and food, have become major users and/or developers of these technologies. The US has succeeded in establishing a considerable lead in these technologies, and several of these industrial sectors, and its continued economic pre-eminence is in part a consequence of this. Information technology and biotechnology firms routinely seek intellectual property right (IPR) protection of their products, technologies and services so as to maximize returns from their often enormous research and development investments. For companies in the other industrial sectors referred to above, much of the value added to their goods and services may come from such IPR-protectable intangible inputs as knowledge and creativity or attributes like reputation. But it is not only IPR-protected *products*, *technologies* and *services* that are major exports of developed countries like the US; it is also the *rights* themselves in the form of licences to use patented processes, techniques and designs, copyrights, trademarks and franchises (Coleman 1997).

With respect to the US, Gadbaw and Richards (1988, cited in Evans 1996) estimate that the percentage of the country's exports with a high intellectual property content rose from 9.9 per cent in 1947 to 27.4 per cent in 1986. It is a fairly safe assumption that this figure has increased since then, as it has done for most other technologically advanced developed countries, and for global trade in general. Moreover, Ryan (1998) states that:

> *US multinational manufacturing enterprises increasingly transfer intellectual property internationally through the industrial processes that they sell abroad. Exports, as*

measured by royalties and licensing fees, amounted to about $27 billion in 1995, while imports amounted to only $6.3 billion. At least $20 billion of the exports are transactions between US firms and their foreign affiliates.

This balance of payments surplus is far higher than for any other country.[2]

In spite of the market dominance of these knowledge-rich corporations, they are highly vulnerable in that the marginal costs of reproducing such goods as software packages, CDs, videos and medicines tend to be very low. With the exception of pharmaceuticals, multiple reproduction of these goods requires only low-cost equipment and minimal (if any) technical know-how. In the many countries where IPRs such as patents, copyright, trademarks, and trade secrets are unavailable or enforcement is weak, imitators can quickly and inexpensively copy these products and sell them at home and abroad. Frequently, drug companies that need to make time-consuming and expensive research and development commitments to create new products have their medicines copied and sold at lower prices by other firms. And plant breeding companies find their non-hybrid plant varieties being replanted or sold in countries where intellectual property protection for such products is either weak, non-existent, or simply not enforced. The US International Trade Commission (1988, cited in Boyle 1996) has estimated that US corporations are victims of foreign 'intellectual piracy' amounting to losses of between US$40 and US$60 billion per year. Such numbers cannot be trusted, in part because they include sales figures for goods manufactured and sold in countries where they are not IPR-protected anyway. Even so, there is no doubt that unauthorized copying – both illegal and legal – takes place on a tremendous scale in many countries (and not only in developing countries).

However, these corporations are by no means passive victims. In fact, they are highly effective lobbyists, and their campaigns have influenced both domestic and foreign policy (eg see Paine and Santoro 1995; Ryan 1998). One example is when they dissuaded President Bush from signing the CBD, a decision he made partly due to the Convention's ambiguities regarding IPRs. Just as the US has pioneered the expansion of IPR protection to cover the products and processes of the new technologies, US companies played a major part in determining the framework of TRIPS, with Japanese and European commercial interests playing an important supporting role (Drahos 1995; Nijar 1996a; Ryan 1998). That the US government and its allies were so determined to ensure that trade-related IPRs were a major agenda item during the GATT Uruguay Round supports the assertion of Boyle (1996) that 'the protection of information "value-added" in products is one of the key elements in the foreign policy of the developed world'.

The successful negotiation of TRIPS, given the ambivalent if not hostile stance of many developing countries, requires an explanation. The aggressive position of the US and its insistence that the Uruguay Round agreements be accepted in their totality or not at all were certainly critical. The broad agenda of the Uruguay Round was also key since it provided opportunities for linkage-bargain diplomacy (see Haas 1980) that WIPO, with its exclusive focus on IPRs, did not allow. Hard bargaining by the US, Europe and Japan on IPRs could thus be linked to concessions in such areas as textiles and agriculture, where exporting countries in the developing world were eager to achieve favourable agreements (Ryan 1998; Sell 1998). According to McGrath (1996):

> *the United States saw that tying obligations to protect intellectual property rights to other trade commitments under GATT would provide the desired vehicle for pressuring recalcitrant trading partners. So, having recruited support from other developed nations, 1985 to 1989 saw the United States employing various methods to 'encourage' in particular the less developed countries (LDCs) and newly industrialised countries (NICs) to accept the insertion of TRIPS into GATT.*

Developed countries regarded WIPO as an unattractive forum for such negotiations, not only because of its exclusively IPR-specific agenda, but also because it has no enforcement or dispute settlement mechanisms except through the treaties that it administers, and these treaties provide very little provision for compliance.

Nevertheless, it is not entirely accurate to characterize IPRs as a North versus South issue. The developing world is highly heterogeneous in terms of countries' levels of industrialization, and social and political development. Some countries, especially in Africa, are virtually devoid of a manufacturing sector and have become poorer and more indebted in recent years. Others, especially in Asia, have extremely dynamic export-oriented industrial economies (albeit affected by the recent economic downturn) and are likely to have their own IPR-protected products and technologies. Therefore, the IPR-related interests of different developing countries in international trade negotiations vary considerably. Second, the domestic IPR-related interests both within and between different industrial sectors may vary widely. For example, one sector in an otherwise underdeveloped country may be a significant producer and exporter of high-technology goods or services, and/or may be heavily dependent upon the flow of proprietary technologies from overseas. Therefore, just as there are bound to be disagreements *between* developing countries over the appropriate stance that should be taken in trade negotiations, countries may be divided *internally* as well. In India, for example, many farmers (though not all) are resistant to TRIPS (see p76), yet copyright protection of computer programs is a relatively uncontroversial issue. There is little doubt that one of the main reasons is that India is relatively advanced in this field of technology and is likely as a consequence to have a large number of potential domestic beneficiaries.

NOTES

1 As of 4 March 1999.

2 Even some of the major developed countries have a balance of payments deficit for royalties and licence fees. According to IMF figures, countries with a balance of payment surplus in 1995 included the US (US$20.66 billion) and UK (US$1.71 billion). Other countries with a deficit included Japan (–US$3.35 billion), Germany (–US$2.66 billion), India (–US$68 million [1992 figure]) and Brazil (–US$497 million) (Maskus 1998). This is a puzzling finding, especially considering the heavy R&D commitments that are well-known features of the private sectors of Germany and Japan. Patel and Pavitt (1995) believe there is a simple explanation: 'German and Japanese firms exploit their technological advantage mainly through exports, whilst US and UK firms rely much more on direct foreign investment, which results in a higher volume of measured royalty income'. So Germany and Japan have just as much reason as the US and UK to favour strong and enforceable IPR protection in overseas markets.

3 BIODIVERSITY-RELATED ASPECTS OF THE GLOBAL INTELLECTUAL PROPERTY RIGHTS REGIME

As was explained in Chapter 2, the key international IPR agreements relevant to plants, biodiversity and trade are the TRIPS Agreement and the UPOV Convention. This chapter presents the most relevant provisions of these agreements and discusses some of their wider implications.

THE TRIPS AGREEMENT

The TRIPS Agreement is now the key international agreement promoting the harmonization of national IPR regimes.[1,2] As explained earlier, the reason for the inclusion of IPRs in the Uruguay Round agenda had much to do with the effective lobbying of industrial concerns, mostly in the United States, and the attraction to the developed countries and corporations of the existence of a dispute settlement mechanism within GATT that WIPO lacked.

Objectives and General Principles

The purpose of the TRIPS Agreement, as stated in the preamble, is to introduce new rules and disciplines for global trade concerning the provision of:

- adequate standards and principles concerning the availability, scope and use of trade-related intellectual property rights;
- effective and appropriate means for the enforcement of trade-related intellectual property rights;

- effective and expeditious procedures for the multilateral prevention and settlement of disputes between governments.

Protection and enforcement of IPRs should, according to Article 7 (*Objectives*), 'contribute to the promotion of technological innovation and to the transfer and dissemination of technology, to the mutual advantage of producers and users of technological knowledge and in a manner conducive to social and economic welfare, and to a balance of rights and obligations.' This means that national IPR regimes need not be modelled on those of the US, Europe or Japan, and may be flexible and country-specific so long as they comply with the minimum standards set out in Parts II and III of the Agreement (see Box 3.1). Just as social and economic welfare are considered as priority matters, Article 8 Paragraph 1 gives priority not only to the public interest in sectors of vital importance to social, economic and technological development, but also to public health and nutrition. For most developing countries, agriculture is certainly one such sector.[3]

It seems paradoxical to suppose that a market intervention, which is what IPRs are, should enhance trade liberalization (see Box 3.2). Whether IPRs do have this effect is a question this study will not attempt to answer. Neither will it discuss the question of whether social and economic welfare is greater with or without a national IPR regime. The fact is that WTO members are required to implement minimum IPR standards, and so attention must be drawn to the task of designing the national regime so that it best serves the needs of each country in terms of public welfare and the interests of producers and users of technological knowledge. However, it is by no means easy to ensure that the rights and obligations of these producers and users are well balanced in support of the social, economic and developmental objectives that governments intend their IPR laws to pursue. In some technological fields, legislators and patent offices may be experienced and impartial enough to ensure that an optimal balance is achieved, although it is difficult to be certain that this is true. It is far more difficult to achieve this with new technologies, especially if governments are unduly pressured by powerful economic interests.

Even in developed countries where biotech patenting is quite well established, this optimal balance has proved to be very difficult to achieve. Sometimes the rights granted to patent owners appear to be more extensive than can be justified in terms of the public interest. For example, Heller and Eisenberg (1998) warn of an emerging IPR problem in the US in the field of biomedical research which they call the 'tragedy of the anticommons'. Specifically, this refers to a situation in which the increased patenting of premarket, or 'upstream', research 'may be stifling life-saving innovations further downstream in the course of research and product development' (ibid). One way this can happen is based on the fact that developing future commercial products such as therapeutic proteins or genetic diagnostic tests often requires the use of multiple patented gene fragments. However, there is an increasingly high number of patents on isolated gene fragments. The cost of R&D will be affected by the existence of so many of these patents because a company intending to develop such products will need to acquire licences from other patent holders, and thus will incur large (and possibly prohibitive) transaction costs. Since the first patent for gene fragments of the type known as expressed sequence tags (ESTs) was awarded to Incyte Pharmaceuticals in 1998 (McFarling 1998), this problem could become more serious.[4]

In the field of agro-biotechnology, a related problem is that patents sometimes contain claims which appear to be excessively broad (Crespi 1995; Roberts 1995; van Wijk 1995a). A good example is US patent 5,159,135 awarded in 1992 to Agracetus for *all* transgenic cotton. The patent claims covered any variety of cotton produced by means of any gene transfer technology (Gibbs 1994). However, the patent system and the courts can sometimes respond positively to such problems by means of pre-grant opposition,[5] post-grant re-examination requests and litigation. In 1994 this patent was cancelled by the US Patent and Trademark Office (PTO) 'on the basis that other researchers already knew what was disclosed in the patent application as being novel and new' (NBIAP/ISB 1995). The cancellation followed complaints about the patent's excessive breadth from other companies, the US Department of Agriculture, NGOs, and a re-examination request made on behalf of an anonymous party (NBIAP/ISB 1994). Also, Calgene's attempt to acquire a 'genus patent' on transgenic *Brassica* failed when the PTO 'denied the broadest claims and awarded the company rights only to *Brassica* cells transformed using Calgene's method' (ibid).[6] Another broad patent owned by Novartis which covered all insect-resistant corn containing *Bacillus thuringiensis* (Bt) technology was only invalidated after the company had taken Monsanto and DeKalb Genetics (a Monsanto affiliate) to court for patent infringement. It should be pointed out that the limited time allotted for patent examinations in countries like the United States means that the legally enforceable breadth of patents is likely to be determined in the courts. Litigation requires substantial financial commitments well beyond the means of many individuals and smaller companies (Barton 1993).

Great care must be taken to ensure that the rights provided are neither insufficient nor excessive in terms of enhancing social and economic welfare. As the situations and examples described above indicate, there are dangers that an excess number of patents or over-extensive breadth in the scope of individual patents can create perverse incentives which may reduce the rate of innovation. Although the PTO and US courts ought to be gaining experience in

---

BOX 3.1 MAIN CONTENTS OF THE AGREEMENT ON TRADE-RELATED ASPECTS OF INTELLECTUAL PROPERTY RIGHTS

Part I General Provisions and General Principles

Part II Standards Concerning the Availability, Scope and Use of Intellectual Property Rights
1   Copyright and Related Rights
2   Trademarks
3   Geographical Indications
4   Industrial Designs
5   Patents
6   Layout-Designs (Topographies) of Integrated Circuits
7   Protection of Undisclosed Information
8   Control of Anti-Competitive Practices in Contractual Licences

Part III Enforcement of Intellectual Property Rights
1   General Obligations
2   Civil and Administrative Procedures and Remedies
3   Provisional Measures
4   Special Requirements Related to Border Measures
5   Criminal Procedures

Part IV Acquisition and Maintenance of Intellectual Property Rights and Related Inter-Partes *Procedures*

Part V Dispute Prevention and Settlement

Part VI Transitional Arrangements

Part VII Institutional Arrangements; Final Provisions

---

establishing the right balance, the very real danger of a tragedy of the anticommons in some fields of biotechnological (and possibly other) research suggests there may still be much to learn even in the United States. Indeed, Allen Littman (1997) warns that 'the neutral balance between patent holders and the public domain created by the constitutional and statutory system has been shifted by the United States Court of Appeals for the Federal Circuit to one that unduly favours the patent holder, and needs to be brought back into balance'. Other countries might be advised to heed these concerns and to take a wait-and-see approach before removing their restrictions on life-form-related patents, irrespective of any ethical concerns they may have about such patents.

Article 1 (*Nature and Scope of Obligations*) makes clear that whilst members are required to implement the provisions of TRIPS, more extensive protection and enforcement of IPRs are not precluded. Therefore, the absence of, for example, any mention of traditional ecological knowledge, does not disallow a member from

BOX 3.2 IPRs AND TRADE LIBERALIZATION: A CONTRADICTION IN TERMS?

When discussing the objectives of the TRIPS Agreement, one is faced with an apparent contradiction, which is that whereas the role of the WTO is to promote trade liberalization, intellectual property rights are essentially a market intervention. If IPRs impede the operation of free market competition,[8] how can their promotion be justified?

Historically IPRs such as patents and copyrights have been justified on either consequentialist or deontological grounds (see Schrecker *et al* 1994). The consequentialist justification is that when inventors, authors or artists have an exclusive right to reproduce and sell their works, society benefits. This proposition is based on two assumptions. First, it assumes that such a right encourages inventors to invent and authors to write. Second, it presupposes that the greater the quantity of inventions and creative works released into the public domain, the more the public benefits through economic or cultural enrichment, or (in the case of medicines) greater physical well-being. Thus advocates of this justification tend to say either that IPRs are rewards for inventors and artists for their contribution to the public good or that they are incentives that encourage creative endeavour. Deontological arguments derive from considerations of rightness and wrongness. For example, it may be argued that using somebody's invention or creative work without his or her permission is morally wrong, perhaps because it is in some way harmful to that person or because it is a means of unjust enrichment.

Consequentialist arguments tend to influence national IPR laws more than deontological ones,[9] and the TRIPS Agreement emphasizes development and public welfare objectives. The limited scope of IPRs, the fact that most of them are time-restricted (or at least need to be renewed), and the exclusion of some manifestations of creativity such as discoveries of natural phenomena, are evidence that IPRs seek to strike a balance such that the size of the rewards and incentives to rightholders is optimal in terms of the public good. In this way, a market intervention that permits limited property rights over valuable intangibles is felt to be consistent with rules that promote trade liberalization.

It should be understood, though, that all justifications – whether consequentialist or moral – for the scope, duration, and even the existence, of IPRs are contestable. Numerous attempts have been made to evaluate the economic efficiency of patent rights by such means as determining the optimal breadth of the rights granted (eg Merges and Nelson 1990; Scotchmer 1991; Scotchmer and Green 1990), their duration (eg Nordhaus 1969; Scherer 1972), the extent to which patents induce increased R&D expenditure (eg Taylor and Silberman 1973), and the welfare losses caused by the temporary monopolies provided (eg Plant 1934). Yet none of these assessments provides a trustworthy guide to the level of IPR protection that would be the most economically or socially optimal for any legal jurisdiction, even less the world as a whole.[10] According to an Oxford University Law Professor, David Vaver (1991), '[i]t seems impossible to argue that the current laws encourage just the right amount of research, creativity and financing, and just in the right areas'.

Moreover, concepts central to justifying IPRs such as inventiveness, creativity and authorship are subject to a range of conflicting definitions, all of which may be legitimately questioned.

enacting legislation to protect such a category of knowledge. For example, Kenya passed an Industrial Property Bill in 1989 that allows petty patents relating to traditional medicinal knowledge, ie, for 'herbal as well as nutritional formulations which give new effects'.[7] There is no conflict whatsoever between such a provision and TRIPS. However, other WTO members are not required to recognize rights in other countries that go beyond the minimum standards established by TRIPS.

By virtue of Article 3, members accept the principle of *National Treatment*, ie that each country must treat nationals of other Members at least as well as it treats its own nationals. In other words, IPR protection and enforcement must be non-discriminatory as to the nationality of rights holders.

Article 4 upholds a related key principle: *Most Favoured Nation*. This means that any concession granted by a Member to another Member must be accorded to all other Members 'immediately and unconditionally'. So if Argentina, say, agrees to take special measures to prevent the pirating of a US seed company's products, but turns a blind eye when the company is British, Swiss or Japanese, such inconsistency of treatment will violate this principle.

The following intellectual property rights covered by TRIPS are of relevance to plants and plant varieties: patents, geographical indications, undisclosed information (or trade secrets) and trademarks.

Patents

The patents section of TRIPS has been the subject of considerable debate. According to the first paragraph of Article 27 (*Patentable Subject Matter*), 'patents shall be available for any inventions, whether products or processes, in all fields of technology, provided that they are new, involve an inventive step and are capable of industrial application'. Newness or novelty is a conventional requirement in patent law; after all, an 'invention' that is not new is by definition not an invention at all.[11]

Paragraph 1 also requires that patents be available and patent rights enjoyable 'without discrimination as to the place of invention, the field of technology and whether products are imported or locally produced'. This provision is very favourable for corporations who dislike the idea that technological fields can be excluded from patentability and fear the imposition of requirements that patent protected goods be manufactured in those countries where they hold patents (Dutfield 1997b).

Ordre public *and morality*[12]

Certain defined exclusions are allowable (see Table 3.1 for a summary of these exclusions), the most significant being in Paragraphs 2 and 3. Paragraph 2 states as follows:

> *Members may exclude from patentability inventions, the prevention within their territory of the commercial exploitation of which is necessary to protect* ordre public *or morality, including to protect human, animal or plant life or health or to avoid serious prejudice to the environment, provided that such exclusion is not made merely because the exploitation is prohibited by their law.*

The terms '*ordre public*'[13] and 'morality' are not defined in TRIPS although human, animal or plant life or health and the environment are referred to. In fact, this is the only reference to environment in the whole of TRIPS (WTO-CTE 1996a). The language of Article 27.2 follows very closely that of the European Patent Convention,[14] yet even in Europe, the true meaning and potential extent of the *ordre public*/morality exclusions remain unresolved (Nuffield Council on Bioethics 1995). According to the European Patent Office, an invention is 'immoral' if the general public would consider it so abhorrent that patenting would be inconceivable (Llewelyn 1995). As yet, though, the EPO has not decided how it should interpret the meaning of 'abhorrent', nor indicated what evidence opponents of a patent should provide to demonstrate that the general public regards the invention as immoral.

Opposition to the patenting of genetically modified organisms (GMOs) on the grounds of morality and *ordre public* has been expressed by members of Western societies on the grounds that releases of GMOs and genetically-engineered food products may cause ecological damage and even be prejudicial to human health or animal welfare. Representatives of many indigenous and traditional societies have condemned monopoly protection of products derived from communally-held resources on the grounds that this is economically exploitative and morally and spiritually repugnant.[15] Members of such societies have also expressed the view that the patenting of life-forms – that is to say whole plants and animals, and functional or structural components of life-forms such as gene sequences, proteins and cells – is inherently immoral (Posey and Dutfield 1998).[16] It seems plausible, then, for patenting life in general to be outlawed on moral or *ordre public* grounds in countries where such views are especially prevalent. However, legal experts tend to assume that TRIPS-compatibility requires governments to apply the exclusion narrowly on a case-by-case basis rather than to broad classes of patents such as life-forms in their broadest sense (Moufang 1998). Otherwise, such patents would have been specifically outlawed by TRIPS or, at the very least, the option to outlaw them would have been explicitly indicated (Roberts 1996). There again, some commentators feel that the lack of clarity in the language of Article 27 makes it impossible to predict how member states and the WTO's dispute settlement mechanism will interpret and enforce Paragraph 2 (Costa e Silva 1996).

'Patenting life' and the sui generis *option*

Paragraph 3 states that members may also exclude from patentability:

(a) diagnostic, therapeutic and surgical methods for the treatment of humans or animals;

(b) plants and animals other than micro-organisms, and essentially biological processes for the production of plants or animals other than non-biological and microbiological processes. However, Members shall provide for the protection of plant varieties either by patents or by an effective sui generis *system or by any combination thereof. The provisions of this subparagraph shall be reviewed four years after the entry into force of the WTO Agreement.*

With respect to *products*, plants and animals may be excluded from patentability. As regards *processes*, essentially biological processes for the production of plants or animals may also be excluded. Patents must be available for microorganisms as *products* and for non-biological and microbiological *processes* for producing plants or animals. Patent protection need not be available for plant varieties but an effective IPR system is still obligatory. This may be an UPOV-type Plant Breeders' Rights system, another *sui generis* alternative, or some combination of systems. As indicated, this provision is subject to review (see p92).

The question arises of how 'plant varieties' can be distinguished from 'plants' and whether a transgenic plant is a 'plant' or a 'plant variety'. This is very important given the increased application of genetic engineering to crop research.

In fact, defining and legally interpreting the term 'plant variety' is not easy. The UPOV Convention provided two definitions. According to the 1961 version, a plant variety is 'any cultivar, clone, line, stock or hybrid which is capable of cultivation'. The 1991 revision contains a more detailed definition according to which a plant variety is:

a plant grouping within a single botanical taxon of the lowest known rank, which grouping, irrespective of whether the conditions for the grant of a breeder's right are fully met, can be:

– defined by the expression of the characteristics resulting from a given genotype or combination of genotypes,

– distinguished from any other plant grouping by the expression of at least one of the said characteristics, and

– considered as a unit with regard to its suitability for being propagated unchanged (Article 1(vi)).

The European Patent Convention expressly excludes plant *varieties* from patentability.[17] A ruling of the Technical Board of Appeal of the European Patent Office in 1995 (Greenpeace v Plant Genetic Systems NV) determined that a claim for plant cells *contained in a plant* is unpatentable since it does not exclude plant varieties from its scope (Llewelyn 1995). To support its decision, the Technical Board referred to a plant variety as:

> *any plant grouping within a single botanical taxon of the lowest rank which, irrespective of whether it would be eligible for protection under the UPOV Convention, is characterised by at least one single transmissible characteristic distinguishing it from other plant groupings and which is sufficiently homogeneous and stable in its essential characteristics ... Plant cells as such cannot be considered to fall under the definition of plant or of plant variety ...*

In Europe this implies that transgenic plants *per se* are not patentable because of the plant variety exclusion. Because of Article 27, a similar interpretation in the TRIPS context would mean a requirement for either a patent or a *sui generis* system to protect such plants. However, it should be emphasized that the situation has not been fully resolved in Europe in spite of the 1995 TBA judgement, which might well be overturned.

One might assume that defining 'micro-organism' should be relatively straightforward. A conventional definition that few biologists would dispute is 'any of various microscopic organisms, including algae, bacteria, fungi, protozoa, and viruses'.[18] However, Philip Grubb (1999), an Intellectual Property Counsel at Novartis, recently extended this definition to include 'animal and plant cells'. It does not seem at all reasonable to argue that a single cell from a multi-cellular organism is itself an organism. An even more dubious definition comes from Josef Straus of the Max-Planck Institute for Foreign and International Patent, Copyright and Competition Law (1998). In direct contradiction to the European Patent Office, whose Opposition Division declared DNA to be 'not "life", but a chemical substance which carries genetic information',[19] he states that:

> *if micro-organisms are mandatorily declared subject matter eligible for patent protection, naturally occurring biochemical substances, such as sequences of nucleotides (DNA),* per argumentum a maiore ad minus *are also to be regarded as subject matter, for which WTO Members have to offer product patent protection.*

Since a DNA sequence cannot possibly be classed as a micro-organism in any scientific sense, there is no justification for arguing that WTO members must allow them to be patented merely because they have to allow micro-organisms to be.

Articles 28 and 29 refer to the specific rights conferred on patent owners and the conditions on applicants, and are standard patent law provisions. Article 30 allows for exceptions to exclusive patent rights, if these exceptions 'do not unreasonably conflict with a normal exploitation of the patent and do not unreasonably prejudice the legitimate interests of the patent owner'. An example of one exception provided in many countries is 'acts done for experimental purposes' (WTO-CTE 1996a).

Article 31 (*Other Use Without Authorization of the Right Holder*) lays down conditions for restricting exclusive rights of patent owners through compulsory licensing[20] or for government use.[21] Although legal commentators tend to emphasize the limitations on compulsory licensing, Halewood (1997) argues persuasively that TRIPS allows countries quite broad discretion in legislating for mandatory domestic local working and compulsory licensing. According to Nijar (1996a), compulsory licensing is compatible with TRIPS for such reasons as protection of public health and nutrition; and promotion of the public interest in sectors of vital importance to socio-economic and technological development, including protection of indigenous technologies, protection of farmers' rights, and generally all that which would adversely affect the socio-economic fabric of developing societies. Interestingly, the American Seed Trade Association (in Schapaugh 1989, cited in Correa 1994) recommended that compulsory licensing provisions should apply:

> *when the scope of a [plant-related] patent is so broad as to encompass within its scope varieties or parts of plants not yet developed. Examples of such patents would include patents with claims direct to:*
>
> *(a) characteristics of crops;*
>
> *(b) genetic components that act as agents for expression of characteristics of crops, or that serve to regulate or control further steps of synthesis of plant material; or*
>
> *(c) processes of genetic manipulation.*

This is an interesting possibility, though it might be better simply to disallow such patents in the first place.

Geographical Indications

Geographical indications 'identify a good as originating in the territory [of a member], or a region or locality in that territory, where a

Table 3.1 *Patenting in TRIPS: compulsory and optional exclusions*

Compulsory exclusion	Optional exclusion
Inventions that are not new, do not involve an inventive step, or are incapable of industrial application	Diagnostic, therapeutic and surgical methods for the treatment of humans or animals
Failure to disclose the invention in a manner clear and complete enough to be carried out by a person skilled in the art	Inventions, the prevention of the commercial exploitation of which is necessary to protect *ordre public* or morality
	Animals and plants (including plant varieties)
	Essentially biological processes for the production of plants or animals
	Failure to provide information concerning corresponding foreign applications and grants

given quality, reputation or other characteristic of the good is essentially attributable to its geographical origin' (Article 22.1). Geographical indications are similar in function to trademarks, the difference being that the former identifies a product with a particular territory, whereas the latter identifies a product with a company or brand (Moran 1993).

Members are required to permit legal action enabling traders to prevent: (a) the designation or presentation of a good (such as a trademark) that suggests, in a manner that misleads the public, that the good in question originates in a geographical area other than the true place of origin; and (b) any use which constitutes unfair competition (Article 22.2, 22.3). Article 23 deals solely with wines and spirits, which is indicative of the influence of the major wine and spirit-exporting countries in negotiating TRIPS, especially France. The application of the provisions of Section 3 are to be reviewed periodically by the Council for TRIPS (Article 24).

See page 85 for discussion on utilization of geographical indications.

Trade Secrets

The inclusion of this section in TRIPS was strongly opposed by developing countries, who did not consider undisclosed information to be a form of IPR. However, Switzerland and the US, who were concerned to safeguard trade secrets internationally, successfully persuaded other governments to accept their proposal for such protection (Blakeney 1996). Because no previous convention provides for protection of undisclosed information, the strategy adopted by the two countries was to argue that such protection is a necessary measure for countries to fulfil their obligations to suppress unfair competition as required by Article 2 of TRIPS (which requires Members to comply with the section of the Paris Convention dealing with unfair competition).

Members must enable natural and legal persons to prevent 'information lawfully within their control from being disclosed to, acquired by, or used by others without their consent in a manner contrary to honest commercial practices.' Acts contrary to honest commercial practices that are mentioned include breach of contract and breach of confidence. To be protected, information must be secret (ie not generally known among or readily accessible to persons within the circles that normally deal with the kind of information in question); have commercial value because it is secret; and have been subject to reasonable steps to keep it secret.

Members are also required to prevent disclosure of data that pharmaceutical and agrochemical producers must submit to the government as conditions for approval of the marketing of new products. US dissatisfaction with Argentina's measures to comply with this obligation is one of the main reasons for the recent imposition of its retaliatory sanctions (Dutfield 1997b).

It can be argued that trade secrets do not serve the public interest as well as patents. This is because, while society may benefit from availability of the product or technology associated with a trade secret, this kind of IPR keeps technical information that would be disclosed in a patent application outside the public domain. Nevertheless, trade secret law is important for the seed industry and is commonly used to protect the inbred parent lines of hybrids, since if these are accessed by competitors, the same hybrids could be developed by these rivals.

See page 86 for further discussion of trade secrets.

Trademarks

A trademark is a marketing tool that is often used to support a company's claim that its products or services are authentic or distinctive compared with similar products or services from another trading entity. In the words of Article 15.1 of TRIPS, a trademark is 'any sign, or any combination of signs, capable of distinguishing the goods or services of one undertaking from those of other undertakings'. It usually consists of a distinctive design, word, or series of words, usually placed on the product label. Registered trademarks must be renewable indefinitely (Article 18). The trademark owner has the exclusive right to prevent third parties from using identical or similar marks in the sale of identical or similar goods or services where doing so would result in a likelihood of confusion (Article 16.1).

See page 89 for further discussion of trademarks.

Other Provisions Relating to Agriculture

The developing country WTO members (and the former centrally-planned economies) have five years from the date of entry into force of The Agreement Establishing the WTO to apply most of the TRIPS provisions (ie until 2000), and the least developed countries have eleven years (until 2006). These grace periods are very important, allowing countries time to develop IPR regimes that are socially, culturally, economically and environmentally sound. However, *all* countries must have applied Articles 3, 4 and 5 (dealing with national treatment and most-favoured-nation treatment) within one year of the entry into force of the WTO Agreement.

Article 70.8 (*Protection of Existing Subject Matter*) requires that members that do not provide patent protection for pharmaceutical and agricultural chemical products in accordance with these permitted grace periods provide a facility by which applications for such inventions can be filed (ie a 'mailbox' system). Paragraph 9 requires that where a product is the subject of a patent application, exclusive marketing rights shall be granted for a period of five years after obtaining market approval in that member state or until a product patent is granted or rejected there, whichever period is shorter, if a patent and marketing approval have been obtained in another member state.

In November 1996 the US requested the WTO Dispute Settlement Body to establish a panel because of the alleged failure of India to provide: (a) a mailbox system for the filing of patent applications for pharmaceutical and agricultural chemical products; and (b) legal authority for the granting of exclusive marketing rights (EMRs) for such products. The Panel and Appellate Body concurred that India had failed to comply with its obligations in this regard, and the parties in dispute agreed to accept the decision. In March 1999, India finally amended its patent law to provide the mailbox facility and exclusive marketing rights, but with the exception that EMRs would not be allowed for products based on Indian traditional systems of medicine (*Economic Times* 1999).

THE UPOV CONVENTION

The International Convention for the Protection of New Varieties of Plants (the 'UPOV Convention') was signed in Paris in 1961 and entered into force in 1968. It was revised in Geneva in 1972, 1978 and 1991. The 1978 Act entered into force in 1981, and the 1991 Act entered into force in April 1998. The Convention established the International Union for the Protection of New Varieties of Plants, which is based in Geneva. UPOV has 38 member states of which 29 are parties to the 1978 Act and 8 are parties to the 1991 Act.[22]

UPOV provides a framework for intellectual property protection of plant varieties. These rights are most often referred to as plant variety rights or plant breeders' rights (PBRs). To be eligible for protection, the plant variety must be:

- *distinct*, ie, distinguishable by one or more characteristics from any other variety whose existence is a matter of common knowledge;
- *stable*, ie, remain true to its description after repeated reproduction or propagation;
- *uniform* in its relevant characteristics (UPOV 1991), or *homogeneous* with regard to the particular feature of its sexual reproduction or vegetative propagation (UPOV 1978); and
- *novel*, ie, not have been offered for sale or marketed, with the agreement of the breeder or his successor in title, in the source country, or for longer than a limited number of years in any other country.

UPOV 1978 defines the scope of protection as the breeder's right to prior authorization for the following acts:

- the production for purposes of commercial marketing;
- the offering for sale; and
- the marketing of the reproductive or vegetative propagating material, as such, of the variety (Article 5).

The 1991 version extends the scope of the breeders' rights in two ways. First it increases the number of acts for which prior authorization of the breeder is required so that these include:

- production or reproduction;
- conditioning for the purpose of propagation;
- offering for sale;
- selling or other marketing;
- exporting;
- importing;
- stocking for the above purposes (Article 14).

Second, such acts are not just in respect of the reproductive or vegetative propagating material as with the 1978 version, but also encompass harvested material obtained through the use of propagating material, and so-called 'essentially derived' varieties.

However, the privilege of breeders both to use protected varieties as an initial source of variation for the creation of new varieties and to market these varieties without authorization from the original breeder (the 'breeders' exemption') is upheld in both versions. One difference though is that the 1991 version states that if a new variety is deemed to be essentially derived from a protected variety, the owner of the protected variety enjoys the same rights over the *essentially derived* variety as if the two varieties are identical. Dhar and Chaturvedi (1998) raise a concern that determination of whether a new variety is essentially derived from an earlier one will likely be made not during the examination but through agreement between breeders or litigation. According to the authors:

> *this implies that this critical issue would be settled by the relative strengths of the parties involved, an eventuality that would not favour developing countries like India who have long been involved in major programmes of plant breeding.*

It is often assumed that the 1978 version allows a farmer to re-sow seed harvested from protected varieties for his or her own use. In fact, such a 'farmers' privilege'[23] is not referred to at all. The Convention establishes *minimum* standards such that the breeder's prior authorization is required for *at least* the three acts mentioned above. Although the farmers' privilege is not compulsory, many countries that are members of the 1978 Convention do indeed uphold it.[24]

The 1991 version is more specific about this matter. Whereas the scope of the breeder's right includes production or reproduction and conditioning for the purpose of propagation (Article 14), governments can use their discretion in deciding whether or not to uphold the farmers' privilege. According to Article 15, the breeder's right in relation to a variety may be restricted:

> *in order to permit farmers to use for propagating purposes, on their own holdings, the product of the harvest which they have obtained by planting ... the protected variety....*

There is therefore a strong likelihood that governments will act upon Articles 14 and 15 by further restricting or eliminating farmers' privilege, but this remains to be seen.

UPOV 1991 extends protection from at least 15 years to a minimum of 20 years and from the propagating part of the variety (the seed) to the whole plant. The revised Convention is silent on the matter of double (ie both patent and PBR) protection whereas the earlier version stated that 'member states may not protect varieties by both patent and special rights'. Even so, many countries expressly forbid the patenting of plant varieties, including (as we saw earlier) most European countries.

Supporters of UPOV argue that the 1991 revision encourages breeders to investigate minor crops and to bring whole new species into cultivation. Opponents, however, point out that even if this is true, small farmers will still be worse off if they lose their privilege to re-sow seeds from their harvested crops.[25] According to Verma (1995), in most developing countries a very large proportion of the population depends on agriculture for employment and income, and many of these farmers are smallholders. For such farmers, 'seed saving from their harvest for further propagation, selling and exchanging of seeds is a common practice' (ibid).

Supporters also deny that the 1991 revision is a move towards patent-like protection. (see Table 3.2 for a comparison of UPOV 1978, 1991, and patents). According to Peter Lange of ASSINSEL, plant variety protection and patents differ in quite fundamental ways, not just in terms of criteria for protection, but also of how the rights and obligations of producers and users are balanced. He argues that 'breeding (including genetic engineering) is always based on what already exists, requires a broad range of variability and demands the free use of material' (Lange 1997). Moreover:

> *Since the purpose of plant variety protection is not to protect an invention, for instance a specific property in plant material, but the creation (including the discovery) of a new plant variety (that is to say a unique new 'shuffled' genotype with a corresponding phenotypical expression)..., there must be the continuing possibility of using the protected material of competitors to develop new varieties with a new and unique genotype (for example, by crossing – that is to say a new 'reshuffle'), without there being dependency [on the authorisation of plant variety right holders]. (*ibid)

As yet, the overwhelming majority of UPOV members are in Europe, North America, Latin America and Australasia. This seems to reflect the fact that in many developing countries, especially in Africa, the private sector's involvement in plant breeding and seed supply is quite limited. Moreover, in many of these countries traditional communities are responsible for much of the plant breeding and seed distribution, as they have been for centuries. For example, Indian farmers produce two-thirds of the country's annual seed requirement (Verma 1995).[26] Consequently, until recently there would have been few domestic beneficiaries of a PBR system, especially if state involvement in breeding was also quite limited. However, the interest of developing countries in joining UPOV is increasing and one can expect that many more of them will become members in the next few years.

Table 3.2 *Comparison of main provisions of PBRs under UPOV 1978 & 1991 & patent law*

Provisions	UPOV 1978	UPOV 1991	Patent law
Protection coverage	Plant varieties of nationally defined species	Plant varieties of all genera and species	Inventions
Requirements	Novelty Distinctness Uniformity Stability Variety denomination	Novelty Distinctness Uniformity Stability Variety denomination	Novelty Inventive step (or non-obviousness) Industrial application Enabling disclosure
Protection term	Min 15 years	Min 20 years	20 years (OECD)
Protection scope	*Minimum scope:* Producing for purposes of commercial marketing, offering for sale and marketing of propagating material of the variety.	*Minimum scope:* Producing, conditioning, offering for sale, selling or other marketing, exporting, importing, stocking for above purposes of propagating material of the variety. Plus, some acts in relation to harvested material if obtained through an unauthorised use of propagating material and if the breeder has had no reasonable opportunity to exercise his right in relation to the propagating material.	*In respect of the product:* Making, importing, offering for sale, selling and using the product; stocking for purposes of offering for sale, etc. *In respect of a process:* Using the process; doing any of the above-mentioned acts in respect of a product obtained directly by means of the process.
Breeders' exemption	Yes. However, hybrids (and like varieties) cannot be exploited without permission from holder of rights in the protected inbred line(s).	Yes. However, hybrids (and like varieties) cannot be exploited without permission from holder of rights in the protected inbred line(s). Plus, essentially derived varieties cannot be exploited in certain circumstances without permission of holder of rights in the protected initial variety.	No
Farmers' privilege	In practice: Yes	Up to national laws	No
Prohibition of double protection	Any species eligible for PBR cannot be patented	No	Up to national laws

Source: Derived from van Wijk et al (1993) with further information provided by Heitz (pers comm 1998)

NOTES

1 As of 10 February 1999 134 countries undertake to implement TRIPS by virtue of their membership of the WTO.

2 Its intent is to guarantee minimum standards rather than harmonization per se, but the effect will also be to make national IPR systems more similar to each other.

3 'Members may, in formulating or amending their laws and regulations, adopt measures necessary to protect public health and nutrition, and to promote the public interest in sectors of vital importance to their socio-economic and techno-logical development, provided that such measures are consistent with the provisions of this Agreement' (TRIPS Article 8.1).

4 According to Jonathan King, a molecular biology professor at the Massachusetts Institute of Technology and member of the Council for Responsible Genetics (in McFarling 1998), '[t]he attempt to obtain patent protection of tags violates the intent of patent law, violates the spirit of patent law and uses the patent system exactly opposite its true intent...It is the suppression of invention and the constraining of discovery.'

5 Possible only in countries where patent applications are published before they are granted.

6 To provide some clarification on procedures concerning the drafting and exami-nation of patent claims, Heitz (1998) states that: '[t]he claims must [also] follow a precise order, from general to specific. In this regard, the patent drafters provide for the risk of one or more claims being invalidated: the next 'surviving' claim will then define the scope of protection. In the case of patents on genes, it is thus standard practice to first claim the gene and subsequently a plant containing the said gene. The 'dependent claim', however, does not extend the scope of protec-tion, but only characterizes it further.'

7 Industrial Property Bill (1989) Kenya Gazette Supplement 92 (bills No 18), 1399-1459) in Gollin (1993).

8 In the sense that they prohibit the unauthorized manufacture and sale of identi-cal products.

9 This generalization holds in spite of the existence of authors' 'moral rights' in many national IPR laws.

10 With respect to patent duration, the eminent economist Jagdish Bhagwati remarked at an NGO roundtable meeting in Geneva in November 1998 that the 20 year minimum term of protection required by TRIPS 'had no basis in economics' (*Bridges*, 1(6), p.1). For one thing, product life cycles within different industrial sectors can vary tremendously. It is said, for example, that semiconductor products now have an average life cycle of only 12–16 months (Hall and Ham 1999), which is shorter than the time it takes to process a patent application in many jurisdictions.

11 But see page 68 concerning the problematic nature of the novelty requirement in some legal jurisdictions.

12 See Schrecker et al (1994), Sterckx (ed.) (1997) and van Overwalle (ed) (1998) for comprehensive discussions concerning the morality, *ordre public* and ethical aspects of patenting life-forms.

13 According to Gervais (1998), the French term 'ordre public' is better translated as 'public policy' than 'public order'.

14 *Article 53 – Exceptions to patentability*
European patents shall not be granted in respect of: (a) inventions the publication

or exploitation of which would be contrary to 'ordre public' or morality, provided that the exploitation shall not be deemed to be so contrary merely because it is prohibited by law or regulation in some or all of the Contracting States; (b) plant or animal varieties or essentially biological processes for the production of plants or animals; this provision does not apply to microbiological processes or the products thereof.

15 For example, see the statements and recommendations of the United Nations Development Programme-funded consultations with indigenous peoples that took place in 1994 and 1995 (UNDP 1995).

16 For example, in 1995 indigenous peoples in the Pacific region acted upon these sentiments by producing a 'Treaty for a Lifeforms Patent-Free Pacific and Related Protocols'.

17 The same exclusion is contained in the European Union's 'Directive 98/44/EC on the Legal Protection of Biotechnological Inventions'.

18 *The Concise Oxford Dictionary*, 8th ed (1991).

19 *Howard Florey/Relaxin*, 1995.

20 Defined by Downes (1995) as the compulsory transfer of patent rights for a price set by the government.

21 Defined by the WTO Committee on Trade and Environment (1996a) as use by the government or a contractor working for the government.

22 As of 22 January 1999. Belgium and Spain are Parties to the 1972 revision.

23 Although this term is frequently used by breeders, most farmers would probably prefer this practice to be characterized as a 'right' rather than a 'privilege'.

24 One exception is France, but there has only been one instance of legal action being taken against offending farmers (A Heitz pers comm 1988).

25 It is worth noting that most seed used in the developing world is farm-saved. Even in many developed countries, for some crops farm-saved seed provides a large proportion of the seed that is planted (Tripp 1997).

26 '[O]nly about 7% of wheat seed and 13% of rice seed planted in India is from the formal sector' (Turner, M.R. (1994) Trends in India's seed sector. Paper presented at Asian Seed 94, Chiang Mai, Thailand, 27–29 September, cited in Tripp 1997).

4 IPR-RELATED ASPECTS OF THE CONVENTION ON BIOLOGICAL DIVERSITY

The Convention on Biological Diversity (CBD) came into force in 1993 and now has 175 State Parties.[1] The CBD has three main objectives (Article 1), which are: (i) the conservation of biological diversity; (ii) the sustainable use of its components; and (iii) the fair and equitable sharing of the benefits arising out of the utilization of genetic resources, including by appropriate access to genetic resources and by appropriate transfer of relevant technologies, taking into account all rights over those resources and to technologies, and by appropriate funding.

Agreeing a text acceptable to both governments in the biodiversity-poor industrialized world, and those of biodiversity-rich developing countries, was a difficult and contentious process. Some developing countries felt that influential conservation organizations and developed country governments were expecting them to protect their forests and forgo the economic benefits from selling timber or converting them to other uses without providing adequate financial compensation. These countries felt that a *quid pro quo* for biodiversity preservation was fair and necessary. Realizing the potential economic value of their biodiversity wealth and needing to improve their scientific, technological and financial capacities to exploit it, they wanted to be able to regulate access to their resources and receive benefits such as technology transfers in return for the granting of access. Developed countries and transnational corporations wanted as few restrictions as possible on access to biological resources. Perhaps not surprisingly, most uses of the words 'right' or 'rights' in the CBD are to affirm that they belong either to states or to intellectual property owners. It is commonly supposed that these IPR owners are corporate patent-holders. In fact, in the CBD there is no *explicit* reference to who such rights holders should be. They could be governments, private individuals, community holders of traditional knowledge and technologies, or companies. The key provisions in the CBD relating to IPRs are in Articles 8, 16, 17 and 18 (Table 4.1), and more indirectly, in Article 15.

ARTICLE 16

The only direct references in the CBD to IPRs are in Article 16 on *Access to and Transfer of Technology* (Glowka et al 1994). In paragraphs 16.1 and 16.2, State Parties undertake to provide and/ or facilitate access and transfer of technologies to other parties under fair and most favourable terms. The only technology referred to is biotechnology, but Article 16 is concerned with any technologies 'that are relevant to the conservation and sustainable use of biological diversity or make use of genetic resources and do not cause significant damage to the environment' (Article 16.1).

Recognizing that technologies are sometimes subject to patents and other IPRs, provision of such technologies must be on terms which recognize and are consistent with the *adequate and effective* protection of intellectual property rights. Adoption here of the clause beginning 'adequate and effective protection' was specifically to establish a link with the TRIPS Agreement, which also uses this language (ibid).

Paragraph 16.5 requires the parties to co-operate to ensure that patents and other IPRs 'are supportive of and do not run counter to' the CBD's objectives. This reflects disagreement about whether or not IPRs support the CBD's objectives, and implicitly accepts that conflicts may well arise between IPRs and the CBD such as those considered in Chapter 5, and that 'subject to national and international law' these conflicts should be eliminated.

Nevertheless, there is great resistance among many people in the private sector to accepting that IPRs have anything to do with the destruction of biodiversity or unsustainable practices. An investigation conducted in Switzerland on the views of firms and universities in that country utilizing genetic resources revealed little support for the need for legislative reforms such as changes to IPR laws in support of the CBD or for any other reason (CBD Secretariat 1998).

ARTICLE 8(j)

Article 8(j) requires the State Parties of the CBD to:

> *respect, preserve and maintain knowledge, innovations and practices of indigenous and local communities embodying traditional lifestyles relevant for the conservation and sustainable use of biological diversity and promote the wider application with the approval and involvement of the holders of such knowledge, innovations and practices and encourage the equitable sharing of the benefits arising from the utilisation of such knowledge, innovations and practices.*

Use of the terms 'knowledge', 'innovations' and 'practices' in addition to 'traditional' is very significant. There is a tendency to assume that 'traditional' implies any or all of such notions as 'time-honoured', 'historical', 'inflexible' and 'static'. On the contrary, 'traditional innovations' would not be an oxymoron in this context. Perhaps the most significant word of all, though, is 'holders', which arguably implies ownership but minimally seems to indicate the existence of legal entitlements.[2]

The Article seems to affirm, then, that the holders ('subject to national legislation') have *rights* over their knowledge, innovations and practices, *whether or not they are capable of being protected by IPRs*. If they are not capable of being protected by the existing IPR system, there still an obligation for governments to safeguard these entitlements either through a new IPR law or by other legal or policy measures. These duties should also extend to users of traditional knowledge, innovations and practices. Minimally giving effect to these obligations should be through prior informed consent and observation of codes of conduct, such as those developed by some scientific organizations.[3]

This interpretation that these communities have legal entitlements over their knowledge, innovations and practice just as companies have over their inventions (Costa e Silva 1995) is reinforced by Article 18.4, which affirms the need for Contracting Parties to 'encourage and develop models of cooperation for the development and use of technologies, including traditional and indigenous technologies...'. Since it is agreed that indigenous and traditional technologies have a role to play in biodiversity conservation, there is no justification for assuming (as many tend to do) that such technologies have a lower status than other technologies relevant to the Convention; nor should they be any less morally entitled to legal protection (Posey 1996).

It is very important, though, that the requirement to respect, preserve and maintain traditional knowledge not be justified *solely* by its instrumental value. Traditional knowledge should not be

Table 4.1 *IPR-related provisions of the CBD (emphases added)*

Article		Theme
16	Access to and Transfer of Technology	*'Access to and transfer of technology referred... to developing countries shall be provided and/or facilitated under fair and most favourable terms, including on concessional and preferential terms where mutually agreed, and, where necessary, in accordance with the financial mechanism established by [the CBD]. In the case of technology subject to patents and other intellectual property rights, <u>such access and transfer shall be provided on terms which recognize and are consistent with the adequate and effective protection of intellectual property rights.</u>'* (Para. 2)
16	Access to and Transfer of Technology	*'Each Contracting Party shall take legislative, administrative or policy measures, as appropriate, with the aim that Contracting Parties, in particular those that are developing countries, which provide genetic resources are provided access to and transfer of technology which makes use of those resources, <u>on mutually agreed terms, including technology protected by patents and other intellectual property rights,</u> where necessary, through the provisions of Articles 20 and 21 [ie financial resources and the financial mechanism] and in accordance with international law ...'* (Para. 3)
16	Access to and Transfer of Technology	*'The Contracting Parties, <u>recognizing that patents and other intellectual property rights may have an influence on the implementation of this Convention,</u> shall cooperate in this regard subject to national legislation and international law in order <u>to ensure that such rights are supportive of and do not run counter to its objectives.</u>'* (Para. 5)
8	*in situ* Conservation	*'Each Contracting Party shall, as far as possible and as appropriate ... <u>respect, preserve and maintain</u> knowledge, innovations and practices of indigenous and local communities embodying traditional lifestyles relevant for the conservation and sustainable use of biological diversity and promote their wider application <u>with the approval and involvement of the holders</u> of such knowledge, innovations and practices and encourage <u>the equitable sharing of the benefits</u> arising from the utilization of such knowledge, innovations and practices.'* (Para. J)
18	Technical and Scientific Cooperation	*'The Contracting Parties shall ... encourage and develop methods of cooperation for the development and use of technologies, <u>including indigenous and traditional technologies,</u> in pursuance of the objectives of this Convention.'* (Para. 4)

| 17 | Exchange of Information | *'The Contracting Parties shall <u>facilitate the exchange of information, from all publicly available sources</u>, relevant to the conservation and sustainable use of biological diversity, taking into account the special needs of developing countries.' (Para. 1)* |
| 17 | Exchange of Information | *'... exchange of information shall include exchange of results of technical, scientific and socio-economic research, as well as information on training and surveying programmes, <u>specialized knowledge, indigenous and traditional knowledge as such and in combination with [biotechnology]</u>. It shall also, where feasible, include <u>repatriation of information</u>.' (Para. 2)* |

respected, preserved and maintained merely *because* it is relevant to biodiversity conservation and sustainability; even less because some of it has industrial application. A great deal of traditional knowledge has no commercial potential whatsoever, but this does not make it any less worthy of respect or protection. The disappearance of traditional knowledge may be a tragedy for the world, but above all, it is a tragedy for those peoples and communities of the world that depend upon the integrity of their knowledge systems for their cultural and even physical survival (Dutfield 1999a).

ARTICLE 17

Article 17 deals with exchange of information *from all publicly available sources* relevant to conservation and sustainable use of biodiversity. Paragraph 2 specifically refers to specialized knowledge, indigenous and traditional knowledge as such and in combination with technologies including biotechnology, and also to the possibility of repatriation of information. This Article assumes that publicly available information should be freely exchanged. However, the intellectual property rights of indigenous and traditional communities have rarely been respected and a great deal of traditional knowledge was collected, recorded and placed in the public domain without their prior informed consent. Therefore, this Article should be implemented in ways consistent with and supportive of Article 8(j). So, for example, traditional knowledge holders should not be coerced or tricked into making their knowledge public and should be fully informed of the IPR-related and other consequences of doing so.

ARTICLE 15[4]

Article 15 on *Access to Genetic Resources* reaffirms the sovereign rights of states over their natural resources, an established principle of international law. Specifically, it also assigns to national governments the authority to determine access to genetic resources. Thus, such access is subject to the prior informed consent of the provider country and the fair and equitable sharing of benefits. National access/benefit-sharing (ABS) laws base their provisions upon such nation state sovereignty rights. For example, the preamble of the Philippines bioprospecting law[5] notes that the national constitution 'provides that wildlife, flora and fauna, among others, are owned by the State and the disposition, development and utilization thereof are under its full control and supervision'. According to the *Ley que Protege la Biodiversidad en el Ecuador*: 'The Ecuadorian State is the holder of the property rights over species that comprise the country's biodiversity, which are considered national properties and for public use.'[6] Costa Rica's *Ley de Biodiversidad* states that 'The State will exercise complete and exclusive sovereignty over the elements of biodiversity'.[7,8] By exercising such rights it is intended that these countries will be better able to capture the benefits from industrial use of their biogenetic resources while conserving and sustainably utilizing biodiversity.

Prima facie, this Article has little to do with information, knowledge or IPRs. In fact, it is central to the CBD and to these issues, strengthening – at least to a degree – the bargaining position of developing countries *vis-à-vis* developed countries and transnational corporations. This is well understood by a number of countries developing national and regional ABS legislation, such as the Andean Community member countries and Costa Rica. The Andean Community's *Common System on Access to Genetic Resources* and Costa Rica's new Biodiversity Law both to some extent subordinate IPRs to ABS regulations (see Chapter 8).[9]

Some indigenous peoples' organizations have expressed concern about this application of the national sovereignty principle to genetic resources (IAI-TPTF 1996; see also Dutfield 1997a). But a more commonly-held view in many developing countries is that governments must take control over genetic resources not so much for nationalistic reasons but because, if they do not, local communities will be even more vulnerable to the influence of transnational corporations than they are already (eg Gene Campaign and Forum for Biotechnology and Food Security 1997; Nijar 1996b). There is little doubt that governments are in a far stronger position to bargain with transnational corporations than domestic non-governmental institutions and local communities. On the other hand, a statist approach that assigns the gatekeeper role exclusively to government entities may not be the most efficient way to monitor a country's biological diversity, especially in areas inhabited by indigenous and local communities. It might well also lead to infringements of the legitimate entitlements of these communities. A decentralized approach that empowers democratic local-level institutions with at least some rights to control access and that encourages their participation is likely to be preferable. One might add that channelling the benefits from the trade in genetic resources to encourage environmentally-friendly practices through such institutions is much more likely to result in favourable outcomes than the more top-down and coercive conservation approaches that are still common in many parts of the world (see Colchester 1997; Pimbert and Pretty 1997).

NOTES

1 As of 15 January 1999 (including the European Community).

2 '[W]hen the Convention discusses knowledge, innovations and practices and entitles local and indigenous communities to be their *holders*, it links these concepts with the vocabulary for the definition of the proprietor of an intellectual property right' (Costa e Silva 1995) [emphasis in original].

3 A good example is the International Society for Ethnobiology's 'Code of Ethics and Standards of Practices', and the Biodiversity and Ethics Working Group of Pew Conservation Fellows' 'Proposed Guidelines for Researchers and Local Communities Interested in Accessing, Exploring and Studying Biodiversity'.

4 For the most comprehensive overview of the various possible approaches for implementing Article 15, see Glowka (1998).

5 Executive Order 247 ('Prescribing Guidelines and Establishing a Regulatory Framework for the Prospecting of Biological and Genetic Resources, Their By-Products and Derivatives, for Scientific and Commercial Purposes; and for Other Purposes').

6 'El Estado Ecuatoriano es el titular de los derechos de propiedad sobre las especies que integran la biodiversidad en el país, a las que se considerara como bienes nacionales y de uso publico' (Article 1).

7 'El Estado ejercerá la soberanía completa y exclusiva sobre los elementos de la biodiversidad' (Article 2).

8 It is perhaps more in keeping with the spirit of the CBD to affirm national patrimony over biodiversity rather than *full ownership* since the latter concept includes the absolute right to destroy (Lerch 1998).

9 In contrast, the Philippines' 1995 bioprospecting law deliberately kept IPRs outside its purview (C. Barber pers. comm.), although the law still has some implications for the exercise of IPRs (see Bragdon and Downes 1998).

5 IPRs and Biodiversity: Conflict or Synergy?

In view of the importance of IPRs in international trade, the role of transnational corporations in the negotiating history of the TRIPS Agreement, and the specific requirements it contains, it is hardly surprising that certain aspects of intellectual property rights have attracted a great deal of debate. The extension of the scope of patent rights to cover life-forms has aroused strong feelings among those who argue that it is immoral or unethical to 'own life'. These sentiments are expressed by people not just in developed countries where 'patenting life' is already quite common, but also in those developing countries where such patents are not yet allowed but might be in the near future. Equally strong sentiments are expressed by representatives of the life science firms who argue that such patents are essential to generate innovation in highly expensive and risky fields of scientific research. The question of whether IPRs support or undermine the three objectives of the CBD is shrouded in polemics to the extent that it is sometimes difficult to distinguish the truth from the rhetoric. It is upon this matter that this chapter will attempt to shed some light.

Some commentators feel that the availability of IPRs, especially patents, stimulates industrial interest in natural products. They argue that when linked to contracts or other agreements between genetic resource users and providers, IPRs can support national and local capacity building and conservation (eg Iwu 1996; Lesser 1998; Reid *et al* 1993). On the other hand, serious concerns have been expressed that IPRs and the extension of such rights to cover life-forms not only act as a disincentive to conserving biodiversity but are directly harmful to biodiversity. Box 5.1 summarizes the most common perspectives on the links between patent law and the objectives of the CBD.

Box 5.1 Summary of Perspectives on Links between Patents and the CBD's Objectives

Views on the relationships between the patent system and the CBD's objectives vary widely. It may be helpful to present some positions which may be referred to as: (a) the pro-patent view; (b) the anti-patent view; and (c) a pragmatic or sceptical realist view that lies somewhere between these perspectives.

(a) *The pro-patent view* is that the availability of patents *supports* the CBD's objectives because as long as corporations are free to apply for patents and other IPRs they will be more willing to invest in natural product research and to engage in benefit sharing arrangements with genetic resource providers, such as members of local communities. By these means, IPRs can help to provide incentives for sustainable development, conservation and sustainable use of biodiversity (Iwu 1996; Reid *et al* 1993). Moreover, corporations tend to be more willing to transfer proprietary technologies to countries where these technologies can be protected than to those where IPR protection is unavailable or inadequately enforced.

(b) *The anti-patent view* is that patents create perverse incentives which encourage the destruction of biodiversity, the monopolies they establish[1] are inherently unfair and/or immoral, and that they legitimate and support 'biopiracy' (the unauthorized commercial exploitation of the knowledge and biological resources of indigenous peoples and/ or developing countries). Many such critics in principle oppose the patenting of 'inventions' based closely on traditional knowledge even if the patent holders have undertaken to share benefits with the communities concerned.[2]

(c) *A pragmatic view* is that while there are serious difficulties with reconciling the CBD's objectives with TRIPS, yet implementation of the CBD cannot wait for a patent-free world, even assuming such a world were necessarily an improvement upon the existing one. Far better to work with existing IPR regimes or propose realistic reforms while remaining cognisant of the pitfalls and limitations of IPRs as means to further CBD implementation.

Attempts have been made to use patent law in pursuit of the objectives of the CBD. The case studies below describe agreements which recognize the rights of holders of traditional knowledge, while seeking to guarantee equitable benefit sharing and provide incentives for conservation and sustainable use of biodiversity. Case Study 5.1 presents an example from South India of an agreement involving a botanic garden, a pharmaceutical company and a tribal group. A major obstacle to the success of the agreement is the state government's failure to recognize the territorial and resource rights of the local people concerned. This is not the fault of the patent holding institution or the company, of course, but it underlines the fact that equitable benefit sharing and sustainable use of biodiversity cannot easily be achieved when such basic rights are not recognized.

CASE STUDY 5.1 THE KANI AND JEEVANI[3]

In 1995 the Tropical Botanic Garden Research Institute (TBGRI) of Trivandrum in Kerala State granted Arya Vaidya Pharmacy an exclusive seven-year licence to manufacture and sell a product based on extracts of a sub-species of the *Trichopus zeylanicus* plant called 'Jeevani'. Garden scientists learnt of the plant's health-giving properties from members of the tribal Kani people, who inhabit the forested Western Ghat region of the State (Pushpangadan *et al* 1998). It is clear that the TBGRI could negotiate such an agreement and share the resulting licence fee and royalties with the Kani *because* it owns a patent. Even though the TBGRI is the legal IPR-holder and its contracts are with the company and not with the Kani, its promise to share the licence fee and royalty payments with the Kani is a *de facto* recognition of the latter's IPRs. Two serious problems arise, however. First, although the Kani set up a trust registered with the State to receive the funds, they are dependent on the State government's consent to transfer the funds to the trust. The government was extremely slow to proceed, and the TBGRI – a public sector institution – was made to wait over three years for permission to make the transfer (Bagla 1999). Moreover, the Kerala Forest Department has even been requesting a share of the licence fee and royalties. Second, the Kani do not have legal title to the land they occupy, which belongs to the Forest Department, and the latter has prevented the Kanis from harvesting *Trichopus* growing in the locality. Outsiders attracted to the plant by the high prices are coming to the area and illegally uprooting *Trichopus* even though, as the Kani themselves are aware, the leaves can be picked without need for uprooting or killing the plant.

Case Study 5.2 shows how the IPRs of indigenous people can be protected through a non-IPR instrument (in this case a know-how licence) that is part of a broader arrangement allowing a pharmaceutical company to patent inventions related to the know-how of this indigenous group, but with certain agreed-upon restrictions attached to the right to patent. The success of the strategies described in these case studies arguably strengthens the position of those who feel there is much to gain by working within existing patent law. But those who are sceptical that such benefit sharing is really 'equitable', or who on principle oppose the patenting of 'inventions' based closely on traditional knowledge, are unlikely to concur. Proponents of the strategies described in these two case studies might counter that the community members themselves, if adequately informed, and not outsiders, should be the judges of how equitable or successful the agreements are. Nevertheless, one should still bear in mind the tremendous mismatch in bargaining power between an indigenous community and companies, especially large corporations with their own legal departments.

It may be concluded that such benefit sharing agreements are probably easier to achieve with medicinal plants and pharmaceuti-

---

CASE STUDY 5.2 THE AGUARUNAS AND THEIR KNOW-HOW AGREEMENT WITH SEARLE

Legally-binding agreements such as contracts and licences can be used to guarantee benefit sharing with local communities. In Peru, the Aguaruna people have negotiated a know-how licence with Searle (the pharmaceutical division of Monsanto). The Aguaruna pass on medicinal plants and knowledge (ie 'know-how') to the company and in exchange receive an annual know-how licence fee. This fee will increase to reflect success in research and development even before a product ever reaches the market. Such payments are often referred to as milestone payments. The licence is non-exclusive in that it does not affect the right of any Aguaruna communities to use, share or sell or otherwise transfer plants or knowledge whether or not they are parties to the agreement. According to Brendan Tobin, legal counsel for the Aguarunas, a trust fund will be established to distribute the benefits, and a board appointed to administer the fund from within the Aguaruna people including representatives of both participating and non-participating communities (Tobin 1997a).

One of the main advantages of such an arrangement is that legal ownership of biological resources is not a precondition for the communities to benefit. The agreement implicitly accepts their property rights over knowledge *about* the resources irrespective of whether they legally own them.

---

cals than with seeds and plant varieties. Whereas a new medicine is likely to be derived from a single active principle isolated from a particular species or at least a mixture of a small number of plants, a new plant variety may descend from dozens of varieties from many dispersed locations. Compensating many countries and/or communities will involve much higher transaction costs and the share of benefits to each recipient is likely to be correspondingly modest.

This chapter considers possible conflicts and synergies between certain characteristics or effects of IPRs and achievement of the CBD's three objectives by investigating relationships IPRs on the one hand and (i) conservation and sustainable use of biodiversity; (ii) transfers of technologies relevant to conservation and sustainable use of biodiversity; and (iii) the rights of traditional knowledge holders.

LINKS BETWEEN IPRS AND CONSERVATION AND SUSTAINABLE USE OF BIODIVERSITY

Assertions have been made that there is a link between the availability and adoption of patent or plant breeders' right protection, and the replacement in many areas of the world of complex, diverse agroecosystems containing a wide range of traditional crop varieties with monocultures of single agrochemical-dependent varieties.[4] This section will address this issue first with reference to IPRs in general, especially patents, and then specifically to plant breeders' (or plant variety) right protection.

Before continuing, it needs to be understood that this is a highly complex issue, and an objective evaluation of the various assertions frequently made pro and contra IPRs is hard to achieve when there is such a dearth of reliable empirical evidence (as opposed to anecdotal evidence and pure speculation). What can be presumed with some certainty is that it is most unlikely that the erosion of agro-biodiversity can be attributed to a single cause such as IPRs. In fact, one recent study of the relationships between biodiversity and agriculture does not implicate IPRs at all, whether as a proximate or an underlying cause of agro-biodiversity erosion (see Table 5.1). Nevertheless, the vital importance of this issue merits careful consideration of the arguments presented by commentators who maintain that IPRs do indeed provide perverse incentives which encourage activities that are prejudicial to biodiversity.

Patents and IPRs in general

The following two sets of questions need to be considered:

1   Do intellectual property rights encourage the spread of monocultural agriculture? And if so, does this cause erosion of biodiversity?
2   Is the increasing production and sale of seed-agrochemical 'packages' (such as transgenic crops sold with pesticides and/or herbicides for which they have built-in resistance) harmful to biodiversity? And if so, are IPRs an inducement for companies to produce these kinds of 'package'? In other words, is this an IPR issue?

IPRs and monocultures

With respect to the first set of questions, one of the most plausible critiques of IPRs is by Walter Reid (1992), who identifies a strong connection between IPRs and a bias towards centralized research, and believes that this has an impact on agro-biodiversity.[5] He finds that the prevailing policy framework for the use of genetic resources for food and agriculture favours 'centralised crop breeding and the creation of uniform environmental conditions, and discourages agro-ecological research or local breeding tailored to local conditions.' IPRs enhance incentives to develop seeds that will have a large potential demand. To ensure maximum demand for their products, the seed companies will tend to focus their research on commonly utilized high-value crops and develop varieties that can be cultivated as widely as possible. To do so means either breeding through

Table 5.1 *Addressing causes of biodiversity losses linked to agriculture*

Problems	Proximate causes	Underlying causes (for all problems)
Erosion of genetic resources (livestock and plants) • Leads to disease/ insect pests • Loss of insect diversity	Spread of High Yielding Varieties (HYVs) and monocultures Biases in breeding methods Weak conservation methods	Demographic changes Industrial/Green Revolution Model that stresses uniformity Disparities in resource distribution and in control of land Pressures and influences of seed/agrochemical companies Policies that support HYVs, uniformity and chemicals (subsidies, credit, market standards) Producers/companies focus on short-term returns to neglect of longer-term social factors Disrespect for local knowledge and structural inequities
Erosion of insect diversity	Heavy use of pesticides Use of monocultures Loss of organic material	Policies that support HYVs, uniformity and chemicals (subsidies, credit, market standards) Demographic changes
Erosion of soil diversity • Leads to fertility loss • Productivity decline	Heavy use of agrochemicals Poor tillage practices Use of monocultures	Policies that support HYVs, uniformity and chemicals (subsidies, credit, market standards) Demographic changes
Erosion of habitat diversity (social and private costs)	Extensification in marginal land Drift/spillover from chemicals	Demographic changes
Erosion of indigenous methods for using agrodiversity	Replacement by uniform species	Disrespect for local knowledge and structural inequities

Source: Derived from Thrupp (1997), with changes suggested by Takase (pers comm 1998)

selection of genes for maximum adaptability, or introducing the new seeds while also promoting farming practices that reduce environmental heterogeneity. The biodiversity-erosive effects of this IPR-supported bias towards centralized crop breeding programmes are: (i) decreased crop diversity; (ii) decreased spatial genetic diversity; (iii) increased temporal genetic diversity;[6] and (iv) increased use of external inputs.

It is important to point out that monocultural agricultural systems are not inherently biodiversity-erosive. It is true that they may cause biodiversity loss if they replace more biologically-diverse ecosystems. But *if* a monocultural system produces higher yields per harvest and/or more harvests per year compared to a more polycultural agro-ecosystem it replaced, pressure to open up biologically-diverse ecosystems to cultivation *may* be reduced as a consequence.

Kothari and Anuradha (1997) conclude that IPRs alone cannot be held responsible for the loss of agro-biodiversity, but that IPRs are bound to encourage the displacement of a wide diversity of traditional local varieties in favour of a small number of widely adapted hybrids and homogeneous modern varieties. Moreover, they point out that one of the lessons of the Green Revolution is that the development of new varieties by the seed industry is unlikely to match the loss of traditional varieties after these new varieties are introduced.

IPRs and crop-agrochemical linkages

With respect to the second set of questions, it is true that seed companies often develop hybrids and other modern varieties that depend upon applications of agrochemicals (such as fertilizers, herbicides and insecticides) to achieve high yields. A common accusation is that excessive use of these chemicals is encouraged and other plants growing nearby are killed as a result. However, IPRs are unlikely to be directly responsible for this trend in crop breeding, which dates back to the time when the Green Revolution began, and earlier still in some countries. The Green Revolution is frequently blamed for the development and spread during the 1950s and 1960s of high-yielding wheat and rice varieties requiring heavy applications of agrochemicals, but the varieties most commonly associated with the Green Revolution were developed by public crop breeding institutions and were not IPR protected.

However, the IPR link appears stronger in the case of genetically modified crops. In recent years, life-science corporations (often originally chemical companies that have bought seed companies) have increasingly been creating transgenic plants with built-in resistance either to herbicides marketed by the same company (see Bell 1996; Kloppenburg 1988) or to insect pests. In the former case, both the herbicide and the seed for which it is designed are likely to be patent-protected. For example, the development of Monsanto's Roundup Ready soybeans, canola and cotton has enabled the market for Roundup herbicide to expand at a time when the patent on the latter product is soon to expire (McNally and Wheale 1996). Monsanto's patent on the gene for Roundup resistance and all plants containing this gene has many more years to run, and Roundup Ready seed buyers are contractually obliged to purchase Roundup herbicide as part of the 'package'. An example of a crop with built-in resistance to a pest (rather than a herbicide or pesticide) is Monsanto's NewLeaf potato, which claims to provide *total* protection against the Colorado beetle (Magretta 1997). Another is Novartis' patented Bt corn, which is designed to resist the European corn borer pest.[7]

The position of the large life-science corporations such as Monsanto and Novartis is that genetic engineering can reduce or even obviate pesticide use. Monsanto's claim is that when they produce packages of herbicides and plants resistant to these herbicides, their aim is not to ensure that farmers will need to increase herbicide use. Their main interest is to ensure that farmers use *their* herbicides. If these are more effective than alternative products, overall herbicide use may decrease. According to the company, 'Roundup herbicide can reduce the number of weed treatments and can also help reduce tillage to conserve soil moisture and reduce erosion of valuable topsoil'.[8]

Environmentalists and some scientists counter that genetically-engineered herbicide resistance has negative environmental effects.[9] Among the claims commonly made are that use of herbicide-resistant transgenic plants may: (a) encourage excessive use of herbicides which may kill other plant varieties and species (Bell 1996); (b) accelerate the development of resistance among pests (Jenkins 1998); and (c) create the possibility of herbicide resistant genes crossing over to other plants including the weeds being targeted. This could create 'superweeds' which would render the herbicide ineffective in the long term, and cause ecological impacts that cannot easily be predicted. It may also be possible that transgenic plants themselves could become 'weeds' if the added characteristic gives them a competitive advantage over neighbouring wild species (de Kathen 1996), though this is unlikely in the case of the most highly domesticated crop species. Some critics also allege that herbicides are far more toxic than the manufacturer companies are willing to admit, and that the health of both farmers and consumers could be affected (McNally and Wheale 1996; Tappeser and von Weizsäcker 1996).

Concerns are also expressed that increased use of hybrids and other modern varieties specifically designed for use with other proprietary agricultural inputs such as fertilizers and pesticides may have serious social impacts, especially in developing countries. These crop-herbicide-pesticide linkages can be considered to represent a shift towards capital intensive agriculture that increases the costs of farming and may therefore be detrimental to small farmers (Verma 1995). Consequently, critics maintain that farmers must have the right to choose whether or not to accept these packages and should not be subjected to aggressive sales promotion campaigns.

Even if we accept that these concerns are well-founded, are IPRs implicated just because plants (whether transgenic or not), herbicides and pesticides can be patented? Corporations in these technological fields tend to claim that without IPR protection they would have no incentive to invent or to innovate. This suggests that these products would not exist without IPRs. But this does not mean that the national patent office is the appropriate place to deal with marketing approval for such products. Most countries have an agency with jurisdiction over such matters, and such a body is probably much better placed than the patent office to decide whether plant-herbicide-pesticide packages are in the public interest or not.

A more indirect way that IPRs may encourage such allegedly environmentally-unfriendly R&D is that IPRs are sometimes said to stimulate industrial restructuring in ways that make such R&D more attractive to industry than it would otherwise be. Two US rural sociologists, Frederick Buttel and Jill Belsky, argued (1987), for example, that the 1970 US Plant Variety Protection Act increased expectations of seed industry profits and thereby helped to stimulate an upsurge in acquisitions and mergers involving seed companies such that many seed producers became subsidiaries of large agrochemical firms. These:

> *multinational parents of seed companies have larger fertiliser, herbicide, insecticide, and fungicide product lines that generally are far more important in terms of total revenue and profit than are seeds…[a]ccordingly, many agrochemical-based seed company subsidiaries might be hesitant to emphasise plant breeding goals that would threaten fertiliser and pesticide product lines.* (ibid)

Consequently:

> *a substantial amount of plant research in private firms has been aimed at developing various types of seed-chemical packages that reinforce rather than threaten sales of agricultural chemicals.* (ibid; see also Sehgal 1996)

The so-called 'terminator technology' patent (Case Study 5.3) has aroused tremendous controversy following allegations that the widespread application of such technologies – known as Variety-specific Genetic Use Restriction Technologies (V-GURTs) – would threaten the customary seed saving and exchanging practices of traditional farming communities throughout the world. The technology has already been condemned by the Indian government because of its alleged social and economic impacts on farmers. In this case, it is not so much the patent that has been criticized as the technology that it describes. Even so, this case is a TRIPS-related issue. As stated earlier, TRIPS Article 27.2 allows countries to exclude from patentability inventions whose commercial exploitation must be prevented to protect *ordre public* or morality, but such exclusion cannot be made 'merely because the exploitation is prohibited by law'. This means that a decision by a country to ban the technology is insufficient in itself to permit the country to exclude the technology from patentability. In addition, the government could be called upon to provide an explanation of why commercial use of the technology is either immoral or contrary to *ordre public*. Of course, even if the patent is granted, the patent will have no value in a country where the technology it describes is illegal. Yet, the patent owners might still be able to contest the ban on the grounds that it is a barrier to trade that conflicts with the WTO's rules. In such a case, the government concerned could use the *ordre public* exclusion to demonstrate that such a ban conforms to GATT Article XX and is therefore legal.[10]

Environmental objections to the technology so far are purely speculative. Even so, the patent was discussed at the 4th meeting of the Conference of the Parties (COP) to the CBD, and referred to in the Decision on agricultural biodiversity.[11] In the context of the precautionary approach, the COP requested the Subsidiary Body on Scientific, Technical and Technological Advice (SBSTTA) to:

consider and assess, in light of contributions to be provided by Parties, Governments and organizations, whether there are any consequences for the conservation and sustainable use of biological diversity from the development and use of new technology for the control of gene expression, such as that described in United States patent 5723765, and to elaborate scientifically based advice to the COP.

In a recent submission to the WTO's Committee on Trade and Environment, the Secretariat of the CBD (WTO 1998) states that:

The possible outcome from this decision [ie IV/6 on Agricultural Biological Diversity] ... could include consideration of ways in which the environmental soundness of a technology can be properly assessed in the process of granting a patent.

Burdening the patent system in this way may not be the most appropriate or effective approach. The award of a patent is not in itself an authorization to commercialize the technology, product or process, and patent offices are not usually required to evaluate technologies described in patent applications in terms of their environmental soundness anyway. Indeed, patent offices are not the right places for such evaluations to be made since decisions on allowing or banning technologies should ideally be made in open and democratic forums, which patent offices are clearly not meant to be.[12] The relevant technology assessment/regulatory agencies are probably in a better position to call upon greater expertise anyway.

It seems likely that a range of similar genetic technologies will be developed and adopted in the coming years. In June 1999 an expert paper (Jefferson *et al* 1999) annexed to a report prepared by the CBD Secretariat (1999) was presented and discussed at the 4th meeting of SBSTTA. The paper drew a distinction between Variety-specific GURTs and Trait-specific GURTs (T-GURTs), which are also technically feasible. The terminator technology is an example of the former since it prevents a variety from being propagated by farmers without seed purchase. T-GURTS would be somewhat more benign from the farmers' position in that only the value-added transgenic trait developed by the company would be protected. Farmers would have to pay to activate the trait but would not be prevented from planting harvested seed.

Plant Variety Rights

With respect to plant variety rights, two criticisms are sometimes made about the UPOV Convention based on the requirement that protected varieties must be distinct, stable, uniform and novel. The first concerns the uniformity/homogeneity and stability requirements, the second is based on the distinctness and novelty criteria.

First, although it is easier and less expensive to acquire a plant variety right than a patent[13] – so it is conceivable that local communities could apply for a plant variety certificate for some of their crop varieties[14] – the uniformity/homogeneity and stability requirements mean that only breeders of genetically uniform varieties can use the system. Local communities, whose landraces (or traditional cultivars) may be rich in intra-varietal genetic diversity (due in part to the preference of communities for versatility and adaptability), are unable to acquire protection because of this genetic diversity. Not only is this inequitable, but as an incentive to breed genetically-uniform varieties, it is alleged that the Convention is in conflict with the aims of the CBD.

Second, it is sometimes suggested that the distinctness and novelty standards are too low. Given that professional breeders can be expected to have far greater financial resources, legal experience and scientific facilities than local communities, there is a danger that traditional cultivars will be misappropriated with minimal if any modification. For example, the Canadian NGO RAFI claims to have uncovered 147 cases of mostly public institutions seeking PBR protection for varieties acquired from the CGIAR network (RAFI 1998b,c,d). Many of these varieties, it is alleged, are landraces that have been subjected to little, if any, additional breeding. Moreover, since landraces are usually acquired from *ex situ* collections rather than from the farmers directly, benefit sharing with the original providers is precluded.

In response to the first criticism, the point about the inequity of

CASE STUDY 5.3 THE TECHNOLOGY PROTECTION SYSTEM ('TERMINATOR TECHNOLOGY')[15] PATENT

In March 1998, the US Department of Agriculture (USDA) and Delta & Pine Land Co were awarded a US patent entitled 'Control of plant gene expression'. Applications are pending in *at least 78 other countries*. The technology described in the patent can produce transgenic plants with a 'lethal gene' whose seeds are incapable of germinating. According to the patent, 'in this way, accidental reseeding, escape of the crop plant to areas outside the area of cultivation, or germination of stored seed can be avoided.' The main purpose of the technology is to make it impossible for farmers to save, replant or sell seed. Consequently, farmers will have to purchase seeds at the start of each growing season as they already (usually) have to do with hybrids.[16] According to a spokesman from the USDA, the aim is for the technology to be 'widely licensed and made expeditiously available to many seed companies' in order 'to increase the value of proprietary seed owned by US seed companies and to open up markets in Second and Third World countries'. The President of Delta & Pine Land told RAFI that the patent 'has the prospect of opening significant worldwide seed markets to the sale of transgenic technology for crops in which seed currently is saved and used in subsequent plantings.'

The development of this technology seems to reflect the increased determination of the private sector (in this case with the assistance of a public agency) to eliminate the replanting of proprietary seeds, which is also reflected in licensing agreements that forbid customers to save and replant their patent-protected seeds. Such agreements would of course become unnecessary if this technology became widely used.

The patent and the technology protection system were swiftly condemned by Third World activists and their supporters as well as some Northern farmers. According to Farhad Mazhar of the South Asian Network for Food, Ecology and Culture, 'this patent is profoundly immoral. It will fundamentally change both the biology and economics of agriculture to the detriment of the poor.' Camila Montecinos of the Centro de Educación y Tecnología (Chile) denounced it as 'an immoral technique that robs farming communities of their age-old right to save seed and their role as plant breeders'.

The technology has obvious attractions for seed companies concerned to protect their non-hybrid proprietary seed products. It seems likely, then, that it will be widely used once it comes on the market, especially for seeds sold in countries where it is difficult to prevent seed saving. So do farmers in developing countries stand to benefit from wider use of the technology? The inventors argue that the technology will encourage greater investment in the development of new varieties of self-pollinated crops like wheat and barley for which hybridization is economically unattractive. Moreover, investment may also be encouraged in crops for which the existing market is quite small. If it is true that seed-saving discourages breeders from producing new varieties, then the inventors may be right. However, critics counter that even if they are right about this, such additional investments will not *on balance* benefit farmers in developing countries. This is due to the serious socio-economic effects they predict will follow if the technology is widely adopted. At a time when commercial seed companies dominate seed supply in the North and are increasing their activities in the South, the critics argue that companies armed with this technology could eliminate the age-old practice of seed saving which enables hundreds of millions of resource-poor farmers and farming communities to subsist.

An interesting possibility, though, is that if saving seeds from harvested varieties is precluded entirely, local communities will be encouraged to return to their traditional cultivars (assuming they still exist). Just as breeders need to use proprietary seeds as raw materials in the development of new varieties, many local communities also practise breeding in the field using both modern varieties and landraces. Being unable to save seed to breed from makes this more difficult and may act as a further disincentive to purchase technology protected seed.

In October 1998, the Consultative Group on International Agricultural Research (CGIAR) pledged not to develop crops using this technology. According to a Reuters report dated 30 October 1998, Ismail Serageldin, Chairman of the CGIAR, said that 'crops with such "suicidal tendencies" would be a nightmare in the developing world, where farmers, as a matter of course, retain part of each harvest as seed for next year'. He was also reported as saying that instead of using the technology, 'the group preferred to focus on high-yielding, disease-resistant plant varieties that retain their vigour for generations – a boon to poor farmers who cannot afford to buy seed and whose best hope for higher income is to boost output.' One might add that such varieties should require a minimum of chemical and other expensive inputs.

the system could be rebutted by saying that there is little if any evidence that local communities are interested in acquiring plant variety protection for their cultivars. Moreover, while traditional cultivars may contain *characteristics* with widespread utility (and characteristics *per se* cannot be the subject of a plant variety right), it is not necessarily true that landraces are more versatile and adaptable than modern varieties. Landraces may be suitable only in highly localized conditions, in which case they are unlikely to have enough commercial potential to justify seeking IPR protection. In any case, commercial breeders are deterred from using landraces by the amount of extraneous genetic material which must be bred out of them before the desirable attributes can be used.

With respect to the allegation that the Convention provides incentives that are inimical to biodiversity, if there are such perverse incentives, it is not so much because of any encouragement to breed uniform varieties *per se*, but because these varieties cause loss of biodiversity through their widespread cultivation and/or their forming monocultures in places that previously were more genetically diverse. This is a very complex issue, but for the allegation to have merit, *minimally* the following propositions would need to be true: (a) that the widespread cultivation of new varieties instead of landraces is driven by the independent decisions of breeders to develop varieties that are popular with as many farmers as possible *because* they can be cultivated widely and/or grow best in monocultural conditions; and (b) that these decisions would not be made if plant variety protection were unavailable. In fact, these decisions are not made independently. Commercial breeders must respond to the demands of farmers, who in turn must heed market signals from consumers, food retailers or other purchasers or users of their crops. According to a preliminary study produced for the Secretariat of the CBD for consideration of the 3rd meeting of the COP (CBD Secretariat 1996a), other policies that might encourage the use of new crop varieties and the loss of landraces include: (a) government farm credits and subsidies, and extension services; (b) the policies and programmes of international agencies and donor institutions; (c) the marketing and research and development policies and programmes of transnational corporations; and (d) the increasingly concentrated corporate control of pesticide and agro-biotechnology research and distribution. It is worth adding here that the trend towards cultivation of genetically uniform varieties is due also to the seed certification requirements of many countries. Often these apply more stringent uniformity standards than even the UPOV Convention (Louwaars 1999).

In response to the second criticism of the Convention, the novelty criterion makes clear that varieties cannot be protected if they have been bred by others. Given the relative ease of acquiring plant variety rights as compared to patents, the less rigorous novelty criterion, and the fact that there is no prior art search, it is of course possible for a landrace (or a variety resulting from a mere 'cleaning' of a landrace) to 'slip through the net'. However, given the general lack of commercial potential for landraces and their immediate derivatives, this is probably not a significant concern, especially when we consider that the vast majority of the 40,000 or so plant variety titles in force worldwide are the result of breeding work done on commercial varieties of a previous generation.

In short, it seems impossible to prove that the UPOV Convention provides any significant perverse incentives for biodiversity loss. The problem for critics is the lack of systematic empirical studies on both patents and plant variety rights. One of the few is a study on the relationships between stronger IPR protection and seed supply in five Latin American countries[17] which attempted to clarify:

> *the effects of plant variety rights on: (i) investments in plant breeding in private seed companies; (ii) international transfer of plant material; (iii) access to public germplasm; and (iv) the distribution of seed among farmers (Jaffé and van Wijk 1995; van Wijk 1995b).*

The study found that in Argentina, where plant variety owners enforce their rights themselves and have done so effectively in recent years,[18] during the early 1990s breeders experienced an increased flow of royalties as the unauthorized seed trade plummeted. Although the companies themselves expressed uncertainty that the increased R&D during this time was a consequence of the enhanced royalty receipts, they tended to agree that plant variety right protection had maintained some breeding programmes that might otherwise have been reduced or even abandoned.

With respect to exotic germplasm, it was not clear that stronger plant variety right protection had increased the diversity of plant material available to breeders, seed traders and farmers. IPR protection in the recipient country seemed to facilitate the acquisition of breeding lines and high quality propagating material from developed countries, but is irrelevant in the case of germplasm from the International Agricultural Research Centres since these institutions have a policy of not claiming IPR protection over the varieties they hold (see p105). However, companies with licences from overseas breeders to produce proprietary varieties may sometimes have to contend with parallel import restrictions. For example, in 1994 Argentinean strawberry plant growers were forbidden to export their plants to Europe because the US breeder and the European licensees did not want these plants to compete with those that were already produced in Europe (ibid).

Increasingly the public agricultural research centres in all five countries are using plant variety right law to protect their new varieties. Van Wijk assumes (but without producing any conclusive evidence) that dependence on the commercial success of these varieties and increasing instances of joint research projects with the private sector will probably restrict free access to their varieties.

As to seed saving and the seed trade black market, the former is still permitted in all five countries whereas the latter is illegal everywhere (but only in Argentina is it effectively enforced). IPR legislation in most of these countries, then, has not prevented exchanges of seeds harvested by farmers. This of course may change if enforcement is tightened up. Van Wijk (1996) expects that flows of improved genetic material *will* increase in line with stronger IPR protection, but believes that while commercial farmers might benefit from this, middle and lower income farmers are less likely to because of the restrictions on seed saving and exchanging.

Van Wijk identifies three advantages of seed saving and 'informal exchange' for middle and low income farmers:

1 *Lower seed costs*
   This is certainly the case for self-pollinating crops and may sometimes be true for hybrids. However, van Wijk concedes that

'the cost advantage of saving seed is eroded by the deterioration of saved seed, causing yield losses over time. Deterioration is especially rapid with hybrids, but even here, the wide gap between new seed prices and the cost of seed-saving has encouraged some farmers in Latin America to save hybrid maize for a second generation'. It must be borne in mind, though, that the purchase of seed is one among several agricultural inputs that must be paid for, and even poor farmers may decide to pay a higher price for better quality seed if they expect a bigger harvest to result.

2 *Access to informal credit*
Sometimes grain dealers provide farmers with high grade seed not for cash but as credit in kind which can be paid off at harvest time with double the quantity of grain received by the farmer.

3 *As a check against seed price increases*
If seed companies try to raise prices, farmers can respond by increasing their seed saving.

Given that breeders are unlikely to find such activities acceptable, it seems probable that sooner or later they will unite to form an association and enforce their legal rights. However, it may be that the further spread of hybrids[19,20] and the wider use by seed companies of seed purchase/licensing agreements[21] and production contracts (Hamilton 1994) will eliminate illicit seed trading and on-farm seed-saving if breeders fail to achieve this through stronger and more enforceable IPR protection.

In conclusion, there is a clear need for further research and case studies that clarify the links between IPRs and biodiversity erosion. However, the evidence so far indicates that IPRs are at most one of several factors that together cause biodiversity erosion. Even so, the very possibility of grave negative environmental and social impacts justifies serious consideration of how the precautionary principle might be applied in the IPR context.

IPRs AND TRANSFER OF TECHNOLOGIES RELEVANT TO CONSERVATION AND SUSTAINABLE USE OF BIODIVERSITY

Technology transfer is a complex matter which lies mostly outside our subject-area. However, in the context of this study, elucidating the links between IPRs and transfer of relevant technologies requires brief consideration of three related questions:

1 Does the existence of effective IPR protection in recipient countries on balance facilitate, hinder or have no effect on the transfer of technologies?

2   What categories of technology are relevant to the conservation and sustainable use of biological diversity or make use of genetic resources and do not cause significant damage to the environment?

3   To what extent are these technologies in the public domain and freely accessible anyway?

Technology transfer and developing countries: general observations

First it is important to be clear what is meant by 'technologies', and then to outline the mechanisms by which they are normally transferred. According to Crespi and Straus (1996), technologies are 'industrial and agricultural processes and products, and the relevant enabling technology for practical realisation'. Technologies may also be conceived as a range of elements such as 'knowledge about plant design, process know-how, plant construction, feasibility studies, production management, marketing, distribution, and so on' (CBD Secretariat 1996b). An implicit presumption in the CBD is that technology transfers must take place in a North–South direction. However, the Convention also acknowledges the existence of 'indigenous and traditional technologies', which probably flow in a less predictable pattern, but are quite likely often to be South–North. In the biodiversity context traditional technologies include the following: (i) know-how concerning preparation, processing, or storage of useful species; (ii) knowledge of formulations involving more than one ingredient; (iii) knowledge of individual species (planting methods, care, selection criteria, etc); (iv) knowledge of ecosystem conservation (methods of protecting or preserving a resource that may be found to have commercial value); and (v) classification systems of knowledge, such as traditional plant taxonomies (Posey and Dutfield 1996).

Industrial technologies are conventionally transferred through such formalized means as: foreign direct investment (FDI); turnkey projects; joint ventures; wholly owned subsidiaries; licensing; technical-service arrangements; joint R&D arrangements; training; information exchanges; sales contracts; and management contracts (CBD Secretariat 1996b). Of these, FDI accounts for over 60 per cent of technology transfer flows to developing countries (ibid). However, norms for the transfer of indigenous and traditional technologies are still in a process of development, though protocols, research guidelines, codes of ethics, standards of practice, contracts, know-how licences and material transfer agreements are increasingly being used.

IPRs are relevant to all of these mechanisms of technology transfer though not of course to every transfer. According to the CBD, access to and transfer of technology must be 'provided and/or facilitated under fair and most favourable terms' but:

where subject to patents and other intellectual property rights, such access and transfer shall be provided on terms which recognize and are consistent with the adequate and effective protection of intellectual property rights (Article 16.2).

The private sector plays a key role in technology transfer, yet it is governments that are required to implement the CBD. Therefore, while governments can act as facilitators[22] by, for example, helping to build capacity and providing financing so that developing countries are in a position to make best use of technologies transferred to them, the providers of technologies will mostly be companies.

The extent to which effective IPR protection in recipient countries facilitates, hinders or has no effect on the transfer of technologies is difficult to ascertain. If we limit our discussion to biotechnology, since R&D costs can be enormous and the marginal costs of copying the resulting products may be extremely low, it seems logical that IPR availability would be a prerequisite, at least with proprietary technologies. Companies take the position that they cannot be expected to give away or license cheaply technologies that have cost them millions of dollars to develop. Following this argument, the only way that companies would have an incentive to transfer proprietary technologies is by having the freedom to charge licence fees high enough to reflect the costs of innovation, or alternatively by means of FDI or joint ventures where they would remain in control of these technologies.

However, a counter-argument can be made that the *overall* effect of IPRs will inhibit technology transfers and thus make it harder for provider countries to add value to their genetic resources. The views of the critics who argue that IPRs inhibit technology transfer and reinforce North–South inequalities can be summarized as follows: As an intervention in the free market, patents restrict the number of people who could otherwise freely make, use, sell or import the protected products and processes, and enable owners to avoid a situation where the price of their products or processes is driven down towards the marginal cost of reproduction. But just as the geographical distribution of biodiversity-richness is heavily skewed in favour of technologically poor developing countries, the global distribution of patent owners is unbalanced, this time in favour of developed countries. Patent Cooperation Treaty statistics show that the vast majority of 'world patents' are filed and held by companies based in North America, Western Europe or Japan (Table 5.2). Since such companies are the main users of patent protection and will at least in the short term be the major beneficiaries of new patent laws in developing countries, critics might argue that the best way for developing countries to acquire technologies and ensure that the products derived from these technologies are affordable to poor people may be either through compulsory licensing (see page 23, above) or non-recognition of patents.

Table 5.2 *Geographical origin of Patent Cooperation Treaty patent applications filed in 1997*

Region	Country	Number of patents filed	Percentage of total
North America	US	22,736	41.78
	Canada	1,075	1.98
Total North America		*23,811*	*43.76*
Western Europe/EU	Germany	7,436	13.66
	UK	3,939	7.24
	France	2,496	4.59
	Sweden	2,188	4.02
	Netherlands	1,749	3.21
	Switzerland	1,101	2.02
	Finland	873	1.60
	Italy	797	1.46
	Denmark	642	1.18
	Austria	373	0.69
	Norway	367	0.67
	Other	867	1.59
Total Western Europe/EU		*22,828*	*41.93*
East Asia and China	Japan	4,845	8.90
	South Korea	304	0.56
	China	157	0.29
Total East Asia and China		*5,306*	*9.75*
Eastern Europe	Russia	419	0.77
	Other	313	0.58
Total Eastern Europe		*732*	*1.35*
Australasia	Australia	881	1.62
	New Zealand	166	0.31
Total Australasia		*1,047*	*1.93*
All other regions		*698*	*1.28*
Total number of applications		**54,422**	**100.0**

Source: Derived from figures published on World Intellectual Property Organization website

Moreover, the concentration of technology ownership is becoming even more skewed as large corporations in the life science/biotechnology sectors increasingly access rival companies' IPR-protected technologies through cross-licensing, or by purchasing or merging with these companies. Such life science giants as Monsanto and Novartis, which dominate more than one industrial field, are the result of mergers and acquisitions involving companies in such sectors as chemicals, seeds, biotech and pharmaceuticals (see Kloppenburg 1988; Sehgal 1996; Suppan 1998). Thus, there has been a concentration of high-value IPR-protected technologies and products in the hands of a small number of conglomerates with annual turnovers higher than the GNPs of several developing countries. Given the economic power of these companies it may be more difficult than ever for developing countries to negotiate favourable terms for technology acquisition, though it must be conceded that empirical data are lacking to prove this assumption.

Empirical studies on the links between stronger IPRs, investment flows, R&D and technology transfers have proved inconclusive. A study by Keith Maskus (1998) claimed some evidence of a positive correlation, while conceding that IPRs are one of several factors that may enhance technology transfers, and also that strengthening IPRs can involve costs as well as benefits for developing countries (see also UNCTAD 1996a; World Bank 1998). A World Bank study was even more cautious and recommended further research before firm conclusions could be made (Primo Braga and Fink 1999). Evidence from Turkey (Kirim 1985) found that the banning of pharmaceutical patents appeared to have no significant effects on levels of direct foreign investment, technology transfers or domestic innovation. Similarly, Kondo (1995), taking manufacturing industry as a whole, found no evidence to support the notion that foreign direct investment levels in Brazil are greatly affected by patent protection.

It is sometimes suggested that one reason why patents facilitate technology dissemination is that most patents are no longer in force and the described inventions are therefore in the public domain. For this reason texts of expired patents constitute a storehouse of non-proprietary technical information. This is basically true, but it is important to be cognizant of two facts.

First, it may not be the case that a patent fully discloses the invention to the extent that a person skilled in the art can manufacture it. Moreover, 'in the public domain' is not synonymous with 'freely available'. According to Stuart Macdonald of Sheffield University (1998):

> *Legal fiction maintains that all the information needed to re-create the invention is contained in the patent specification. The fact is that the specification is forced to refer again and again to other information, information that is in the*

> *public domain, which means that it is available somewhere but must be acquired from these sources before the information in the specification can be used. Much of this information will be tacit and uncodified information [ie know-how].*

Moreover, 'the information contained in patent specifications is available only to those who consult them directly, or who pay others more adept at arcane classifications and the language of lawyers to do so' (ibid).

Second, many developing countries lack the institutional capacity enabling them to harness and apply new technologies (CBD Secretariat 1996b). Building such capacity is of course a priority, but the assessment of indigenous and traditional technologies existing domestically should not be overlooked either. In many cases, these may be more appropriate and will almost certainly be less expensive.

Transfer of CBD-related technologies

With respect to technologies relevant to the conservation and sustainable use of biological diversity, which make use of genetic resources, and/or do not cause significant damage to the environment, there seems to be general agreement that many of them are already in the public domain (FAO 1996; Juma et al 1994; WTO-CTE 1996a), either because the patents have expired or because they were never IPR-protected anyway. The note by the Secretariat of the CBD to the 2nd meeting of the Subsidiary Body on Scientific, Technical and Technological Advice (SBSTTA) refers to *in situ* and *ex situ* conservation technologies and sustainable use technologies (CBD Secretariat 1996b). Often these are interlinked or even identical.

In situ conservation and sustainable use technologies include aerial survey equipment, Geographic Information Systems, fencing equipment, and 'technologies associated with low-external input agriculture, integrated pest management, re-vegetation and other on-farm management techniques' (ibid). Soft technologies may take the form of 'know-how, management routines, and behavioural patterns and attitudes' (ibid). *Ex situ* conservation and sustainable use technologies include 'tissue culture, field-based propagation, protoplast fusion, and cryopreservation' (ibid). Common mechanisms for transferring such technologies include: 'joint R&D, the training of nationals in foreign universities and other institutions, [and] technology partnerships undertaken under biodiversity-prospecting arrangements' (ibid). In addition, organizations exist that provide technology transfer brokerage services.[23]

In spite of this section's emphasis on public domain technologies and knowledge, the licensing of IPR-protected inventions (and plant varieties) is undeniably important as a means to facilitate transfers of technology to developing countries. In the case of IPR-protected plant varieties, licensing can enable developing country recipients to acquire valuable know-how and access to inbred lines, and enhance their technology-absorbing capacity by such means as training and transfer of production techniques. The proceedings of a 1990 seminar organised by UPOV provide two examples of how plant variety protection facilitated technology transfer (UPOV 1991) (although the recipient in each case was not a developing country but a former centrally-planned economy).

The main concern of developing countries is that the licence fees and royalties can be financially burdensome, and this is why compulsory licensing can be an attractive option for these countries (albeit an often unpopular with IPR-owning companies) (see page 23).

IPRs AND THE RIGHTS OF TRADITIONAL KNOWLEDGE HOLDERS

It is sometimes asserted that intellectual property rights – in terms of their characteristics or their effects – are inequitable or even exploitative of indigenous peoples, whose knowledge, innovations and resource management practices are considered to play a key role in the conservation and sustainable use of biodiversity. Is this true? Two questions must be considered when discussing the relationship between IPRs, especially patents, and the rights of the holders of traditional knowledge, innovations and practices. First, do IPRs have characteristics that are inherently unjust or which lead to injustices *vis-à-vis* traditional knowledge holders? Second, to what extent can IPRs be used to protect their rights? This section begins by presenting the arguments of defenders of strong patent systems based upon those of the developed countries and then considers views that are more critical. It should be noted that this section deals mainly with patents.

Are IPRs inimical to indigenous and local people's rights?

Defenders of strong patent systems are likely to argue that companies holding patents derived from knowledge acquired from local communities cannot prevent members of these communities from continuing to use their knowledge, and moreover such companies have never attempted to do so. For example, just because a US company holds a patent for, say, a stable storage form of neem pesticide, this does not prevent Indian farmers from continuing to use neem as a pesticide as they have done for generations. Defenders may also assert that as long as the patent requirements of usefulness, novelty and inventive step are strictly upheld by patent offices, there is no reason for local communities to feel exploited since if their knowledge were simply copied there would be no invention to patent. Both of these arguments are essentially correct, although the turmeric patent case discussed below shows how the theory and practice of patenting may sometimes differ.

A recent study by two political philosophers, Anthony Stenson and Tim Gray (1997), took the controversial position that moral entitlement theories do not justify indigenous peoples'[24] IPRs over their knowledge. The problem with their analysis is that they based it on a simplistic conception of traditional knowledge, assuming that it is *by definition* collectively held and generated *and* part of the public domain.[25] This makes their argument appear more plausible than it should. To argue that *traditional* knowledge when defined this way should enjoy a privileged legal status *vis-à-vis* other public domain knowledge originating from *non-traditional* sources such as public or private sector research programmes does indeed *prima facie* seem problematic from a moral entitlement-based perspective.

However, what should not be overlooked is the question of *how* traditional knowledge usually falls into the public domain. Indigenous peoples have for centuries endured abuses of their basic human rights, and they still tend to be politically, economically and socially marginalized. It would therefore be naïve to suppose that it has ever been normal practice for their knowledge to be placed in the public domain and disseminated, with their prior informed consent *and* with respect for their customary laws and regulations concerning access, use and distribution of knowledge. It can plausibly be argued, then, that unconsented placement of knowledge into the public domain does not in itself extinguish the legitimate entitlements of the holders and may in fact violate them.

Second, while Stenson and Gray's argument is relevant to cases of widely-distributed and long-documented traditional knowledge such as that which is related to neem, a great deal of knowledge is more localized in its distribution and may be held only by small numbers of people or even an individual (see below).

Third, it is unreasonable to suggest that indigenous peoples have no reason to complain as long as their knowledge is not directly copied in a patented invention. The outrage felt by many indigenous peoples in South America about the US plant patent on a sacred plant, ayahuasca (see COICA 1996), is legitimate, and makes clear that resorting to the arguments of Western thinkers who justify IPRs, like Hegel and Locke,[26] is irrelevant and even dangerous unless the existence of non-Western property concepts is acknowledged first.[27]

Nevertheless, Stenson and Gray usefully demonstrate that advocates of indigenous peoples and local communities' rights need to be consistent in their argumentation.[28] For example, let us assume that the traditional knowledge about neem had been forgotten by most Indians so that only a few farmers still held the knowledge.

Would the use of their knowledge by a company as a lead for a patented invention make these people victims of intellectual piracy? If the farmers were identifiable, one could possibly build a strong case that the company's act was economically exploitative by using some of the arguments provided earlier. But – unlike the turmeric case – it is more difficult to argue that it is intellectual piracy. This is because to be consistent one would also have to argue that a temporary monopoly right to an incremental improvement (which is what a patent essentially is) is inherently exploitative of *all* people past and present that had contributed to the state of the art (or more accurately all the states of the arts) relevant to the patent. Such a position is difficult to sustain and is highly inappropriate in this case (see Menon 1993). The state of the art includes not only the knowledge that neem seed extracts are an effective pesticide, but also the industrial techniques that can be applied to produce neem derivatives that are in one way or another more useful than the natural product.[29]

Following a more critical perspective, it is tempting to draw an analogy between the taking of indigenous peoples'[30] knowledge without permission and patenting inventions based upon this knowledge, and seizing their territories and displacing them from their homelands. In each case, it seems that territories, ecosystems, plant varieties (whether domesticated or not) and traditional knowledge are treated as if they are *res nullius* (the property of nobody) before their 'discovery' by explorers, scientists, governments, corporations, and conservation organisations (Dutfield 1999b). During the Colonial period, sparsely populated 'wildernesses' were regarded as being to all legal intents and purposes vacant prior to colonisation.[31] Settler societies, such as in Australia, built up legal systems based upon the *terra nullius* (the land of nobody) doctrine.[32] According to such a view, open access is the rule for land, traditional knowledge and resources, whereas enclosure is the rule as soon as these are proved to have economic value.

The analogy is powerful and persuasive even if it is conceded that whereas lands and territories are finite, new knowledge is constantly being generated and is, at least in theory, inexhaustible. Nevertheless, the analogy does seem to reflect indigenous peoples' views – based as they are upon bitter historical experience – more accurately than the conventional (and Western) arguments favouring intellectual property rights for holders of useful knowledge (as presented in Box 3.2). Also, it accurately reflects the sentiments of indigenous peoples who see Western law as an imposition which seems to negate their own custom-based regulations. After all, if indigenous peoples in WTO member states are required to accept the existence of patents that they are economically prevented from availing themselves of, why shouldn't their own knowledge-related regimes be respected by others? *It is perhaps this point, that one type of IPR system is being universalized and prioritized to the exclusion of all others, that causes the most legitimate disquiet among those peoples and communities that are least able to benefit from what to them is an imposed system.* It is of course reasonable to argue that if indigenous peoples are not affected by the Western IPR system it can hardly be called an imposition. At least two immediate responses can be given. First, a number of countries (eg the US and Japan) do not recognize undocumented traditional knowledge held abroad as prior art (see below). Therefore it is legally permissible simply to copy this knowledge and apply for a patent. Second, patents with overly broad claims encompassing non-original products or processes are sometime mistakenly awarded. Due to poverty, most indigenous groups are in a weak position to challenge patents in the courts on the grounds that their knowledge or, say, folk varieties, have been fraudulently or erroneously claimed.

The following patent case studies illustrate a number of very real concerns about patents in the context of traditional knowledge. The turmeric case (Case Study 5.4) may be atypical since there was so obviously no real invention and the decision to grant the patent was clearly a mistake by the patent examiner. The system proved to be self-correcting in the sense that the patent was revoked, yet it required the active intervention of a foreign government agency to ensure that this happened. Even the most controversial of the multiplicity of neem patents display more inventiveness, but the neem case study (5.5) shows that patented inventions which relate closely to public domain traditional knowledge can be challenged successfully if they are considered to lack novelty and/or an inventive step. The quinoa patent (Case Study 5.6) is an example of how the breadth of a patent's claims may be construed as encompassing the traditional plant varieties.

Comparing these examples also shows some of the various ways that inventions may be derived from traditional knowledge and how the entitlements of traditional knowledge holders may vary as a result. In the turmeric case, the 'invention' *was* the traditional use of the plant, and it is because this traditional use had been documented that the invention was ultimately deemed to lack novelty. At least some (and possibly most) of the neem-related inventions embody uses identical to those of Indian farmers but the products and/or methods of extraction are different. In such cases it can safely be assumed that the existence of relevant traditional knowledge was a (but not *the*) *sine qua non* for the inventions. In the case of the quinoa patent, traditional knowledge was not a *sine qua non* for the invention except in the sense that the development and continued existence of quinoa varieties can be attributed to the efforts of past and present Andean peoples. The main problem with this patent is that it seems to appropriate part of the public domain by dint of the excessive breadth of what it claims rather than that it 'pirates' tradi-

CASE STUDY 5.4 THE TURMERIC PATENT

In March 1995, a US patent on 'Use of Turmeric in Wound Healing' was awarded to the University of Mississippi Medical Center. The claim covered 'a method of promoting healing of a wound by administering turmeric to a patient afflicted with the wound', such wounds including surgical wounds and body ulcers. According to Agarwal and Narain (1996), in India the powder of the turmeric plant is 'a classic grandmother's remedy' which 'has been applied to the scrapes and cuts of generations of children'.

In mid-1996 the Council of Scientific and Industrial Research of India (CSIR) requested the US Patent and Trademark Office to revoke the patent on the basis that turmeric powder is widely known about and used in India for its wound-healing properties, and that a great deal of scientific research has been carried out by Indian scientists that confirms the existence of these properties. One could easily suppose that the patent was awarded because the applicant had omitted to mention related traditional use of turmeric and to cite the relevant literature. After all, there is a limit to the amount of time patent office examiners can devote to examining each application for novelty, inventive step and usefulness. However, the patent description helpfully states that: 'Turmeric, a yellow powder developed from the plant *Curcurma longa*, is commonly used as a food colorant in many Indian dishes and imparts a bitter taste ... Although it is primarily a dietary agent, turmeric has long been used in India as a traditional medicine for the treatment of various sprains and inflammatory conditions.' No method for extracting the active principle was described. Instead, the patent simply declares that 'turmeric is a natural product that is readily available in the food store.'

Given the admission that turmeric has long been used to treat inflammatory conditions, it is difficult to see how this patent could have passed the tests of novelty and non-obviousness during the examination.

This patent was revoked after the CSIR's challenge on the basis of its absence of novelty. CSIR did not succeed by proving that many Indians already use turmeric as a wound-healing agent, but because it was able to provide relevant scientific literature.[33] Patent examiners in the US are not required to accept the evidence of traditional knowledge held outside the US as prior art (ie already known) unless it has been reported (and thereby validated) by scientists and published in learned journals or otherwise made available to the public. The inventors in fact made no explicit claim that the wound-healing agent (ie the turmeric powder) was any different from the one used traditionally by Indians. Ironically, Indians in the US using turmeric to treat their children's wounds were therefore infringing the patent. If the University of Mississippi had been awarded a similar patent in India, tens of millions of people would then have become patent infringers!

Source: Adapted from Dutfield (1997c)

tional knowledge. Even so, it is understandable that local communities should object when patent claims include names of their own folk varieties (as did the quinoa patent), especially when these

CASE STUDY 5.5 THE NEEM PATENTS

The neem tree (*Azadirachta indica*) has been the subject of a consider-able number of patents, with more than 40 in the US alone (Appendix 1) and at least 153 worldwide.[34] The inventions described in virtually all of the neem-related patents used public domain traditional knowledge as a starting point. They have aroused considerable controversy, especially in India, where most of the traditional knowledge holders are from. There have been at least two patent challenges: (1) to a European Patent Office (EPO) patent for fungicidal effects of neem oil (Patent No 436 257 B1) owned by W R Grace & Co, and (2) to a US patent for a storage stable azadirachtin formulation (Patent No 5124349) also owned by W. R. Grace (Kocken and Van Roozendaal 1997). The challenge to the former patent has been successful insofar as the Opposition Division of the EPO in September 1997 delivered an interim judgement expressing doubt that the patent can be maintained on the basis of lack of novelty and inventive step.

It is noteworthy that the evidence from Appendix 1 shows that Indian scientific institutions appear to be adopting an 'if you can't beat them, join them' attitude and are increasingly applying for patents, with six US neem-related patents awarded since 1995.

communities depend on exporting these varieties to countries where such a patent is held. A strong case can still be made for compensat-ing the Andean farmers when their knowledge and resources are used in such patent applications, but patent law is unlikely to be the best possible mechanism for benefit sharing given that most patented inventions are not commercially viable while many natural products may not even be IPR-protected.[35]

Even if it is still debatable whether strong patent systems modelled on those of Europe or the US are *inherently* harmful to indigenous peoples and local communities, arguments that such systems *reinforce* existing injustices are convincing. The question to be asked, then, is whether perverse characteristics of the system are integral to IPRs or whether they could be mitigated by rigorous patent examinations or by careful drafting of IPR laws. A strong argument can be made that IPR systems should be available to protect holders of *all* useful knowledge whose dissemination is beneficial to the wider public. To the extent that they cannot do this, they are inherently flawed. But on the other hand, some defects could be corrected without necessarily having to make radical changes. To take one example, the novelty requirement in patent law is sometimes defined in a way that could legalize the misappropriation of tradi-tional knowledge. *Prima facie*, countries which grant patents to the first applicant ('first-to-file' systems) rather than the first inventor ('first-to-invent' systems) appear to be applying a less rigorous defin-ition of novelty since a patent recipient need not be the first person

CASE STUDY 5.6 THE QUINOA PATENT[36]

Quinoa (*Chenopodium quinoa*) is a highly nutritious drought-resistant food crop grown in the cold high-elevation regions of the Andean countries of South America. Indigenous communities in Bolivia and Peru have bred numerous varieties, including Apelawa, named after a village in Bolivia. Although still a little-known food outside these countries, there is a growing demand for quinoa among health-conscious Europeans and North Americans and industrial plant breeders have started to take an interest. In order for plant breeders to produce hybrids from self-pollinating quinoa plants, the male properties of one parent must be eliminated so that plants of two different varieties do not fertilize themselves as well as each other, leaving progeny that are mixtures of the hybrid and the two parental varieties. Use of male sterile plants in the breeding of hybrids can avoid the labour intensive work of removing anthers from plants. In April 1994, a US patent was awarded for *Cytoplasmic Male Sterile Quinoa*. The patent accepts that male sterile quinoa lines have been reported in the literature but claims that 'a reliable system of cytoplasmic male sterility has not been reported, and cytoplasmic male sterile plants have not heretofore been available for commercial production of quinoa hybrids'.

The patent states that 'the cytoplasm conferring the property of male sterility is derived from the Apelawa variety of quinoa'. However, in an Internet exchange between one of the named inventors, Professor Sarah Ward, and Pat Mooney of Rural Advancement Foundation International (RAFI), the former states that she *found* the cytoplasm in question in quinoa plants of the Bolivian Apelawa variety growing in a field in Colorado, USA. The cytoplasm, she argued, does not exist in quinoa plants growing in South America but had been transferred naturally from a related weed species growing nearby (in Colorado). This was not made clear in the patent. Consequently, the failure to indicate the non-Bolivian provenance of the cytoplasm inducing male sterility or to refer to its discovery made it possible to interpret the patent very broadly in ways the inventors may not have intended. For example, the first two patent claims were for a quinoa seed of the variety Apelawa having male sterile cytoplasm and a quinoa plant produced from this quinoa seed. Although it is difficult to see how Andean farmers could be directly affected by the patent, since the existence and value of quinoa plants with the male sterility characteristic were known to many traditional cultivators, it was understandable that those farmers exporting quinoa to the US would feel threatened by these claims. An international campaign involving RAFI and Bolivia's National Association of Quinoa Producers that called for Colorado State University to let the patent lapse was successful when in May 1998 Professor Ward admitted that it had been abandoned.

One of the lessons from this case is that patent applicants should be required (where feasible) to disclose the origins of all source biological material from which the inventions they claim are derived. In cases such as this one, to do so might be in their best interests anyway, as greater openness from the start may avoid subsequent controversies.

to invent something. However, the most well-known first-to-invent patent system is that of the US,[37] and according to the law there:

> *A person shall be entitled to a patent unless –*
>
> *(a) the invention was known or used by others in this country, or patented or described in a printed publication in this or a foreign country, before the invention thereof by the applicant for patent, or*
>
> *(b) the invention was patented or described in a printed publication in this or a foreign country or in public use or on sale in this country, more than one year prior to the date of the application for patent in the United States... (35 United States Code § 102).*

This means that unpublished traditional (or any other) knowledge acquired from abroad but not known in the US can be the subject of a patent application by a company that simply discovers this knowledge (Kadidal 1997). In Europe, on the other hand, where first-to-file systems prevail, the novelty requirement is in this sense more demanding. According to Article 54(2) of the European Patent Convention:

> *An invention shall be considered to be new if it does not form part of the state of the art. The state of the art shall be held to comprise everything made available to the public by means of a written or oral description, by use, or in any other way, before the date of filing of the European patent application.*

Thus, there is no distinction made as to the geographical source of prior knowledge relevant to the invention. This seems to be much fairer.

One last but very important point to make is that farmers in most developing countries (and in some developed countries as well) still tend either to save their own seeds or acquire them from other farmers. In countries where neither the public nor private sectors play a dominant role in seed production or distribution, such as in many African countries, seed saving and sharing will probably continue to be prevalent means of seed acquisition for several years to come. To attempt to eradicate these practices through expansive IPRs would very likely cause serious economic and social impacts for farming communities. It should be noted in this context that, according to the IPR systems of the developed countries, the private property rights afforded by patents and plant variety rights to a varying extent restrict or even eliminate the right to continue such customary practices of seed saving and exchange, and the trend is very much towards further restriction of the former and complete elimination of the latter.

Can IPRs protect traditional biodiversity-related knowledge?

IPR law does not enable all creative or inventive expressions to be protected by IPRs. With respect to patents, only inventions that can be dated and attributed to an individual or small group of people can be protected. In traditional societies, the sources of traditional knowledge may be attributable to individuals, kinship or gender-based groups (E Reichel pers comm 1998), or to single communities. In theory such knowledge may be patentable. However, a great deal of traditional knowledge is not traceable to a specific community or geographical area and is ineligible for patent protection. Whether widely known or not, once traditional knowledge is recorded and publicly disseminated, its use and application are beyond the control of the original knowledge providers. As we saw earlier, if a researcher investigates a piece of published traditional knowledge and then improves upon it in a practical way, the result may well become a patentable 'invention' that this researcher can own.

Patents are essentially blunt instruments that cannot be expected to accommodate the subtleties and complexities of many non-western proprietary systems. These systems are sometimes assumed to be collective or communally-based, but in fact any assumption that there exists a generic form of non-western, traditional collective intellectual rights ignores the intricacies and sheer diversity of indigenous and traditional proprietary systems (Four Directions Council 1996). Implicit in some criticisms of patents is an erroneous assumption that collective and individual *ownership* and *property rights*, including intellectual property rights, are necessarily alien concepts in all traditional societies (see Biothai and GRAIN 1998) which are characterized by a strong sharing ethos. In fact, reviews of anthropological literature reveal that such concepts (or at least close equivalents to them) are quite common (Cleveland and Murray 1997; Griffiths 1993). Any laws that aim to protect property rights, including IPRs, should not therefore be dismissed out of hand. Even so, the strong tendency among many traditional communities is to exchange seeds freely rather than to treat them as commodities to be bought and sold.

At the practical level, the lack of economic self-sufficiency of many traditional communities, the unequal power relations between them and the corporate world, and the high cost of litigation, would make it very difficult for them to protect their IPRs through the patent system (Posey 1996). In the US, for example, it costs about US$20,000 to prepare a patent application (Lesser 1998). This is clearly beyond the financial means of local communities (as well as many independent inventors and small companies) in most parts of the world, especially when we take into account the fact that most patents do not result in the development of a profitable product anyway. How could this situation be justified? First, one could argue that the high expenses of acquiring and enforcing patents do not make the system inherently unfair if patent examinations and legal challenges are unavoidably expensive. Second, it might be asserted that the patent system cannot be blamed because many potential users either lack sufficient financial resources or are unwilling to take the risks of applying for patents in exchange for future gains that may never materialize. Besides, many countries have low-cost petty patent systems that are more accessible to less wealthy rights claimants, and TRIPS does not prohibit these systems.[38]

But if we accept that the purpose of an IPR system is to protect the rights of knowledge holders for the public good, it should be possible for all those who possess useful knowledge with economic or cultural value to secure its protection. To the extent that present-day IPR systems cannot protect traditional knowledge whose dissemination is beneficial to the wider community,[39] ie in terms of its practical utility or its contribution to the cultural heritage of society, these systems are failing to operate optimally in terms of their public policy function. Moreover, it is completely reasonable that the disproportionate legal treatment of commercially useful knowledge held by companies and of similarly useful knowledge held by indigenous peoples should seem unjust to the latter, whose own customary regimes are so frequently ignored. When large industrial concerns in new technological fields find the IPR system cannot protect their innovations, it seems that new forms of IPRs are created in response. Traditional knowledge holders, on the other hand, do not have the political influence to change the system. Moreover, they are rarely successful in ensuring that their own custom-based intellectual property rights systems are observed by others.[40]

Is it a futile exercise even to try using IPRs to protect traditional knowledge, innovations and practices? Certainly, IPRs should not be considered the *only* means of protecting traditional knowledge,[41] especially when so much of it has limited if any commercial application. However, one should not be completely dismissive about IPRs for two reasons. Firstly, trademarks and geographical indications may be appropriate forms of protection for some products based on traditional knowledge even if they cannot protect the knowledge *per se*. Second, policy makers schooled in the Western legal system are apt to suppose that the only IPRs which exist are the ones referred to in TRIPS and the WIPO-administered conventions. In fact, local and indigenous communities often have very complex custom-based intellectual property systems. Just as local communities can benefit from learning about the western IPR tradition, it is about time that lawyers, policy makers *and* industrial users of biological resources also learned about how traditional communities generate, use, manage and control their own knowledge.

NOTES

1 It should be pointed out that while a patent grants a monopoly to the owner (in the sense of allowing him/her to exclude others from making or selling the product), the ability to charge a monopoly *price* depends upon its reputed superiority to alternative products on the market.

2 For example, see Reyes (1996).

3 For detailed discussions of this case, see Anuradha (1997) and Martin (1998).

4 See Crucible Group (1994) for presentation of pro and contra arguments.

5 Tarasofsky (1997) drew my attention to this article.

6 Due to the need to replace cultivars with new ones every few years.

7 Novartis World Wide Web site (http://www.novartis.com).

8 Monsanto World Wide Web site (http://www.monsanto.com).

9 For excellent assessments of the environmental impacts of agricultural biotechnology see Lappé and Bailey (1999) and Krimsky and Wrubel (1996).

10 'Subject to the requirement that such measures are not applied in a manner which would constitute a means of arbitrary or unjustifiable discrimination between countries where the same conditions prevail, or a disguised restriction on international trade, nothing in this Agreement shall be construed to prevent the adoption or enforcement by any contracting party of measures:
(a) necessary to protect public morals;
(b) necessary to protect human, animal or plant life or health;'. (GATT Article XX [General Exceptions]).

11 Decision IV/6 (*Agricultural Biological Diversity*).

12 The fact that 'open and democratic' forums are more likely to be unduly influenced by special interest groups is of course a legitimate concern.

13 An application for plant variety protection requires the completion of an application form, a description of the variety, and the deposit of propagating material. This material may be used by a government institution to conclusively demonstrate stability and homogeneity through propagation trials.

14 And possibly some of the non-domesticated plants that they utilize as well (Gollin 1993).

15 As named by RAFI. This case study is based on information from US Patent 5723765, RAFI (1998a) and Lehmann (1998).

16 According to Dr Harry Collins of Delta and Pine Land Co. (1998): 'The most common type of germplasm protection system is hybrid seed production. Although primarily a system for increased yield via heterosis (improved performance), it is also a protection system...Because hybrids produce seed that is not uniformly like the parent seed, there is a reduction in overall performance when hybrid seed is saved and replanted'.

17 This study was carried out by the Inter-American Institute for Cooperation on Agriculture and the University of Amsterdam, in collaboration with researchers in those five countries (Argentina, Chile, Uruguay, Colombia and Mexico).

18 Greater enforcement was facilitated by the creation of an association of domestic and foreign breeders.

19 According to Rangnekar (1996), 'technically a hybrid produces a substantial yield increase in its first generation compared to parents. This "hybrid vigour" is not inherited by the progeny. Though the farmer can save and re-use the seed, the economic loss resulting from a yield decrease forces the farmer to purchase fresh seeds for the next crop.'

20 According to Sehgal (1996), 'of the US$15 billion market in commercial seed at present, hybrids account for approximately 40% of sales, and most of the profit'.

21 Such as those of Monsanto.

22 And are required by TRIPS to do so in the case of least developed countries: '[d]eveloped country Members shall provide incentives to enterprises and institutions in their territories for the purpose of promoting and encouraging technology transfer to least-developed country Members in order to enable them to create a sound and viable technological base' (Article 66.2).

23 An example is the International Service for the Acquisition of Agri-biotech Applications (ISAAA), which was established to facilitate the acquisition and transfer of agricultural biotechnology applications, particularly proprietary technology from the private sector to developing countries (see Krattiger and James 1993-94).

24 Referred to by the authors as 'cultural communities'.

25 Although they accept that individuals in communities can be innovative, their basic understanding is that 'the "traditionality" of traditional knowledge – the fact that it is common knowledge, the product of collective experience without a single act of creation – precludes its being seen, from the point of view of an entitlement theory, as intellectual property' (ibid).

26 For a review of such justifications see Hettinger (1989) and Drahos (1996).

27 It is in fact very difficult to avoid ethnocentricity in discussing the application of IPRs to non-Western systems of knowledge. According to Lester Thurow (1997) '[t]he idea that people should be paid to be creative is a point of view that stems from the Judeo-Christian and Muslim belief in a God who created humankind in his own image. It has no analogue in Hindu, Buddhist, or Confucian societies.'

28 Indeed, their paper can be read as a critique of the writings of advocates that resort to excessive use of rhetoric to state their case and tend to have romantic views about 'communities'.

29 Having made this point, it should still be noted that two of the most controversial neem patents – US patents 4,556,562 ('Stable anti-pest neem seed extract') and 5,124,349 ('Storage stable azadirachtin formulation') – both describe fairly basic chemical processes that could conceivably render the invention 'obvious' to one who is skilled in the art (see Kadidal 1997).

30 Use of the term 'indigenous peoples' here means those populations that conform to the definition of 'indigenous and tribal peoples' in the International Labour Organization Convention Concerning Indigenous and Tribal Peoples in Independent Countries (ILO Convention 169). The analogy does not apply so well to other traditional rural populations who may of course be equally oppressed.

31 For example, John Locke considered America to be in a state of nature ('In the beginning all the world was America') in which indigenous modes of governance did not constitute political society, and customary land use was not a legitimate form of property rights. Tully (1993) provides evidence that some British colonists found Locke's ideas convenient in justifying the dispossession of indigenous peoples from their lands. Interestingly, if Locke had recognized (as a few British

colonists of the time did) that indigenous peoples regarded themselves as self-governing nations, his theory of government could have been used to legitimize their violent rebellion against the British (ibid).

32 Even today, traditional forest communities in some countries (eg Latin America) can more easily acquire legal title to their lands if they 'improve' them by removing the trees so that they are no longer 'virgin forests'. The same rules may also apply to colonists.

33 According to Prakash (1998) '[t]he [CSIR] claim had to be backed by written documentation claiming traditional wisdom. CSIR went so far as to present an ancient Sanskrit text and a paper published in 1953 in the *Journal of the Indian Medical Association*.'

34 As revealed by the author's search of the European Patent Office's patent information database on 30 November 1998.

35 According to Leskien and Flitner (1997): 'the principle of benefit sharing certainly requires more than being integrated into IPR legislation, simply because not all applications of plant genetic resources end up being protected by an IPR. Since in many countries plant varieties and other products need to undergo an authorisation or certification procedure before they are allowed to be released, the application for such marketing authorisation could also be used as a trigger for benefit sharing.'

36 This case study is based on information from US Patent 5304718 and the following sources: A. Bonifacio (1997) 'Technical Considerations on Cytoplasmic Male Sterility in Quinoa' [unpublished paper]; exchanges between S. Ward and P. Mooney on the Environment in Latin America Network e-mail listserv; and the two press releases issued by RAFI on 19 June 1997 and 22 May 1998. For a more detailed discussion of the quinoa patent see Garí (1997).

37 Håkansta (1998) explains how 'first-to-invent' works in practice: '[a]ccording to US patent legislation, to be recognised as the first inventor, one must prove two things. The first is that you were the one that developed the idea (conception), and the second that you were the one to execute the idea and developed a product (reduction to practice). If you only fulfil the first of these, you could have the patent right if you can prove that you had the earliest conception date and then worked diligently to reduce the invention to practice – even if your opponent reduced the invention to practice on an earlier date.' This underlines how problematic is the supposition that inventions happen suddenly at a specific moment in time.

38 According to Kadidal (1997) in reference to plant breeding within traditional farming communities: '[i]t has been suggested that [such] a cooperative and incremental inventive culture does not make a snug fit with the utility patent system and its paradigm of *large inventive leaps* by *individual* inventors. Instead it is more appropriate to a system allowing petty patents, which are suited to lesser inventive steps'. It should be clarified, though, that most patented inventions also cover incremental improvements on the state of the art rather than breakthroughs.

39 As acknowledged in the CBD, at least that knowledge which is relevant to biodiversity and sustainable use of biological resources.

40 According to Drahos (1997): '[w]hile new forms of intellectual property in the form of protection for semiconductors or plant varieties have readily been minted for transnational industrial elites both nationally and internationally, the recognition of indigenous intellectual property forms has proceeded slowly or not at all. This selective approach to solving freeriding problems comes into sharp focus when one compares the evolution of protection for the semiconductor chip and protection of folklore. Prior to 1984 manufacturers of computer chips in the US

had complained that existing intellectual property regimes often failed to protect their products. Their chips often failed to clear the patent hurdles of novelty and inventiveness...In 1984 the *Semiconductor Chip Protection Act* was passed...In contrast, the issue of protection for indigenous knowledge has largely remained just that, an issue'.

41 The Government of Australia, in a submission to the Conference of the Parties to the CBD (1996), listed the various mechanisms that had been suggested in various international forums to protect traditional knowledge. These were: (a) operating within existing intellectual property regimes; (b) the creation, through legislation or other means, of new forms of intellectual property rights; (c) funding mechanisms; (d) an equitable sharing of the benefits arising from the contributions, including elements of using traditional knowledge made by indigenous and local communities; (e) contractual agreements such as material transfer agreements; (f) codes of conduct; (g) rights in relation to cultural products and expressions, including cultural property; (h) greater reliance on unconscionable behaviour and unjust enrichment.

6 TRIPS AND THE CBD: BRIDGING THE GAPS

This chapter considers ways in which harmony between the objectives of the CBD and the requirements of TRIPS can be enhanced, particularly in developing countries. To this end, it begins by clarifying the *minimum* standards required by TRIPS for patents and the *sui generis* option for plant varieties, geographical indications, trade secrets and trademarks, based upon the descriptions of these IPRs in Chapter 3. Following this, the chapter discusses how these minimum standards may be implemented in a CBD-friendly fashion. It must be borne in mind that TRIPS does not require national IPR regimes to be identical. Countries have the right to adopt *higher* standards than TRIPS requires. It is also possible for them to address CBD-related concerns such as by imposing certain administrative requirements on the process of applying for IPR protection (such as certification of origin), or creating mechanisms or institutions within a new IPR law (or an amended existing law) to achieve specific objectives, such as benefit sharing.

The chapter emphasizes the *sui generis* option, basing its proposals on an expansive but realistic interpretation of what may be permitted. It should be noted that the *sui generis* system – assuming that countries decide to develop one – may be defined and provided in various legal forms. For example, the system could be a stand-alone plant variety law, or it could be provided by, say, a patent law.[1] Alternatively, the *sui generis* system could be embedded within non-IPR legislation, such as a biodiversity conservation law.[2]

PATENTS

The whole idea of bridging the gaps between the CBD and TRIPS is meaningless to those who see no conflicts between the two agreements. On the other hand, many activists would argue that attempting to harmonize them is futile since the conflicts between the CBD and TRIPS are irreconcilable, especially the section on patents. Other critics of patents are likely to advise for a policy of 'damage limitation', ie proposing that countries incorporate into their patent laws all the exclusions allowed by TRIPS as presented in Table 3.1 (p24).

The 'damage limitation' strategy may be a feasible and realistic option for some countries, although it can hardly be an attractive option for *all* developing countries for the reasons given in Chapter 2, in short, that developing countries vary tremendously in terms of their levels of industrialization and social and political development, and therefore their IPR interests. Also to be borne in mind is the point made earlier that just as there are likely to be wide variations in the IPR interests of different developing countries, the demands of interest groups *within* a country may also vary widely (Dutfield 1997b). For example, although farmers in India are usually assumed to be vehemently opposed to TRIPS, Bhat (1996) reports that one farmers' group in that country supported full implementation of TRIPS as part of the package of WTO agreements, in the expectation that any increase in seed costs would be offset by increased trade revenues from certain commodities whose prices were kept low by government policies in contravention of the WTO requirements. Akhil Gupta notes that two influential farmers' organizations in India take quite opposite views towards TRIPS even though both consist mostly of well-off farmers, and therefore do not represent different socio-economic classes. The Karnataka Rajya Ryota Sangha (KRRS; Karnataka Farmers Association) is vehemently anti-TRIPS, whereas the Shetkari Sangathana (Farmers Union) is very much in favour (Gupta 1997).[3]

Should governments decide that special measures are needed to ensure that patent law is supportive of the CBD's objectives, rather than simply to incorporate all the allowable exclusions, they may wish to consider such actions as:

1 Applying the precautionary principle by: (a) excluding plants and animals from patentability until the environmental and social impacts of allowing such patents can be assessed; and/or (b) adopting an expansive interpretation of *ordre public* and morality.
2 Requiring more exacting standards of novelty or inventive step so that the failure of IPR law adequately to protect traditional knowledge is not compounded by the ability of others to hold patents for inventions closely derived from such knowledge.

Box 6.1 Certificates of Origin

Certificates of origin have been proposed by Brendan Tobin to make patent law more compatible with provisions in the CBD on national sovereignty, prior informed consent, and the rights of indigenous peoples and local communities (Tobin and Ruiz 1996; Tobin 1997b; see also Gadgil and Devasia 1995). According to this proposal, administrative requirements for filing patent applications based on use of genetic resources and/or traditional knowledge should require inclusion of: (i) a sworn statement as to the genetic resources and associated knowledge, innovations and practices of indigenous peoples and local communities utilized, directly or indirectly, in the research and development of the subject matter of the IPR application; and (ii) evidence of prior informed consent from the country of origin and/or indigenous or local community, as appropriate.

National implementation of these requirements would presumably be quite a simple matter. However, international standardization of these conditions could also be effected with the creation of an international certification system. Accordingly, countries providing resources and/or traditional knowledge would issue certificates indicating that all obligations to the source country and the relevant indigenous people or local community had been fulfilled, such as prior informed consent, equitable benefit sharing, and perhaps other conditions imposing limitations on the use of the genetic material or knowledge. Patent applications would then need to include these certificates without which they would automatically be returned to the applicants for re-submission with the relevant documentation. The system would not affect indigenous communities' right to veto access to and use of their knowledge or resources.

Downes (1997b) advises that before putting in place such a national or international system, consideration should be given to a clearer definition of indigenous peoples and local communities, and to whether such communities in developed countries should be included as well.

But it is possible that the imposition of certificates of origin as an additional patent requirement would not comply with the TRIPS Agreement unless it were limited to patents for plants, plant varieties and animals, or the *sui generis* alternative for plant varieties (Leskien and Flitner 1997). In any case, although India (WTO-CTE 1997) has proposed such a system to the WTO, most governments seem reluctant to consider such a system, at least insofar as it would require changes to patent law. A proposed amendment to the European Community biotechnology inventions directive for a kind of certification of origin system was rejected by the European Commission and Council of Ministers, which deemed that it would have gone beyond the requirements of the CBD. However, both the Andean Pact's Decision 391 (Common System on Access to Genetic Resources) and Costa Rica's new Biodiversity Law introduce such a system in their respective countries (see pp108–13).

3 Developing databases of traditional knowledge, innovations and practices which national patent offices can access when testing patent applications for novelty and inventive step (see pp121–4).
4 Including special administrative requirements in the process of applying for IPR protection, such as certification of origin (see Box 6.1).

Adopting either of these actions should be decided only after broad consultations with all interest groups including, where relevant, the traditional knowledge holders.

OPTIONS FOR THE *SUI GENERIS* SYSTEM

TRIPS is the *only* international agreement that refers specifically to the possibility of a *sui generis* IPR system. Frequently such an alternative (to patents) is assumed to be a system based upon the UPOV Convention, either in its 1978 version or the 1991 revision. But Article 27.3 (b) makes no mention of UPOV and permits countries to design their own plant variety protection system as long as it is considered to be effective. In Box 6.2, Achim Seiler presents a range of possible *sui generis* approaches. It should be noted, though, that only one of them specifically concerns plant variety protection.

Realistic proposals for non-UPOV plant variety protection systems have been few and far between. This is probably one of the reasons why more developing countries are joining UPOV. Nonetheless, it is important to consider alternatives to UPOV so that informed decisions can be made.

In order to devise a *sui generis* system that is consistent with the objectives of the CBD and is TRIPS-compatible, close attention should be paid to the *requirements for* and *scope of* plant variety protection. The possibility of supplementing the system with non-IPR-related provisions designed to support CBD-related objectives or benefit local communities should also be considered.

Requirements for protection

How could a *sui generis* system be devised to resolve the alleged difficulties concerning UPOV's protection requirements? Dan Leskien and Michael Flitner (1997), in their paper for the International Plant Genetic Resources Institute (IPGRI) on options for a *sui generis* system, suggest a number of alternative requirements as follows:

1 *Applying a less strict interpretation of 'uniformity' and 'stability' requirements* so that varieties bred on-farm have a better chance of protection. Leskien and Flitner even suggest that the uniformity and stability requirements could be replaced by a new

---

Box 6.2 Different *Sui Generis* Approaches

Intellectual property rights for communities
This approach could be used to provide communities with IPRs for their informal innovations and biodiversity-related skills that cannot be protected by conventional IPR systems. Many Southern NGOs and indigenous peoples' organisations have the criticism that in vesting those rights in communities, the commodification and monopolization of life forms will be even more strongly established worldwide.

Community intellectual rights and collective rights
This strategy could be pursued to protect the rights of indigenous communities from being usurped by foreign interests. All biodiversity-related rights of local communities (farmers as well as indigenous peoples) are to be protected by adequate legislation, which the state has to abide by. The primary objective is to prevent biopiracy. It is not intended to be in full compliance with the TRIPS stipulations (see Chapter 8).

Modified plant variety protection
This approach is grounded on the stipulations of the plant variety protection system, as laid out in the UPOV conventions. Slight modifications to improve the situation of farmers are included. Instruments under development are Community or Farmers Rights Funds, which are based on royalties on protected seeds. Other measures are grace periods for filing applications on farmers' varieties and the exclusion of certain categories of farmer-controlled plant materials.

Comprehensive biodiversity legislation
In this case, an encompassing legislation deals with the protection and sustainable use of biodiversity. It aims at the definition of coherent policy measures in the national context. Aspects covered range from the question of access to genetic resources, biosafety, IPRs and communal rights (see Chapter 8 for the Costa Rica example).

Sectoral community rights regime
Following this approach, a regulation system is designed especially to deal with the interests of local communities concerning specific categories of biodiversity. National legislation does not encompass all the biodiversity-related problems coherently but concentrates only on specific areas which have to be protected, for instance medicinal plants and the related indigenous knowledge systems. Such a pragmatic approach does not exclude attempts to implement broader legislation.

Source: Reproduced from Seiler 1998

---

requirement, that of identifiability, which would 'emphasise the legal need to identify the protected subject matter instead of the specific physical properties a plant has to have'. Accordingly, less genetically uniform new (or hitherto not widely used) varieties could become eligible for protection. Presumably this might provide an incentive for breeders to rely less on elite germplasm and to seek out less researched and more genetically diverse germplasm.

2   *Differentiating between homogeneous/uniform varieties and heterogeneous and traditional varieties* in extent of rights available. The latter varietal types could still be protectable if they are clearly identifiable but, since broader claims would result, the rights should be weaker (ibid). One possible danger of allowing broader claims in this way is that corporate bioprospectors rather than local communities would take advantage of this and 'jump the queue' by promptly submitting applications for discovered landraces (or those they already hold in their collections). For this reason, the *sui generis* system should incorporate a certificate of origin system as described above to safeguard local communities from unauthorized appropriation and/or to incorporate benefit-sharing requirements.

Scope of the protection

The scope of protection of UPOV 1978 is somewhat weaker than that of UPOV 1991 and might be preferable for developing and least developed countries that have no experience of administering a plant variety right system and find it difficult to identify possible beneficiaries of an IPR system for plant varieties. Upholding the farmers' privilege would lessen possible intrusion on the customary practices of local communities. Therefore, a *sui generis* system using UPOV 1978 as its model in terms of scope of protection but with different protection requirements as described above might be more appropriate than a patent or UPOV 1991-type system for some countries. However, countries that wish to join UPOV are now required to accept the 1991 version.

Additional provisions

Leskien and Flitner refer to various additional components to balance the IPRs granted to plant breeders with the interests of society as a whole and/or to local communities. Genetic resource access and benefit-sharing regimes may restrict the IPRs allowable in accordance with certain objectives, such as benefit-sharing. Other possibilities are the establishment of community gene funds, registers and public defenders or ombudsmen, although these need not be part of the *sui generis* law.

Community gene funds might be financed through a levy on the gross value of seeds sold. If genetic material in these seeds can be traced to a locality, the communities could be rewarded for their efforts in conserving the genetic material in question. In cases where provenance cannot be established, Leskien and Flitner suggest that funds could then be used to support *in situ* conservation in priority regions where biodiversity is particularly threatened. However, for the reasons given in Chapter 1 when discussing the apportioning of benefits, it may be unrealistic to suppose that such a fund would be very large or could benefit single communities to any significant extent. Moreover the transaction costs incurred in the tracing of beneficiaries and distributing of benefits would probably be too high for community gene funds to serve as an effective benefit-sharing mechanism.

Community innovation registers or an international germplasm tracing register are possible means of identifying contributors to IPR-protected plant varieties and might also help to prevent unauthorized appropriation (see also pp121–4).

A *public defender or ombudsman office* could be set up at national or international level to intervene in disputes between local communities and governments or companies to help the former to defend their rights over their own genetic resources and knowledge (see also Posey 1996; RAFI 1994; Shelton 1995).

A few interesting model *sui generis* systems have been proposed with Article 27.3 (b) in mind, notably Dan Leskien and Michael Flitner's plant variety protection seal model and Bees Butler and Robin Pistorius' remuneration system. But perhaps the best elaborated model is the Gene Campaign's Convention of Farmers and Breeders. These are briefly presented and analysed below.

1   *The plant variety protection seal model*[4] (Leskien and Flitner 1997) would grant the right holder an exclusive right to a seal or certificate for a variety that has fulfilled the requirements laid down in the *sui generis* system (eg distinctness and identifiability). The difference between such a seal and a trademark is that the seal would not only constitute the variety's denomination but would also certify full compliance of the variety with the protection requirements. Only the use of the seal in combination with the registered denomination and the material of the variety would be the exclusive right of the holder and those having the holder's authorization.

Once seed has been sold by the seal owner or others authorized by the owner, there will be no further restrictions on use and sale of the variety. Thus farmers would be allowed to save and sell seed. Leskien and Flitner argue that, in spite of this, the seal holders could still enjoy a competitive advantage especially if the protection requirements of the *sui generis* system were adapted to the needs of farmers. Given that the rights are not as strong as those provided by the UPOV Convention or patents, Leskien and Flitner suggest that the duration of the right could be made longer than the minimum protection terms required by UPOV or the TRIPS patent provisions.

However, it seems very doubtful that seal holders really could sustain a comparative advantage for any length of time when other breeders (or farmers) can so easily produce and sell the same variety. Therefore, the system would almost certainly be highly unpopular with plant breeders, who, if the system came into existence, would very likely respond by focusing more of their research on developing genetically-uniform hybrids and crops that lend themselves to hybridization.

2　*The 'remuneration without ownership/property right' model* (Butler and Pistorius 1996) is designed with the following objectives: (i) to remunerate innovative plant breeding and provide incentives to encourage the development of novel plant varieties; (ii) to allow farmers access to varieties available on the commercial market and to save, sell, exchange, and use these varieties for breeding purposes, without violating private property rights; and (iii) to provide incentives to preserve, create and enhance biodiversity. Butler and Pistorius propose that the system should follow the example of a Dutch law in force between 1941 and 1966 by eliminating the concepts of 'ownership' and 'property rights' in plant genetic resources and relaxing the conditions for the registration of new varieties. The model would require all farmers to pay a tax on each crop based on the number of hectares they planted in each crop variety. The funds collected this way would be used to pay plant breeders a remuneration for breeding new varieties, with payment based on the proportion of total hectares planted each year for 25 years. The right of farmers to save, sell and use seed for breeding purposes would not be restricted. According to the two authors, although breeders are likely to be concerned about these freedoms, in developing countries they may have little to lose from not being able to enforce exclusive rights to their varieties. This is because most of the seed trade in developing countries is in the informal sector, and farmers often cannot afford new commercial varieties.

Butler and Pistorius also acknowledge that estimating the areas of cropland planted in a particular variety could be difficult. One might go further and suggest that the costs of monitoring and enforcement could be so huge as to make the system unworkable, especially in large countries and those that lack an effective seed certification system. Besides, TRIPS states that IPRs are private rights, yet this system does not allow the breeders even to control the level of remuneration due to them. Therefore, it may well be considered unacceptable by the TRIPS Council.

3　*The Convention of Farmers and Breeders (CoFaB)* (Gene Campaign 1999) is by far the best conceived and most realistic of the three models. In Article 1, the purpose of CoFaB is stated as follows:

> *to acknowledge and to ensure that farmers have rights*
> *ensuing from their contribution to the identification,*
> *maintenance and refinement of germplasm and that*
> *breeders of new plant varieties have rights over the*
> *varieties that they have bred.*

With respect to the requirements for protection, CoFaB is quite similar to UPOV in that the new variety must also be distinguishable, stable and homogeneous. However, while UPOV also requires that varieties must be distinguishable from any other variety 'whose existence is a matter of common knowledge', CoFaB seeks to clarify the meaning of 'common knowledge' so that no knowledge within local communities relating to a 'new' plant variety, whether documented or not, can legally be misappropriated. According to Article 6 (a):

> *Common knowledge may be established from oral or*
> *documented reference, in the formal and informal*
> *sector, to various factors such as: cultivation, use and*
> *marketing already in progress, entry in a register of*
> *varieties already made or in the course of being made,*
> *inclusion in a reference collection or precise descrip-*
> *tion in a publication.*

Supplementary text in the paragraph dealing with stability states that:

> *Breeders of new varieties shall try to base the new*
> *variety on a broader rather than a narrower base, in*
> *order to maintain greater genetic diversity.*

This is an interesting requirement though it is difficult to see how it could be turned into a binding obligation. Inclusion of the verb 'try to' implicitly acknowledges that it is intended to encourage rather than oblige breeders to breed genetically-diverse varieties.

When applying for protection, the breeder is required to disclose:

> *the name and source of all varieties used in the breed-*
> *ing of the new variety. Where a landrace or farmer*
> *variety has been used, this must be specially*
> *mentioned.* (Article 6.1 (b))

Also, upon receiving the right, the breeder must:

> *provide the geneology of the variety along with DNA*
> *finger printing and other molecular, morphological*
> *and physiological characteristics.* (Article 7.2)

With respect to the rights of farmers, these are monetary in nature and have no time limit. Basically, they are in the form of funds paid from a National Gene Fund. Decisions on distribution of funds, which may go to communities or individuals as appropriate, will be made by a 'multi-stakeholder body' (Article 2 (3)). Contributions to the NGF will be in the form of fees levied on breeders 'for the privilege of using landraces or traditional varieties either directly or through the use of other varieties that have used landraces and traditional varieties in their breeding program' (Article 2 (1)). In its present form, CoFaB apparently envisages a flat-rate fee for the use of a landrace or traditional variety rather than a weighted sum according to how far a particular landrace/variety contributed to the useful characteristics of the new variety or to its genetic make-up.

Two problems can be identified that ought to be considered in any revision of CoFaB. First, it should be remembered that the final customers of seeds are the farmers. If the seed companies raise their prices to make up for their losses due to the fee payments, the farmers themselves will be the real contributors to the gene fund.[5] Second, new varieties use a very large number of landraces as breeding material and from various countries. For example, the breeding of IR–72, a rice variety developed at the International Rice Research Institute, depended upon landraces that came from India, Vietnam, Philippines, China, Indonesia, Thailand, Malaysia and the United States (see Chrispeels and Sadava 1994). This raises two sets of questions.

First, should only *domestic* landrace providers be compensated? Presumably, this is what would happen, but, whatever, this should be made clear in the text. Alternatively, future CoFaB member states could apply the reciprocity principle by recognizing and compensating communities and individuals only from other member states whose governments agree to do the same.

Second, should community or individual donors be compensated only for their present-day donations of germplasm, or should compensation be paid for – and fees levied on – use of germplasm collected in the past, held in *ex situ* collections, and subsequently acquired by breeders? In case of the latter, how far back in time would collected germplasm continue to be subject to fee payment?

It is noteworthy that the International Plant Genetic Resources Institute (IPGRI) will shortly be publishing a decision check list for countries developing a *sui generis* system (Bragdon pers. comm. 1998). IPGRI will also be holding a workshop in Southern Africa in early 1999 that will bring together representatives of trade, environment and agriculture ministries to discuss the development of *sui generis* systems. In addition Quaker Peace and Service have published two papers concerning Article 27.3 (b) for developing countries so they are better informed about possible courses of action at local, national, and regional levels in the context of the 1999 TRIPS Council review of Article 27.3 (b) (Mulvany 1998 [published jointly with the Commonwealth Secretariat]; Tansey 1999) (see p92).

GEOGRAPHICAL INDICATIONS

Although so far the use of geographical indications has been confined mainly to certain beverages and foodstuffs, the principles of geographical indications could guide laws to protect certain traditional know-how and help to maintain the economic value of locally produced goods including herbal formulations (Bérard and Marchenay 1996; CBD Secretariat 1996a; Downes 1997b; Dutfield 1997).

Perhaps the best known type of geographical indication is the appellation of origin.

Appellation of origin was originally a French system for regulating geographical indications. It applied to products considered to be distinctive due to a combination of traditional know-how and highly localized natural conditions. The system evolved in that country in response to problems of illegal labelling and overproduction (Moran 1993). A government agency validates Appellation d'Origine Contrôlée (registered designations of origin), so that producers of wines, cheeses and other foodstuffs, whose goods are renowned for their distinctive qualities and geographic origins, are protected from those who would undermine or exploit their good reputation by making similar, but false, claims (Bérard and Marchenay 1996). For example, wines from the Champagne region of France are protected this way; local producers acting collectively have prevented the use of the word 'Champagne' on bottles of perfume, English wine, and German shampoo (Freedman 1994). However, some other wine-producing countries do not accept the necessity for an appellations system. In the US, it is considered allowable under certain circumstances to use a French appellation preceded by the origin of the wine (eg Californian Chablis) (Moran 1993).

In July 1992, the European Community adopted a resolution on the protection of geographical indications and designations of origin for agricultural products and foodstuffs other than wines and spirits.

The European Commission's register of geographical indications and designations includes those from EC member countries. According to Schwab (1995), the aim is 'to encourage the diversification of agricultural production and promote products having certain characteristics to the benefit of the rural economy'. Adoption of such regulations implies acceptance of what Moran (1993) calls 'the underlying philosophy of the distinctiveness of local and regional products and some of the assumptions that underlie these arguments'. Thus, 'globalisation of such artisanally-based principles counters the standardisation of products which is normally considered the outcome of the internationalisation of the agro-food industries [and] assists small family firms to resist the industrialisation and corporatisation of production'. It is interesting to consider whether this type of intellectual property right could be used to resolve a recent controversy, the Basmati rice case (Case Study 6.1).

A model law developed in 1985 by the UN Educational, Scientific and Cultural Organization (UNESCO) and WIPO is somewhat relevant. In Section 6 of the Model Provisions for National Laws on Protection of Expressions of Folklore against Illicit Exploitation and Other Prejudicial Actions, 'prejudicial actions' include failure to indicate the ethnic and geographic source of an expression of folklore in printed publications and other communications to the public, and deliberately deceiving the public about the ethnic source of a production. Although not explicitly stated in the document, a law to implement the model provisions *could* include traditional cultivars as 'expressions of folklore' to be protected if national law-making bodies felt it desirable to protect such resources.[6]

TRADE SECRETS

The knowledge or know-how of an individual or a whole community might be protected as a trade secret as long as the information has commercial value and provides a competitive advantage, whether or not the community itself wishes to profit from it. If a company obtains such information by illicit means, legal action may be used to force the company to share its profits (Gollin 1993). Conceivably, a considerable amount of indigenous peoples' knowledge could be protected as trade secrets. Restricting access to their territories and exchanging information with outsiders through agreements that secure confidentiality or economic benefits would be appropriate means to this end. It is very likely that knowledge shared by all members of a community may not qualify as a trade secret. However, 'if a shaman or other individual has exclusive access to information because of his status in the group, that individual *or the indigenous group together* probably has a trade secret' (Axt et al 1993).

CASE STUDY 6.1 COULD BASMATI RICE BE PROTECTED BY A GEOGRAPHICAL INDICATION?[7]

Basmati rice is a long-grained aromatic rice variety cultivated in areas of Northern India and Pakistan. Basmati is exported to North America and Europe and commands a high price on account of its high quality. Two corporations in France and the US have been actively appropriating the high reputation of Basmati rice and are in this way threatening a lucrative market for India and Pakistan.

A food company called Etablissements Haudecoeur La Courneuve has been granted two French trademarks using the word 'Basmati': 'Riz Long Basmati' and 'Riz Long Basmati Riz du Monde' (*Economic Times* 1998), and a US company called RiceTec has for several years been selling rice in the US and the Middle East under the name 'Texmati' (Dasgupta 1996). Although this has caused great irritation in India, the germplasm was freely and legally acquired by RiceTec from the International Rice Research Institute (IRRI) in the Philippines (CSE 1996) prior to the entry into force of the CBD.[8] Neither RiceTec or Etablissements Haudecoeur La Courneuve have any benefit-sharing obligations to India and Pakistan under the terms of the CBD (even if the US were a Party).

Further outrage in India and Pakistan was provoked when it was revealed in early 1998 that RiceTec had been awarded a US patent entitled *Basmati Lines and Grains*. Among the various claims are for 'novel rice lines, whose plants are semi-dwarf in stature, substantially photoperiod insensitive, high yielding and produce rice grains comprising characteristics and qualities similar or superior to those of good quality basmati rice grains produced in India and Pakistan'.

The Indian and Pakistani governments are considering how to protect an export market upon which many thousands of farmers depend. They could appeal to the US Patent and Trademark Office to revoke the patent on the basis that the 'invention' described in the patent is spurious, or try to make use of the TRIPS provisions on geographical indications to have the trademarks revoked on the grounds that they are misleading to consumers and/or harmful to the reputation of Basmati rice. Initially, India raised the possibility of challenging the marketing of US produced 'basmati' rice as a violation of TRIPS. However, TRIPS does *not* require a member to protect geographical indications unless they are protected in their country of origin (Article 24.9). But once India and Pakistan have passed an appropriate law, retrospective action becomes possible to prevent firms in other countries marketing rice grown outside the Indian Subcontinent as basmati. However, India and Pakistan still have much to gain from taking prompt legislative measures, because a geographical indication system can have retrospective effect. For example, Cypriot rivals to the sherry producers of the Jérez region of southern Spain were for many years allowed to call their product 'Cyprus Sherry' (sherry being an English corruption of Jérez). Now the same product must be labelled as 'Cyprus Fortified Wine' if producers wish to export it to EC countries. So assuming both countries enact legislation to protect Basmati rice as a geographical indication, what are their chances for success?

The two governments will probably find it difficult to challenge use of the name 'Texmati'. If the US allows such domestically-produced goods as 'Pete's Wicked Bohemian Pilsener' to be sold, and would certainly consider permissible a name like 'California Chablis' for wine produced in that State (Moran 1993), 'Texmati', which connotes Texas more strongly than it does the Indian subcontinent, is probably safe from legal challenges. However, India or Pakistan could certainly take legal action in US or French courts to prevent either company market-ing the rice as if it is genuine Basmati rice and thereby free-riding on a reputation built up over many years by Indian and Pakistani farmers. Otherwise, they could challenge the French and US governments through the World Trade Organization on the grounds that TRIPS Article 22.2 requires members to 'provide the legal means for interested parties to prevent the use of any name in the designation or presentation of a good that indicates or suggests that the good in question originates in a geographical area other than the true place of origin in a manner which misleads the public as to the geographical origin of the good'. Success then depends upon rejection of any claims that Basmati is a generic term, and acceptance of the argument that Basmati is a variety of rice made distinctive, not only by its inherent qualities, but also by its geographical origin *and* local know-how. The taste and quality of Basmati rice, but above all its reputation (since these are to some extent subjective attributions), *must* be inextricably linked to its place of origin. If consumers in countries where Basmati is sold *do not* associate Basmati rice with the Indian subcontinent, then 'Basmati' is no more than a generic term for long-grained fragrant rice.[9]

Another difficulty for India and Pakistan is that Basmati is not a geographical expression *per se*. Consequently, the association with a place is not a strong as, say, Darjeeling tea, whose producers are able to secure very good prices due to its high reputation. This situation is not helped by a frequent failure to label Basmati rice in any way that indicates a strong connection between the product and a place. (Most often only the country of origin is printed on Basmati packets.)[10] Also, Pakistan and India disagree on the meaning of 'basmati'. According to Pakistan, authentic basmati must be grown in Punjab. India argues that the exact location is not so important as long as it is cultivated in the foothills of the Himalayas. The likelihood, though, is that Basmati has not yet become a generic term, and India and Pakistan would have a very strong case *with appropriate national legislation in place first*.

Such legal challenges notwithstanding, the best way for Basmati rice growers to increase exports and secure good prices is not through litiga-tion but effective marketing, and this will surely benefit from the availability in India and Pakistan of either a geographical indication system or certification trademarks. These could do much to protect and enhance the reputation of Basmati rice and facilitate international protection from competitors who would unfairly exploit this reputation.

An experimental project based in Ecuador and supported by the InterAmerican Development Bank is ongoing to protect traditional knowledge as trade secrets. The project, *Transforming traditional knowledge into trade secrets*, aims to enable indigenous communities to benefit from bioprospecting through effective trade secret protection of their knowledge (Vogel 1997). Knowledge from communities wishing to participate in the project will be catalogued and deposited in a restricted access database. Each community will have its own file in the database. Checks will be made to see whether each entry is not already in the public domain and whether other communities have the same knowledge. If communities with the same knowledge were to compete rather than collaborate, there would be a price war that would benefit only the corporate end-users. To overcome this danger, the project envisages the creation of a cartel comprising those communities bearing the same trade secret. The trade secret can then be negotiated in a Material Transfer Agreement (MTA) with the benefits shared between the government and the cartel members. This is undoubtedly an interesting project, but it is still too early to draw any firm conclusions as to its success.

TRADEMARKS

A kind of trademark that exists in the laws of some countries, and which TRIPS does not disallow, is the certification trademark. Certification marks can be used by small-scale producers to guarantee to customers that goods are genuine in some way or another, and perhaps to support production that is conducted in an environmentally-sustainable manner. Certification marks indicate that the claims made by the traders have been authenticated by an organization independent of the individual or company making or selling the product. This is likely to be a regional trade association that has registered its own collective mark. In Britain, the makers of a British cheese called Stilton are entitled to use the 'Stilton' certification trademark. To be eligible, cheese must be produced in or near the village of Stilton, with the traditional ingredients, and in accordance with the traditional manufacturing techniques. Producers cannot use the mark if they fail to conform to these conditions of manufacture (Dutfield 1997b). In the US, the Intertribal Agriculture Council licenses use of its annually-renewable 'Made by American Indians' mark for the promotion of agricultural or other Indian-made products that have been produced and/or processed by enrolled members of recognized Tribes.

Trademarks, labelling and also independent certification are used in India for marketing Darjeeling tea. Not only does genuine Darjeeling tea carry a special logo which is the intellectual property of the Tea Board of India, but only such tea can be referred to on the packaging as 'Darjeeling', 'pure Darjeeling' and '100% Darjeeling'.[11] The organic Darjeeling tea gardens are certified by two organizations: the Institut für Marketecologie, Switzerland, and Naturland-Verband, Germany, which carry out periodic inspections.[12]

However, labelling has been unsuccessful in some US states in terms of promoting trade in indigenous peoples' products. This may be because customers are unaware of the marks, do not care whether the articles they purchase are genuine (Axt et al 1993), or are confused by the labels. These problems illustrate the difficulties that can arise from the use of trademarks, certification and geographic indications for manufactured goods and artwork. Nevertheless, they can be successful marketing strategies, especially if traders have a clear understanding of why people wish to buy their articles.

NOTES

1 As is the case, for example, with the US Plant Patent Act.

2 As is the case in Costa Rica's *Ley de Biodiversidad* (see p110).

3 According to KRRS leader Dr Nanjundaswamy, '[w]e are going to launch a one-point programme – to drive out the multinationals. Our genetic resources are our national property' (*The Hindu*, 4/3/93, p.9 in Gupta). In contrast, Shetkari Sangathana leader Sharad Joshi said '[w]hat's wrong with Dunkel? [the draft TRIPS Agreement] I prefer to pay royalty for good quality seeds than pick bad subsidised ones.' One might add that neither of these leaders is himself a farmer. Nanjundaswamy was formerly a professor in Germany, while Joshi used to work for the United Nations in Switzerland (Gupta 1997).

4 According to Heitz (pers. comm. 1998), this model is based on an abandoned IPR system devised in Czechoslovakia in the 1920s.

5 Dr Suman Sahai, Gene Campaign's Director, is aware that the National Gene Fund would require funds from other sources and has suggested the levying of sales taxes on non-agricultural goods as one possibility (pers. comm. 1999).

6 For a commentary on the UNESCO/WIPO Model Provisions, see Posey and Dutfield (1996).

7 Portions of this case study reflect the author's contribution to the following publication: Downes, D R and Laird, S A (in press) *Innovative Mechanisms for Sharing Benefits of Biodiversity and Related Knowledge: Case Studies on Geographical Indications, Trademarks and Databases*. UNCTAD, Geneva.

8 Although the company reportedly claimed that the germplasm 'came partly from the World Collection of Germplasm in Aberdeen, Idaho' (Prakash 1998). What the RiceTec spokesperson meant by saying 'partly' is unclear to this author; it naturally leads one to wonder wherelse the germplasm came from.

9 'Basmati' is Hindi for 'the fragrant one'.

10 A notable exception is the UK-based company, Tilda Rice, which states the following on its basmati rice packets: 'Tilda basmati rice has travelled from the foothills of the Himalayas. It has been carefully tended and harvested by hand in an area whose unique soil and climatic characteristics give the area its exquisite and delicate flavour'. This statement evokes a strong connection between the product, a specific geographical location, and the local people's cultivating and harvesting practices. The words 'Tilda Rice' are trademark-protected, but not 'basmati'.

11 Website of the Darjeeling Planters Association (http://www.darjeelingtea.com).

12 Ibid.

7

THE CBD, WTO AND OTHER IPR- AND BIODIVERSITY-RELATED INSTITUTIONS, FORUMS AND PROCESSES

The global IPR regime, as with international law generally, is in a state of continuous evolution under the influence of institutions, forums and processes at international, regional and national levels. The work of the international institutions, forums and processes most relevant to this study is described below with an assessment of how they are likely to influence the global IPR regime in the coming years.

INTELLECTUAL PROPERTY RIGHTS

The WTO

Two WTO bodies are of particular relevance to this study: the Council for TRIPS, which oversees the functions of the TRIPS Agreement, and the Committee on Trade and Environment (CTE). Unlike meetings of the Conference of the Parties to the CBD, neither is open to the public.

The Council for TRIPS

The Council for TRIPS is responsible for: (i) monitoring the operation of TRIPS, and in particular members' compliance; (ii) affording members the opportunity to consult on matters relating to trade-related IPRs; (iii) assisting members in the contest of dispute settlement procedures; and (iv) carrying out other duties assigned to it by the members (Article 68). To date, discussions held by the Council have apparently not delved into the relationships between

TRIPS and the environment, in marked contrast to the Committee on Trade and Environment for which this issue is a key item on its work programme (see below).

According to the built-in agenda of TRIPS, the Council will review Article 27.3 (b) in 1999, and the implementation of the whole Agreement in 2000, and at two-year intervals thereafter. It is noteworthy that the Council may also undertake reviews in the light of any relevant new developments which might warrant modification or amendment of TRIPS (Article 71).

These reviews are an opportunity and a danger (see Box 7.1). They are an opportunity because they could lead to a wider acceptance of alternative plant variety systems devised specifically with the CBD's objectives in mind, and even to the removal of the requirement to patent life-forms. They are a danger in that some developed countries may seek to have Article 27.3 (b) removed entirely from TRIPS so that there will be virtually no restrictions at all on the patenting of life-forms (Downes 1998; Roberts 1996). This appears to be the strategy of the US government. A US government communication to the WTO General Council dated 19 November 1998 noted in reference to the 1999 review that the TRIPS Council is 'to consider whether it is desirable to modify the TRIPS Agreement by eliminating the exclusion from patentability of plants and animals and incorporating key provisions of the UPOV agreement regarding plant variety protection' (WTO General Council 1998). That this ignores the options both of leaving Article 27.3 (b) unaltered and of developing *sui generis* systems that do not incorporate key provisions of UPOV would appear to be a deliberate attempt to pre-empt the agenda of the review. In all likelihood, though, such attempts to revise TRIPS will not be made until the whole agreement is reviewed in 2000 or, which is more likely, during the Millennium Round of inter-governmental trade negotiations that is expected to be launched at the WTO Ministerial Conference in Seattle in November-December 1999. This is because the US and its allies will then be able to link their demands concerning to Article 27.3 (b) to negotiations about other trade-related matters. Developing country governments should take heed of these possibilities and develop a coordinated strategy.[1]

The Committee on Trade and Environment (CTE)

The 1994 Marrakesh Ministerial Decision on Trade and Environment, which set out the CTE's terms of reference, required the CTE, which was formally established by the General Council the following year, to consider the relevant provisions of TRIPS 'as an integral part of its work'. To this effect, Item 8 of the CTE's work programme is *The Relevant Provisions of the Agreement on Trade-Related Aspects of Intellectual Property Rights*.

BOX 7.1 OPTIONS FOR THE REVIEW OF ARTICLE 27.3 (B)

Although there has been no formal discussion in the WTO of the options that countries may consider, informally many options are being discussed, including:

1 Doing nothing, simply reviewing progress in implementing the sub-paragraph and leaving the wording as it is, retaining some ambiguity. This would provide countries with maximum flexibility within the existing agreement, particularly because the exact meaning of most of the terms has yet to be agreed, or defined by international jurisprudence. By agreeing to do nothing, it also reduces the risk of negative changes being imposed.

2 Extending the exclusions to patentability to include all living organisms and the associated knowledge for their conservation and sustainable use. This is the option favoured by many developing countries whose genetic wealth and the food and livelihood security of their citizens could be threatened by monopoly ownership of biological resources through patents. It is a low-cost option removing the need to defend their resources and know-how through litigation. Benefit-sharing arrangements should be agreed through the FAO/CBD negotiations in the International Undertaking and the CBD itself, which may prove a better arrangement for developing countries.

3 Removing the obligation to provide plant variety protection or ensuring that measures adopted are carefully tailored to a country's own needs – the *sui generis* option. Most developing countries do not require this as a priority. The reciprocal arrangements with developed countries for the use of their protected plant varieties or germplasm, which have been produced mainly to meet the needs of northern temperate industrial agriculture, are not usually to the advantage of the majority of farmers in developing countries. With the exception of a few industrial export-oriented commodities, such as flowers, the priority for the majority of people is for the local development of varieties adapted to the needs of sustainable agricultural practices in labour intensive holdings.

4 Deletion of the whole sub-paragraph, which would provide for no exclusions to patenting of living organisms and their accompanying intellectual property – an option favoured by some industrial countries. This would favour the biotechnology industry, which would be able to insist that all countries impose and recognize their patents, and their right to patent material irrespective of its origin.

Source: Reproduced from Mulvany 1998

Traditional and indigenous knowledge has been discussed during several CTE meetings, and a few governments have argued in favour of the need to reform the patent system and to protect indigenous knowledge, such as through trade secrets and *sui generis* systems consistent with CBD Article 8(j). For example, the Nigerian delegation opposed the patenting of life forms and argued that TRIPS must be construed to 'accord recognition to traditional interest and right holders' (WTO-CTE 1996b). An Indian representative argued that:

> *the worst casualty, in an IPR regime for plant varieties, was the knowledge, innovations and practices of indigenous and local communities embodying traditional lifestyles relevant for the conservation and sustainable use of biodiversity, highlighted in Article 8 (j) of the Biodiversity Convention (ibid).*

In November 1996, the Committee adopted its Report to the Singapore Ministerial Conference (WTO-CTE 1996c). The Report concluded that further work was needed to appreciate better the relationship of the relevant provisions of TRIPS to environmental protection and sustainable development and whether and how these provisions relate to:

> *The creation of incentives for the conservation of biological diversity, the sustainable use of its components, and the fair and equitable sharing of the benefits arising from the utilization of genetic resources including the protection of knowledge, innovations and practices of indigenous and local communities embodying traditional lifestyles relevant to the conservation and sustainable use of biodiversity.*

Such critical views as those presented above imply that WTO members could not achieve a consensus and that some have for the time being agreed to disagree.

The 1996 Ministerial Declaration seemed to indicate an unwillingness among WTO members to await the results of further work by the CTE, stating that 'each Member should carefully review all its existing or proposed legislation, programmes and measures to ensure their full compatibility with the WTO obligations' (Paragraph 12). This statement should be considered in the light of two articles of the CBD: (a) Article 16.5, which recognizes that 'patents and other intellectual property rights may have an influence on this Convention' and requires States to co-operate 'subject to national legislation and international law in order to ensure that such rights are supportive of and do not run counter to its [ie the CBD's] objectives'; and (b) Article 22.1, according to which:

> *The provisions of this Convention shall not affect the rights and obligations of any Contracting Party deriving from any existing international agreement, except where the exercise of those rights and obligations would cause a serious damage or threat to biological diversity [emphasis added].*

The issue of supersession in the case of two international agreements with provisions and aims that may be in conflict arises here.[2] Which agreement has priority? International law does not provide a definitive answer in this particular case (see Cameron and Makuch 1995), and the CTE deliberations evince a strong disagreement among members about the relationship of multilateral environmental agreements (MEAs) like the CBD to WTO rules. Ashish Kothari and R V Anuradha (1997) argue that Article 22.1 may well provide grounds for applying the precautionary principle to an IPR regime or a GATT obligation.

The World Intellectual Property Organization

Most international conventions pertaining to intellectual property rights are administered by the World Intellectual Property Organization (WIPO). WIPO was established in 1967, although its origins can be traced to the Paris and Berne Conventions adopted in 1883 and 1886, respectively. WIPO's primary objectives are to administer international treaties on intellectual property laws; to provide assistance to member states in promulgating intellectual property laws; and to seek harmonization of national laws, aiming to promote the protection of intellectual property throughout the world. WIPO administers, *inter alia*, the following IPR treaties:

- Paris Convention for the Protection of Industrial Property (1883, Stockholm Revision, revised most recently in 1967 at Stockholm);
- Berne Convention for the Protection of Literary and Artistic Works (1886, revised most recently in 1971 at Paris and amended in 1979);
- Madrid Agreement Concerning the International Registration of Trademarks (1891, revised most recently in 1967 at Stockholm and amended in 1979);
- Lisbon Agreement for the Protection of Appellations of Origin and their International Registration (1958, revised in 1967 at Stockholm and amended in 1979);
- Patent Cooperation Treaty (1970, amended in 1979 and modified in 1984);
- Budapest Treaty on the International Recognition of the Deposit of Micro-organisms for the Purpose of Patent Procedure (1977, amended in 1980).

Unlike the WTO and its GATT predecessor, WIPO does not have a dispute settlement mechanism. As we saw earlier, this is one of the main reasons why the developed countries worked hard to ensure that one of the outcomes of the Uruguay Round was an IPR agreement promoting minimum standards throughout the world while allowing members to challenge perceived failures of other members to implement these standards.

This does not mean that WIPO is becoming marginal to the global IPR regime. Indeed, WIPO is by far the most important international institution dedicated to IPRs, and is likely to increase its influence as WIPO builds closer links with other institutions such as the WTO and the CBD Conference of the Parties and Secretariat. Moreover, WIPO is collaborating with the WTO to help developing countries to meet their TRIPS obligations by 2000 through provision of technical assistance, for example, 'in preparing legislation, training, institution-building, and modernizing intellectual property systems and enforcement' (Joint WTO-WIPO press release, 21 July 1998).

In early 1998, WIPO established its Global Intellectual Property Issues Division to deal with:

> *The challenges facing the intellectual property system in a rapidly changing world, such as accelerating technological advancement, the integration of the world's economic, cultural and information systems, and the expanding relevance of intellectual property issues in trade, culture, investment, human rights, health and environmental spheres.*[3]

The Division researches and explores various issues including:

1 *New approaches to the use of IPRs for new beneficiaries* with respect to (i) the intellectual property needs of holders of traditional knowledge, innovations, culture and genetic resources, such as in agriculture and medicine; (ii) the feasibility of establishing databases of traditional knowledge; and (iii) the international legal character of IPRs arising from references to intellectual property in multilateral instruments in other fields, such as human rights, the environment, culture, trade, health and investment.
2 *Biodiversity and biotechnology* with a focus on: (i) the role of IPRs in the preservation, conservation and dissemination of global biodiversity; (ii) the IPR aspects of biotechnology; and (iii) the use of IPRs in the transfer of technology under multilateral environmental agreements.
3 *Protection of expressions of folklore* including: (i) the need for, and possible nature and scope of, new or adapted forms of protection for expressions of folklore; and (ii) the use of the existing intellectual property system for the beneficial commercialization of expressions of folklore, such as by way of multimedia and Internet technologies.

The decision of WIPO to undertake these activities, to collaborate with the CBD process, and to carry out extensive consultations with indigenous peoples and local communities, is a positive development (see pp98–99). However, it is difficult at this stage to predict where these activities will lead. It is conceivable that the outcome could be an updated version of the 1985 UNESCO/WIPO *Model Provisions for National Laws on Protection of Expressions of Folklore Against Illicit Exploitation and Other Prejudicial Actions*, which attracted little interest from national legislatures.

BIODIVERSITY: CONSERVATION AND SUSTAINABLE USE

The CBD Conference of the Parties

To review implementation of the CBD, the Conference of the Parties (composed of all those countries that have ratified the CBD) meets at regular (usually 1–2-yearly) intervals. At the 3rd meeting of the Conference of the Parties (COP–3) in November 1996, two of the agenda items were *Implementation of Article 8 (j)*, and *Intellectual Property Rights*. At COP–4 in May 1998, there was no agenda item dealing exclusively with IPRs, but the subject came up in a number of decisions, including the Decision IV/8 on *Access and Benefit Sharing*.

Article 8 (j)

With respect to Article 8 (j), COP–3 agreed on the need to 'develop national legislation and corresponding strategies for the implementation of Article 8 (j) in consultation with representatives of their indigenous and local communities' (UNEP 1997 [Decision III/14]). Pursuant to this, the CBD Secretariat arranged a Workshop on Traditional Knowledge and Biodiversity. The Workshop took place in Madrid, Spain, in November 1997, and was attended by representatives of governments and 148 indigenous and local community organizations. The Report of the Workshop (CBD Secretariat 1997) suggested the following options for recommendations for elements of a workplan for future elaboration under the framework of the CBD:

1 participatory mechanisms for indigenous and local communities;
2 status and trends in relation to Article 8 (j) and related provisions;
3 traditional cultural practices for conservation and sustainable use;
4 equitable sharing of benefits;
5 exchange and dissemination of information;
6 monitoring elements; and
7 legal elements.

Decision IV/9 on *Implementation of Article 8 (j)* and *Related Provisions* recognized 'the importance of making intellectual property-related provisions of Article 8 (j) and related provisions of the Convention on Biological Diversity and provisions of international agreements relating to intellectual property mutually supportive, and the desirability of undertaking further cooperation and consultation with the World Intellectual Property Organization.' The Parties agreed to establish an '*ad hoc* open-ended inter-sessional working group' to address the implementation of Article 8 (j) and related provisions to be composed of Parties and observers including, in particular, representatives of indigenous peoples and local communities. The mandate of the working group includes the following items:

- To provide advice on the application and development of legal and other appropriate forms of protection for the knowledge, innovations and practices of indigenous and local communities.
- To develop a programme of work, based on the structure of the elements in the Madrid report (see above).

As part of the work programme's short-term activities, governments, international agencies, research institutions, representatives of indigenous peoples and local communities and NGOs are invited to submit case studies and other relevant information to the Executive Secretary as background information for the working group on such topics as:

- The influence of international instruments, IPRs, current laws and policies on knowledge, innovations and practices of indigenous and local communities.
- Documented examples and related information on ethical guidance for the conduct of research in indigenous and local communities about the knowledge they hold.
- Matters of prior informed consent, fair and equitable sharing of benefits and *in situ* conservation in lands and territories used by indigenous and local communities.

No reference is made in the decision to the WTO, but WIPO has a key role to play. The COP requested the Executive Secretary of the CBD to compile case studies:

> *relating to Article 8 (j) and intellectual property rights, including existing* sui generis *systems and/or adapted forms of protection to the knowledge, innovations and practices of indigenous and local communities ... for transmittal to the World Intellectual Property Organization and for use in initiatives on legislating on implementation of Article 8 (j) and related provisions.*

Furthermore, the Executive Secretary was requested to seek ways to enhance cooperation with WIPO and encourage Parties to submit information to the Executive Secretary to support such cooperation.

The potential for the COP working with WIPO to influence the international IPR regime in favour of the CBD's objectives and the rights of indigenous peoples and local communities is an intriguing one. It is not inconceivable that the end result could be the elaboration of either: (a) a new IPR treaty to protect traditional biodiversity-related knowledge, innovations and practices; (b) a more general agreement to protect traditional culture and folklore as was suggested in the Plan of Action from the 1997 *UNESCO-WIPO World Forum on the Protection of Folklore* which might include biodiversity-related knowledge; or (c) a Protocol to the CBD to implement protection of traditional biodiversity-related knowledge and/or FAO Farmers' Rights (see p102). Decisions to adopt one or more of these possible actions depends on the will of a majority of countries to give higher priority to the CBD, especially *vis-à-vis* the WTO.

Intellectual property rights

The COP–3 decision on *Intellectual Property Rights* (Decision III/17) called, *inter alia*, for dissemination of case studies on the relationships between IPRs and CBD objectives, including technology transfer and benefit-sharing with indigenous and local communities. It was suggested that these case studies consider matters such as (i) the role and potential of *existing* IPR systems in enabling 'interested parties', including indigenous and local communities to determine access and equitable benefit sharing, and (ii) the development of IPR, such as *sui generis* systems.

Even though COP–4 did not deal with IPRs as an agenda item, Paragraph 10 of Decision IV/15[4] expressed agreement on the need for further work to enhance understanding of the relationship between IPRs, TRIPS and the CBD.[5] Clearly intellectual property remains a topic of interest to the COP given that the relationship between IPRs, TRIPS and the CBD was a major part of the agenda of the June 1999 Intersessional Meeting on the Operations of the Convention.

Access and benefit-sharing

In Decision IV/8 on *Access and Benefit Sharing*, the COP agreed to establish 'a regionally balanced panel of experts appointed by Governments, composed of representatives from the private and the public sectors as well as representatives of indigenous and local communities' to report to COP–5. The mandate of the panel is to develop 'a common understanding of basic concepts and to explore all options for access and benefit sharing on mutually agreed terms including guiding principles, guidelines, and codes of best practice for access and benefit sharing arrangements'. Such options might address the following elements set out in an annex to this decision as follows:

- Prior informed consent in provider countries for access to genetic resources and research and development.
- Clear, established mechanisms to provide such consent, including, *inter alia*, legislative, administrative and policy measures, as appropriate.
- Reference to the country of origin, where available, in relevant publication *and patent applications* [emphasis added].
- Mutually agreed terms including on benefit sharing *and intellectual property rights* and technology transfer, where appropriate [emphasis added].
- Efficient permitting and regulatory procedures that avoid burdensome procedures involving high transaction costs.
- Incentive measures to encourage the conclusion of contractual partnerships.

The first meeting of the panel will take place in October 1999.

By virtue of Paragraph 2 of Decision IV/16 (*Institutional Matters and the Programme of Work*), the COP agreed 'to hold an open-ended meeting to consider possible arrangements to improve preparations for and conduct of the meetings of the Conference of the Parties, taking into account proposals made at the fourth meeting of the Conference of the Parties, *including a preparatory discussion of the item on access to genetic resources* on the agenda of the fifth meeting of the Conference of the Parties' [emphasis added]. This meeting, which took place in June 1999, was mandated to 'explore options for access and benefit-sharing mechanisms and to start work on Paragraph 10 of Decision IV/15 [see page 99, above] and to make recommendations for future work' (IV/8, Para. 1). The meeting, known as the Intersessional Meeting on the Operations of the Convention, also discussed the issue of *ex situ* collections acquired prior to the entry into force of the CBD.[6]

The UNCTAD Biotrade Initiative

The Biotrade Initiative of the UN Conference on Trade and Development (UNCTAD), in collaboration with the Secretariat of the CBD, claims to be 'a new approach to biodiversity conservation and sustainable development' (UNCTAD 1996b). For developing countries to benefit from increased private sector interest in bioprospecting, conducive conditions for an efficient and equitable bioprospecting market need to be established by overcoming the following obstacles: (i) property rights to biological resources that are not well defined or easily protected; (ii) insufficient information about these resources to determine their actual and potential value; (iii) high transaction costs and undeveloped risk spreading mechanisms; and (iv) lack of technical and entrepreneurial resources. The Initiative advocates effective economic instruments and strategic partnerships as a means to bring value to biological resources, achieve appropriate technology transfers, and enhance export capacity for developing countries in such resources.

The Biotrade Initiative makes no assertions that existing IPR regimes are incompatible with conservation, sustainability or equitable benefit sharing. Indeed, the UNCTAD Secretariat paper on the Biotrade Initiative argues that the availability of IPR protection provides incentives for more generous technology transfer and technical assistance arrangements. In spite of this apparently rather conservative approach, the paper proposes that the Conference of the Parties to the CBD consider an international certification system for bioprospecting linked to a code of conduct. Resulting products from bioprospecting and R&D that comply with the code's requirements could then carry this certification. Patent laws could even be amended to require such certification for applications on inventions developed from biological resources. Moreover, in a section dealing with enhancing conservation and sustainable development opportunities, the paper argues that:

> *on equity grounds it is ... essential that information provided by traditional healers, farmers or other local residents which is used to identify potentially valuable biological materials, is obtained through informed consent and results in appropriate compensation.*

The paper goes on to mention that mechanisms have been proposed or are being used to promote equitable sharing, local development and incentives for biodiversity conservation, and these mechanisms will be evaluated by the Initiative. Among such mechanisms to be evaluated are:

- communal intellectual property rights over information concerning uses for components of biodiversity; and
- certification of origin programmes for local suppliers of biological material.

Ideally the Biotrade Initiative should work closely with the CBD Secretariat, WIPO and the FAO to ensure that these institutions can benefit from these evaluations and assist with their wide dissemination.

The Biotrade Initiative approach has encountered some criticisms. One of the main ones is that it is felt to give undue weight to the needs and priorities of corporations in developed countries yet insufficient attention is given to the rights of indigenous peoples. Moreover, by encouraging developing countries to act unilaterally, it is argued that such countries will not be able to achieve favourable bioprospecting agreements as long as companies are free to negotiate separately with neighbouring countries that can supply most of the same resources at a lower price.[7]

It is noteworthy in the context of access and benefit sharing that the Swiss survey referred to on page 34 provides evidence that both public and private sector users of genetic resources in developed countries would accept a code of conduct on access and transfer of genetic resources. It revealed widespread agreement among the Swiss government, industry and universities that such a code might be a beneficial instrument to promote best practice in access and benefit sharing and equitable partnerships between industrialized and developing countries under mutually agreed terms (CBD Secretariat 1998). Most likely, determining the provisions of such a code would require some extensive negotiations among the interested parties.

AGRICULTURE

The Food and Agriculture Organization[8]

Since 1983 the UN Food and Agriculture Organization (FAO) has been developing its Global System for the Conservation and Sustainable Use of Plant Genetic Resources for Food and Agriculture. There are four main components of the Global System:

1 An intergovernmental forum, the *Commission for Plant Genetic Resources* (CPGR).
2 A non legally-binding agreement, the *International Undertaking on Plant Genetic Resources* (IUPGR).
3 An interim financial mechanism, the *International Fund for Plant Genetic Resources*.
4 The Global Plan of Action for the Conservation and Sustainable Utilization of Plant Genetic resources for Food and Agriculture that was adopted by the 1996 International Technical Conference on Plant Genetic Resources.

The objectives of the IUPGR are 'to ensure the safe conservation and promote the unrestricted availability and sustainable utilization of plant genetic resources for present and future generations, by providing a flexible framework for sharing the benefits and burdens'. Included in the IUPGR is the concept of *Farmers' Rights* as an attempt to acknowledge 'the contribution farmers have made to the conservation and development of plant genetic resources, which constitute the basis of plant production throughout the world'. Resolution 5/89 defined Farmers' Rights as:

> *Rights arising from the past, present and future contributions*
> *of farmers in conserving, improving and making available*
> *plant genetic resources particularly those in the centres of*
> *origin/diversity. Those rights are vested in the international*
> *community, as trustees for present and future generations of*
> *farmers, and supporting the continuation of their contribu-*
> *tions as well as the attainment of overall purposes of the*
> *International Undertaking [on Plant Genetic Resources].*

Implementation of Farmers' Rights was principally to be through the
voluntary International Fund for Plant Genetic Resources. Farmers
themselves would not directly benefit from the FAO-administered
Fund, which would be disbursed to governments. In any event, the
Fund failed on account of the lack of contributions.

In May 1992 the Conference for the Adoption of the Agreed Text
of the Convention on Biological Diversity (Nairobi Final Act) adopted
Resolution 3 on *The Interrelationship Between the Convention on
Biological Diversity and the Promotion of Sustainable Agriculture.*
This recognized the need:

> *to seek solutions to outstanding matters concerning plant*
> *genetic resources within the Global System for the*
> *Conservation and Sustainable Use of Plant Genetic Resources*
> *for Food and Sustainable Agriculture, in particular:*
>
> *(a) Access to* ex situ *collections not acquired in accordance*
> *with this Convention; and*
>
> *(b) The question of farmers' rights (FAO 1993).*

The following year, the CPGR Resolution 93/1 called for a revision of
the IUPGR to harmonize the latter with the CBD. To this effect, the
Commission, now called the Commission on Genetic Resources for
Food and Agriculture (CGRFA), has held a series of negotiations to
revise the International Undertaking. If Parties to the CBD so decide,
the revision could be converted into a legally-binding instrument or
protocol to the CBD. A legally-binding IUPGR would ensure that
Farmers' Rights finally have legal recognition. However, the Fourth
FAO International Technical Conference, held in Leipzig in June
1996, made little progress in terms of agreeing a revised IUPGR and
operationalizing the Farmers' Rights concept. Protracted discussions
have continued at five extraordinary sessions of the CPGRFA with
slow, if any, progress.

There are three serious problems with the 'Farmers' Rights'
concept, as it is currently understood, that need to be resolved before
further progress can be achieved:

The first problem is the inadequacy of the term 'farmer' when considering who the beneficiaries of a Farmers' Rights system should be. It is frequently assumed that 'farmers' are by definition cultivators of field crops. In fact, the genetic resources conserved and enhanced by local communities include not only field crops, but also non-timber forest products, medicinal and herbal plants, and animals. Therefore, if the purpose of a Farmers' Rights system is to reward the traditional conservers and improvers of plant genetic resources, the beneficiaries should not be restricted to field crop cultivators. Fisherfolk, hunters, pastoralists, nomads and gatherers, must also be included in any Farmers' Rights system (Posey 1996). The CBD term, 'indigenous and local communities embodying traditional lifestyles', though somewhat vague, is far less restrictive than 'farmers'.

The second problem is that, whether or not Farmer's Rights are envisaged as an IPR system, it is unclear who the rights holders are and how they should benefit. Farmers' Rights, as the term suggests, was originally conceived as a counterpart to Breeders' Rights and is more a political concept than a legal term (Bragdon and Downes 1998). Farmers' Rights are a way of recognizing that plant genetic resources are different from natural mineral resources like coal and oil, since to assume that plant genetic resources are mere gifts of nature fails to give credit to the knowledge and resource management practices of traditional communities past and present that have nurtured many of these resources. However, while plant breeders' rights are intellectual property rights vested in natural or legal persons and are incorporated in the national legislation of several developed countries, Farmers' Rights are vested not in local communities but in the international community as trustee for present and future generations of farmers (ibid). Mechanisms to give practical expression to Farmers' Rights and to compensate farmers still do not exist, and seem unlikely to exist as long as there is so little clarity about the meaning of the concept and a lack of consensus with regard to how communities are supposed to benefit.

The third problem is that not all traditional farmers and farming communities are conservers of genetic resources. Therefore, identifying the deserving beneficiaries of a Farmers' Rights system would be necessary. This is likely to be extremely difficult on practical and political grounds.

Nevertheless, the latest negotiating text of the revision of the IUPGR contains one whole (albeit heavily bracketed) article on Farmers' Rights. If approved, the provisions in this article would, *inter alia*:

• Promote the establishment … of an international *sui generis* system for the recognition, protection and compensation of knowledge, innovations and practices of farmers and traditional communities.

- Ensure that the [individual and/or] collective knowledge and plant genetic resources for food and agriculture held and developed by farmers and [farming / local] communities are protected and promoted by adopting and implementing appropriate legislation [in the form of a collective rights regime] that provides for the adequate protection of traditional or indigenous knowledge, innovations, materials and practices of and by farmers and [farming / local] communities [and promote the equitable sharing of benefits arising from the utilization of their plant genetic resources for food and agriculture].
- Review, assess and, if appropriate, modify intellectual property rights systems, land tenure, and seed laws in order to ensure their harmony with the provisions of this Article.

The link made between IPRs, seed laws and land tenure is an important one given the observation made earlier that equitable benefit sharing and sustainable use of biodiversity are hard to achieve when other rights such as land tenurial rights are not recognized. Nevertheless, it remains to be seen how much, if any, of this text will appear in the adopted version.

The Consultative Group on International Agricultural Research

The Consultative Group on International Agricultural Research (CGIAR) is an informal association founded in 1971 and sponsored by the FAO, the World Bank, the United Nations Development Programme, and the United Nations Environment Programme. The CGIAR supports an international network of 16 international agricultural research centres (IARCs).

The mission of the CGIAR is to contribute, through its research, to promoting sustainable agriculture for food security in the developing countries. The CGIAR network holds the world's largest *ex situ* collections of plant genetic resources, with 600,000 accessions of improved varieties and wild species. These collections, which are held under the auspices of the FAO 'in trust for the benefit of the international community, in particular the developing countries', include up to 40 per cent of all unique samples of major food crops held by gene banks worldwide. The fact that the majority of accessions in the CGIAR system's collections are held in trust is important, because this prevents them from becoming absorbed into national collections or owned by national governments or countries in which they are located.

According to the CGIAR Website,[9] programmes at the IARCs fall into six broad categories:

1   Productivity Research: creating or adopting new technologies (such as the 'dwarf' varieties of wheat and rice that brought about Asia's and Latin America's Green Revolution) to increase productivity on farmers' fields
2   Management of Natural Resources: protecting and preserving the productivity of natural resources on which agriculture depends
3   Improving the Policy Environment: assisting developing countries to formulate and carry out effective food, agriculture, and research policy
4   Institution Building: strengthening national agricultural research systems in developing countries
5   Germplasm Conservation: conserving germplasm and making it available to all regions and countries
6   Building Linkages: facilitating cooperation and technology transfer between advanced research institutions in developed countries and national research programmes in developing countries.

Given the importance of the CGIAR network's work and the size of the collections it holds, its IPR policies are of great significance. The IARCs routinely distribute germplasm to plant breeders through Material Transfer Agreements (MTAs) which expressly disallow recipients to apply for IPRs on the materials transferred. In February 1998, the CGIAR called for a moratorium on the granting of IPRs on all plant germplasm held in trust under the FAO's auspices. Given the importance of the CGIAR networks germplasm collections in international agricultural research, this is a very significant step.

However, an unresolved issue is the fact that the CBD does not apply to accessions collected prior to the entry into force of the CBD (see p102). Negotiations under the FAO-CPGRFA's auspices are ongoing, but the issue is not directly referred to in the latest negotiating text of the revision of the IUPGR. It would appear that a complete resolution to this issue will not be achieved for several more years.

NOTES

1 However, it is also highly possible that the US will concentrate on pressuring developing countries to implement existing obligations rather than seeking to create new ones through raising the minimum standards.

2 See Cameron and Makuch (1995) for a detailed discussion of this issue.

3 This quote and the following section are based on unpublished information provided to the author of this paper by Mr Wend Wendland and Mr Shakeel Bhatti of WIPO.

4 '*The relationship of the Convention on Biological Diversity with the Commission on Sustainable Development and biodiversity-related conventions, other international agreements, institutions and processes of relevance*'.

5 The COP 'emphasizes that further work is required to help develop a common appreciation of the relationship between intellectual property rights and the relevant provisions of the Agreement on Trade-Related Aspects of Intellectual Property Rights and the Convention on Biological Diversity, in particular on issues relating to technology transfer and conservation and sustainable use of biological diversity and the fair and equitable sharing of benefits arising out of the use of genetic resources, including the protection of knowledge, innovations and practices of indigenous and local communities embodying traditional lifestyles relevant for the conservation and sustainable use of biological diversity.'

6 The COP '[r]equests the Executive Secretary to invite information from Parties and relevant organizations in time for the inter-sessional meeting in respect of those *ex situ* collections which were acquired prior to the entry into force of the Convention on Biological Diversity and which are not addressed by the Commission on Genetic Resources for Food and Agriculture of the Food and Agriculture Organization, to help the inter-sessional meeting to make recommendations to the fifth meeting of the Conference of the Parties for future work on resolving the issue of such *ex situ* collections, with due regard to the provisions of the Convention' (Decision IV/8 Para. 2).

7 A debate on the merits of the Biotrade Initiative took place in 1997 on the listservs 'Indknow' (indknow@u.washington.edu) and 'Biodiv-conv' (biodiv-conv@igc.apc.org). Participants included P. Hardison, J. de Castro (Biotrade-UNCTAD), A. Artuso (Biotrade), C. McAfee, B. Potter and J. Moles.

8 This section draws on – but expands upon and updates – related text in Posey (1996).

9 http://www.cgiar.org.

8 GOVERNMENT AND REGIONAL INITIATIVES: SOME CASE STUDIES

Genetic resource access and benefit sharing (ABS) laws are being used by some countries to place conditions on the exercise of IPRs as a way to harmonize them with CBD-related objectives. The most well known law of this kind is the Andean Community's *Common System on Access to Genetic Resources*, which is an initiative of a number of governments acting collectively. A similar law has recently been enacted in Costa Rica, though this is more ambitious in scope and seeks to implement the CBD in its entirety rather than just its provisions relating to access and benefit sharing. The Organization of African Unity member states are considering a draft model law on *Community Rights and Access to Biological Resources*.

ANDEAN COMMUNITY *COMMON SYSTEM ON ACCESS TO GENETIC RESOURCES*

The Andean Community *Common System on Access to Genetic Resources* was adopted in 1996 by the Andean Community member countries (Bolivia, Colombia, Ecuador, Peru and Venezuela).

As may be expected, the Common System proclaims that member countries have sovereign rights over the use and exploitation of their genetic resources and the right to determine conditions of access. However, the Andean Community has gone further than the CBD by extending sovereign rights to the *derivatives* of these resources. A derivative is defined as a molecule or combination or mixture of natural molecules, including raw extracts of living or dead organisms of biological origin, derived from the metabolism of living organisms. This is not the same thing as a synthesized product, which is a substance obtained through an artificial process using genetic information or molecules and which may include semi-processed extracts. Even so, it appears that isolated bio-compounds could become subject to the claims of Andean Community member states even if the compound has been isolated *and patented* by a company outside the Andean Community region. It is by no means certain that such a measure is TRIPS-compatible.

With regard to traditional communities, the Common System recognizes their historical contribution to biodiversity, its conservation, development and sustainable use, and the benefits provided by such contribution. It also acknowledges that the close interdependence between these communities and biodiversity must be strengthened.

The Common System introduces an interesting term, 'intangible component', which means any knowledge, innovation or practice (individual or collective) of actual or potential value associated with a biogenetic resource or derivative, *whether or not it is protected by intellectual property rights*. One of the stated objectives of the Common System is to establish a basis for recognizing and appreciating genetic resources, their derivatives and related intangible components. A legitimate objection to the intangible component concept is that it removes non-IPR-protected knowledge from the public domain. It could be argued that upholding rather than undermining the public domain may be in the better long-term interests of society as a whole. On the other hand, the concept may provide legal support to indigenous peoples and local communities contesting misappropriation of their knowledge and negotiating know-how agreements with companies.

Measures to ensure that these intangible components are recognized and appreciated are included in the access procedures. All such access procedures must include an application and signed contract. Parties to access contracts must be the State, represented by the Competent National Authority, and the applicant. Communities are not mentioned as parties. The Common System suggests various conditions for these applications and contracts, including the strengthening and development of communities with respect to their intangible components. But the contract itself is required to take into consideration the rights and interests of suppliers of biogenetic resources and derivatives and their intangible components. If access to a resource that includes an intangible component is requested, fair and equitable benefit-sharing from the use of such component must be provided in an annex to the contract.

Subsidiary contracts may also be agreed between applicants and other institutions. Again, communities are not specifically mentioned as parties, though they can be as long as they are recognized as owners, holders or administrators of the property on which the biological resources containing the genetic resource are found. In this sense, an argument can be made that the Common System is only supportive of communities' rights to the extent that such communities already enjoy recognition of their land rights and are able to enforce these rights. Instead, it may be better to separate ownership of a resource from knowledge about the resource so that legal recognition of the latter is not dependent upon recognition of the former.

Interestingly, in a section dealing with complementary measures, the Common System states that any rights, including IPRs, to genetic resources, derivatives, synthesized products or related intangible components obtained or developed through non-compliance with these terms of access, shall not be recognized by the member states. Furthermore, the national offices dealing with IPRs are empowered to require applicants to submit a copy of their access contract as a pre-condition for the concession of an IPR. Clearly, this is intended to deal with cases in which patents are acquired in developed countries for products derived from resources found within the Andean Community region and then the same patents are subsequently applied for in Andean Community countries.

The experience of the Andean Community suggests that ABS legislation may become a means by which IPRs can be subordinated to the CBD and rendered more biodiversity- and local-community-friendly. This is a very interesting possibility given the strong external pressures that developing countries may have to contend with when they are drafting new patent laws to comply with the TRIPS Agreement.

THE COSTA RICA BIODIVERSITY LAW

In April 1998, the Legislative Assembly of Costa Rica passed the *Ley de Biodiversidad*, or Biodiversity Law. To date, this is perhaps the most ambitious and elaborate national law to implement the CBD. Interestingly, many of its provisions are clear attempts to reconcile the country's CBD obligations with its TRIPS ones, including the initiation of a process to develop a *sui generis* system to protect the intellectual rights of indigenous peoples and local communities.

The Law's overall objective is to conserve biodiversity, sustainably utilize resources, and distribute fairly the derived benefits and costs (Article 1), but there are 13 objectives in all (see Box 8.1 for a number of these). Its 107 Articles cover the full range of issues contained in the CBD including: (i) Biosafety; (ii) Conservation and sustainable use of ecosystems and species; (iii) Access to genetic and biochemical elements of biodiversity; (iv) Prior informed consent; (v) Protection of scientific and traditional biodiversity-related knowledge through intellectual property rights and/or *sui generis* systems; (vi) Education and public awareness; (vii) Technology transfer; (viii) Environmental impact assessment; and (ix) Incentives.

BOX 8.1 PRINCIPLES AND OBJECTIVES OF THE *LEY DE BIODIVERSIDAD*

General principles

1 *Respect for all forms of life* – all living things have the right to life independent of their actual or potential economic value.
2 *The elements of biodiversity are meritorious* – they have decisive and strategic importance for the country's development and are essential for the domestic, social, cultural and aesthetic use of its inhabitants.
3 *Respect for cultural diversity* – the diversity of cultural practices and associated knowledge of biodiversity elements must be respected and promoted, in conformity with national and international juridical standards, particularly in the case of peasant communities, indigenous peoples and other cultural groups.
4 *Intra- and inter-generational equity* – the State and private individuals will ensure that biodiversity elements are utilized sustainably in such a way that the possibilities and opportunities from their use and the benefits are guaranteed in a just manner for all sectors of society and to satisfy the needs of future generations.

Objectives (selected)

1 To integrate conservation and sustainable use of biodiversity elements into the development of socio-cultural, economic and environmental policies.
2 To promote active participation of all social sectors in conservation and ecologically sustainable use of biodiversity, in pursuit of social, economic and cultural sustainability.
3 To regulate access and facilitate equitable distribution of social, environmental and economic benefits for all sectors of society, with special attention to local communities and indigenous peoples.
4 To recognize and compensate the knowledge, innovations and practices of indigenous peoples and local communities for conservation and ecologically sustainable use of biodiversity elements.
5 To recognize rights arising from the contribution of scientific knowledge for conservation and ecologically sustainable use of biodiversity elements.
6 To promote access to biodiversity elements of biodiversity and technology transfer.
7 To foster international and regional cooperation to achieve conservation, ecologically sustainable use and distribution of benefits derived from biodiversity, especially in frontier areas or shared resources.

Unofficial translation by author

The Law regulates the use, management, associated knowledge, and the fair distribution of the benefits and costs derived from the utilization of biodiversity elements, but with three exclusions (Article 4). These are: (i) human genetic and biochemical material; (ii) non-commercial exchanges between indigenous peoples and local communities of biochemical and genetic resources and associated knowledge derived from their practices, uses and customs; and (iii) the autonomy of universities with respect to field investigations and teaching for non-commercial purposes.

The biochemical and genetic properties of wild or domesticated biodiversity elements are in the public domain (Article 6) and all biodiversity elements *per se* are subject to the exclusive sovereignty of the State (Article 2). Therefore, while the resources themselves may be owned by the State, private landowners or local communities, the *properties* of these elements can be owned by nobody, not even those who discover or may be aware of these properties.

Article 7 deals with definitions. Within the definition of 'biodiversity' is included 'intangible elements', which are: traditional, individual or collective knowledge, innovation and practice with real or potential value associated with biochemical and genetic resources whether or not protected by intellectual property systems or *sui generis* register systems. No explicit distinction is made in this Article between 'traditional' and 'scientific' knowledge and the Law makes clear throughout that holders of each kind of knowledge have equal entitlement to legal protection.

Articles 77–85 are devoted to the subject of intellectual and industrial property rights. This section of the Law begins with a statement recognizing the need to protect knowledge and innovations through appropriate legal mechanisms, and refers specifically to patents, trade secrets, plant breeders' rights, *sui generis* community intellectual rights, copyrights and farmers' rights. Remarkably for a biodiversity law, parameters for the scope of IPR protection permitted by the State are drawn very explicitly. Excepted from IPR protection are the following:

1 DNA sequences;
2 plants and animals;
3 non-genetically modified organisms;
4 essentially biological processes for the production of plants and animals;
5 natural processes or cycles *per se*;
6 inventions essentially derived from knowledge associated with traditional biological or cultural biological practices in the public domain; and
7 inventions which, through their commercial exploitation in monopoly form can affect agriculture and livestock processes or products considered basic for nutrition and health of the country's inhabitants.

In order to ensure that these exceptions are observed, the National Seeds Office and the Intellectual and Industrial Property Registries are required to consult the National Biodiversity Management Commission,[1] a State body set up by this Law, before awarding IPR protection for innovations involving biodiversity elements. In every case, a certificate of origin issued by the Technical Office of the Commission and statement of prior informed consent will have to be presented with the IPR application. Such consent may include that of indigenous authorities in cases where bioprospecting takes place on their lands. Indigenous peoples and local communities are fully entitled to refuse access to their resources and knowledge for any reason.

Articles 82–85 deal specifically with the intellectual rights of indigenous peoples and local communities, implicitly acknowledging that a final solution to this issue has not been reached by its initiation of an 18-month participatory process to elaborate an appropriate *sui generis* system. Even so, the State already expressly recognizes and protects what is referred to as '*sui generis* community intellectual rights', ie the knowledge, innovations and practices of indigenous peoples and local communities. Similar in this respect to copyright, these rights have juridical recognition without the requirement of prior declaration or official registration.

The participatory process, which will include indigenous peoples and peasants, will determine the nature, extent and conditions of the *sui generis* community intellectual right, as well as the form the right will take, who will be entitled to hold the legal right, and who will receive its benefits. By means of this process, a registry will be made comprising those intellectual rights that communities wish to register with the Technical Office of the Commission. Such registration will be voluntary and free. The existence of such right claims in the registry will bind the Technical Office to the obligation to oppose the grant of IPR protection being requested for the same element or knowledge. It is not essential for the right to be officially registered for the refusal to be made, provided that the reason is fully justified.

With respect to technology transfer, the State is committed to implementing CBD Articles 16, 17 and 18, and facilitating access to technologies relevant to conservation and sustainable use of biodiversity without prejudicing intellectual and industrial property rights or *sui generis* collective intellectual rights (Article 88). Moreover, the State will promote the recovery, maintenance and dissemination of traditional technologies and practices useful for conservation and sustainable use of biodiversity.

THE ORGANIZATION OF AFRICAN UNITY DRAFT LEGISLATION ON COMMUNITY RIGHTS AND ACCESS TO BIOLOGICAL RESOURCES

In March 1998, the Scientific, Technical and Research Commission of the Organization of African Unity (OAU/STRC) task force on community rights and access to biological resources met to develop a draft model legislation on community rights and access to biological resources as a basis for national legislation and an Africa-wide convention.

According to the OAU/STRC declaration accompanying the draft legislation:

> *WTO imposes intellectual property rights modelled on the protection of industrial innovations to grant individual monopolies on living things and categorically denies the existence of community collective innovations.*

For this reason:

> *the WTO-based approach is predatory in nature and runs counter to the aspirations of communities which are in the first place the innovators of biodiversity so necessary for the survival of the planet.*

The preamble of the *Draft Legislation on Community Rights and Access to Biological Resources* declares that:

> *The State recognizes the necessity of providing adequate mechanisms which guarantee a just, equitable and effective participation of its citizens in the protection of their collective and individual rights and in making decisions which affect the biological, genetic and intellectual resources as well as the activities and benefits derived from their utilization.*

As yet, the draft includes no definitions, although the declaration considers a 'local community' to be:

> *A section of society in a given area whose means of livelihood are based on the natural resources, knowledge and technologies of and related to its immediate ecosystems. The local community keeps adapting, generating and regenerating those natural resources, knowledge and technologies as its preceding generations had done and, if spared disruption by external forces, as its succeeding generations will do.*

The scope of the legislation embraces biological and genetic resources and related knowledge and their derivatives within the national jurisdiction of the country, but does not apply to traditional use and exchange of biological and genetic resources and related knowledge carried out by and between local communities based on their customary practices (Article 3). Access to resources and knowledge requires prior informed consent of both the State represented by a competent authority and the communities concerned. To oversee implementation and enforcement of the provisions of the legislation, a national inter-sectoral coordination body will be set up comprising representatives from the public sector, scientific and professional organizations, NGOs and local communities. The private sector appears to be excluded.

Article 5 deals exclusively with Community Rights. Local communities are recognized as 'the lawful and sole custodians of the relevant knowledge, innovations and practices', and the State is required to:

> *recognize and protect the rights of the local communities to collectively benefit from their knowledge, innovations and practices ... and to receive compensation for the conservation of biological and genetic resources.*

A certain percentage (to be decided by national legislatures) of benefits obtained from direct or indirect commercial use of a local community's biological and genetic resources will be returned to the community concerned. In the absence of a system to ensure equitable benefit sharing, regulatory measures will be taken by the State through a process of consultation and participation of local communities to develop a collective/community intellectual rights system. It should be added that communities have the right to veto access to their knowledge, technologies and resources.

The Model Legislation is likely to become a document of great significance. In June 1998, a summit of OAU heads of state recommended that member governments:

1 give due attention as a matter of priority to the need for regulating access to biological resources, community knowledge and technologies and their implication for intellectual property rights as entrenched in the international trade regime of the TRIPS Agreement;
2 adopt the draft Model Legislation on access to biological resources and call on Member States to initiate the process at national level involving all stakeholders in accordance with national interest and enacted into law;
3 initiate a process of negotiation among African countries to formulate and adopt an African Convention on Biological

Diversity with emphasis on conditions for access to biological resources and protection of community rights; and
4   develop an African Common Position to safeguard the sovereign rights of Member States and the vital interests of our local communities and forge alliance with other countries of the South on the revision of TRIPS in 1999.

As an awareness-raising exercise, the draft legislation is very important. Nevertheless, it is incomplete since it lacks definitions of the relevant key terms and concepts. Moreover, in its present form, the legislation does not make clear how African countries and their communities can gain substantially from its provisions, and therefore requires further elaboration. The emphasis is very much on controlling access rather than establishing favourable conditions for benefit sharing, conservation and capacity building, and equitable partnerships with the private sector. While controlling access is of course vital, this should be a means to an end rather than an end in itself. One of the main objectives of such legislation should be to enable African countries and communities to capture a greater share of the benefits from the commercial exploitation of their biological resources.

Taking a regional approach to access regulation appears more promising according to economic theory, since supply prices would then be equal in all participating countries and bioprospectors would find it harder to 'shop around'. However, even the Andean Community's regime does not preclude a price war since neighbouring non-member states like Brazil, Chile and Guyana – as well as countries in other continents – will certainly share many of the same resources.

Following the same economic logic, two economists, Joseph Vogel and Timothy Swanson, propose the creation of cartels. Vogel (1998) advocates cartels that would include *all* countries that possess an identical resource. There would be a fixed royalty rate of 13 per cent of sales of products derived from the resources that would be shared among the countries concerned. An additional small percentage (Vogel suggests 2 per cent) would go to the actual supplier country. Although the royalty rate seems high, Vogel believes that such countries have little to lose given the paucity of benefits he believes they currently receive from bilateral bioprospecting contracts. In any case the cartels would not be prevented from lowering royalty rates in the future. There is of course a danger that cartels might have so many members that the benefits going to each one, even at such a high royalty rate, would be very low. One way to improve Vogel's proposal might be to include a mechanism for distributing the benefits in proportion to the efforts individual countries make to conserve and sustainably use biodiversity. It does not seem fair that countries which are the most environmentally destructive should receive an equal share to more responsible countries.

Swanson (1997) believes that cartelization should be linked to a certification system so that only those countries that invest sufficiently in conservation and sustainable harvesting to be designated certified suppliers would be allowed to trade their resources. The idea is that biodiversity-rich countries would have a greater incentive to invest in environmentally friendly practices.[2,3]

NOTES

1 The Commission will consist *inter alia* of government ministers and representatives of the national protected areas system, the university sector, the private sector, and the national peasant (campesino) and indigenous peoples associations.

2 *Bridges* magazine (1997, 1[6], p14) reports that participants at a meeting on 'Biodiversity, Globalisation and Sustainability' organized by the UNEP Regional Office for Latin America and the Caribbean recommended that a Protocol to the CBD be adopted which would create such 'biodiversity cartels'. Kothari (1995) presents an Asian Regional Agreement on Biodiversity which contains a framework for a biodiversity cartel including India and its neighbouring countries.

3 Asebey and Kempenaar (1995) discuss the pros and cons of creating biodiversity cartels.

9 NON-GOVERNMENTAL INITIATIVES AND PROPOSALS

Non-governmental actors such as indigenous peoples' organizations, other grassroots organizations, advocacy groups, and even some academic and scientific institutions, are responding to and seeking to influence international agreements like the CBD, TRIPS and the IUPGR. Their various approaches include: (i) actively opposing trends in intellectual property and international trade law, especially the patenting of life-forms; (ii) advocating equitable benefit sharing from biotechnological research through use of model laws, local/traditional knowledge databases, contracts, or ethical guidelines and codes of practice, and intellectual property rights; and (iii) using emerging international environmental and human rights law as part of a campaign aimed at empowering traditional communities (Sutherland 1997).

Each of the following initiatives illustrates at least one of the above approaches.

COMMUNITY INTELLECTUAL RIGHTS

A model Community Intellectual Rights Act has been devised by Third World Network as a *sui generis* system for protecting the knowledge and innovations of local communities (see Nijar 1996b). The purpose of the act is to prevent the 'privatisation and usurpation of community rights and knowledge through existing definitions of innovation.' Implicit in the Act is an assumption that community knowledge is communally owned and shared, and indigenous peoples do not usually consider knowledge as something that can be owned. 'Local community' means:

a group of people having a long standing social organisation that binds them together whether in a defined area or howsoever otherwise and shall include indigenous peoples, farmers, and local populations, and shall where appropriate refer to any organisation duly registered under the provisions of this Act to represent their interest.

According to Section 1 Paragraph 1, '[t]he local community shall at all times and in perpetuity be the lawful and sole custodians and stewards of *all innovation*' [emphasis added]. It should be noted that since these rights are perpetual, they would go beyond those enjoyed by holders of IPRs. What is more problematic, though, is the definition of 'innovation', which:

shall include any collective and cumulative knowledge or technology of the use, properties, values and processes of any plant variety and any plant or part thereof rendered of any or enhanced use or value as a result of the said cumulative knowledge or technology whether documented, recorded, oral, written or howsoever otherwise existing including any alteration, modification, improvement thereof and shall also include derivatives which utilise the knowledge of indigenous groups or communities in the commercialisation of any product as well as to a more sophisticated process for extracting, isolating, or synthesizing the active chemical in the plant extracts or compositions used by the indigenous people.

In other words, industrial inventions *which derive to any degree from a community's knowledge would legally be considered as innovations belonging to that community for all time.* Such a far-reaching claim is very hard to justify (see Downes 1997a; Menon 1997).[1]

Section 5 of the model CIR Act refers to the possibility of creating *registries of invention*, in which a community might register its innovations as a simple method of declaring their existence to the world. However, similar to copyright law, legal protection does not depend on formal acceptance by a registering authority. Failure to register does not surrender the innovation rights, but doing so may block a patent application for an identical or similar 'innovation'.

In conjunction with the CIR Act, the Third World Network has developed a model Collectors of Biological Resources Act to establish obligations for collectors of genetic resources and traditional knowledge, and a model Contract between the Collector and the Government. According to the Act, a licence would be given for a prescribed period, subject to conditions. Sanctions would be heavy for violators and even directors and employees of companies contravening the Act's conditions could be subject to penal sanctions.

According to the model Contract, the collector would be required to provide:

- plans for prospecting;
- details of types of material to be collected in terms of species and quantities;
- details of the evaluation, storage, and use of the collected material, including the uses to which it would be put;
- explanation of the benefit the host country or community may derive from the collection of germplasm.

Conditions relating to collection and obligations related to post-collection activities would be enumerated, in order that the community or state would receive fair recompense for sharing their resources. An endorsement would be required from the collector's country (an accredited representative) agreeing to indemnify the source country for any losses it may sustain should the collector breach the agreement, plus surrender of the results of any report of studies or experimentation made on the collected specimens. There are strict controls on the right to patent, though none on other IPRs such as trade secrets. According to Paragraph 9.1:

> *No patent application shall be filed within or outside the country in respect of the collected specimens or any part thereof, its properties or activity or any derivatives which utilise the knowledge of indigenous groups or communities in the commercialisation of any product as well as to a more sophisticated process for extracting, isolating or synthesising the active chemical in the plant extracts or compositions used by indigenous peoples or if the same represents the intellectual right of local communities.*

Anil Gupta (1996a) has criticized the CIR Act on two grounds. First, the document implies that local innovation is by definition collective and cumulative, thereby denying the possibility of autonomous and independent innovation by individuals and groups within communities, whose rights are thereby left unrecognized by the Act. Second, he warns that by applying the Act, 'knowledge rich economically poor communities and individual innovators will remain subjugated by those members of the community who may be politically more powerful'. Third, he finds that the definition of community is too broad and ill-defined to be practicable.

SRISTI's LOCAL INNOVATIONS DATABASES

The Society for Research and Initiatives for Sustainable Technologies and Institutions (SRISTI) of Ahmedabad, India, has for several years been developing databases of traditional knowledge and innovations in close collaboration with local community members. Anil Gupta, SRISTI's Director, emphasizes the adaptive and creative nature of so-called 'traditional' systems of knowledge and resource management, and rejects arguments that all traditional knowledge should be treated as communal property. He asserts that entitlements are not equal for all community members. This is because while some individuals within communities possess, conserve, generate and disseminate knowledge, and may deliberately engage in biodiversity-friendly practices, other community members (including some community leaders) may have no interest in innovation or conservation.

Gupta (1996ab) advocates the establishment of a global registration system of local innovations along the lines of SRISTI's local innovations database. Such a system would enable individual and collective innovators to receive acknowledgement and financial rewards for commercial applications of their knowledge, innovations and practices, and in some cases make it possible for individuals or communities to seek IPR protection in such forms as inventors' certificates and petty patents (1996a).[2] Gupta (1998) also proposes that national patent offices should be able to access local innovation databases when carrying out prior art searches and examinations in order that patent applications which appropriate knowledge contained in these databases may be properly tested for novelty and inventive step.

Evidently, the ideal situation for Gupta's proposals to work in practice would be a global registration system that every national patent office could access and universal acceptance that 'prior art' should not discriminate against knowledge held in foreign countries.

PEOPLE'S BIODIVERSITY REGISTERS[3]

The People's Biodiversity Registers programme was originally sponsored by WWF India and co-ordinated with the Centre for Ecological Sciences of the Indian Institute of Science (IISc), and the Foundation for Revitalisation of Local Health Traditions (FRLHT), both in Bangalore. The IISc remains the main promoter of PBRs but many NGOs are now involved in similar projects throughout India.[4] Among the main objectives of the People's Biodiversity Registers programme are (FRLHT 1995):

1   *To provide* a record of local knowledge for the use of present and future generations of village community people.
2   *To promote* the *revitalization* of local knowledge by: (a) recognizing the range of such knowledge; (b) *rewarding* outstanding knowledge, skills, techniques and conservation practices; (c) *validating and promoting* sound local knowledge and resource management traditions; and (d) *promoting* inter-community transfer of knowledge for capacity enhancement.
3   *To alert* conservationists about the need for action concerning threatened resources and the need for protection of local resource rights.
4   *To protect* local biodiversity and knowledge from misappropriation by companies such as through patenting of modified products, processes and biological resources.

The planners envisage a decentralized bottom-up system, recognizing that people must have incentives to participate in the documentation of their knowledge. Promotion of traditional biodiversity-related knowledge primarily for the benefit of local communities is emphasized, while regulation of access to information in the registers is considered a means to achieve this, rather than an end in itself. The long-term goal is a network of decentralized databases, all linked to 'a [consolidated] national database which would give full credit to the origin of information at the level of an individual, a community or a village council' (Gadgil *et al* 1999).

Documents are currently in preparation for villages throughout India. Each study involves a year-long process of talking to local individuals, groups of local people and public meetings. The documentation is carried out mostly with the collaboration of local educational institutions and voluntary organizations. The first People's Biodiversity Register (PBR) was completed and released in 1997.

Copies of each PBR will by held by *panchayats* (local elected councils) and educational institutions, and proposed district level institutions called 'Biodiversity Cells' that will serve as repositories of computerized collections of the PBRs produced within the district (Ghate 1997).

How will the system help to implement the CBD's provisions on traditional knowledge? Placing control of PBRs in the hands of local institutions has obvious advantages in terms of helping to preserve and maintain traditional knowledge, but it is recognized that effective incentive mechanisms are needed to encourage further development of existing knowledge. One idea is to grant *panchayats* the right to charge fees for access to PBRs. Another is to set up a national biodiversity fund, which among other things would provide financial support for *panchayats* and disburse special grants and awards to communities and individuals that make outstanding efforts to conserve biological resources and/or document knowledge (Gadgil 1998).

The proponents of this system argue that the existence of the PBR data banks will encourage mutually beneficial relationships between communities and corporations that will, subject to conditions set by local people, have access to a wealth of information on biodiversity. It is emphasized, though, that community claims over knowledge will not be at the expense of individuals. Individuals desirous to record claims to their own knowledge as a means either of protecting it or of exploiting it commercially can disclose only enough information to establish a claim without sufficient detail to make unauthorized use or commercial application possible. If communities or individuals decide to exchange biological material or knowledge with companies for financial or in kind benefits, the 'biodiversity cells' can assist them in negotiating contractual arrangements. To help create a more level playing field in community–company negotiations, it is intended that they will also channel information on trade in biological resources, such as the volume of trade and prices of medicinal plants, to local communities (Gadgil et al 1999).

Those involved in the programme do not take an anti-patent stand, but they argue that the success of the PBR system depends in part on changes to the patent system. They propose that patent applications based on use of genetic resources and/or traditional knowledge should include a statement as to the origin of genetic resources and proof that the prior informed consent of the holders of traditional knowledge was given.

In both examples of traditional knowledge databases described in this chapter, it is important to consider the difficult question of how far access to databases should be restricted. Access restrictions obviously lessen the possibility of information within them being misappropriated. On the other hand, keeping database information out of the public domain could in some situations make it harder to challenge misappropriation than if such knowledge were made publicly available. For example, a company might acquire knowledge about a medicinal plant directly from an indigenous group without referring to the PBR that also contains it, and then file a patent application on this knowledge. This could happen if the group members were not fully informed about the purpose of documenting their knowledge or if the PBR workers had acquired the same knowledge not from that group but from another community. The validity of such an application would depend on how 'prior art' and 'the public domain' are interpreted in the legal jurisdiction where it is filed. Most likely, if the knowledge had only been recorded in a private database (ie had not been made available to the public through publication) it would not constitute prior art and would therefore have no effect on the application, at least in first-to-file jurisdictions. On the other hand, if the database were publicly accessible, the knowledge would be public domain and therefore unpatentable. It is essential that organizations co-ordinating traditional knowledge register initiatives explain to local communities the full implications and possible dangers of sharing their knowledge with all outsiders *including themselves*. Fortunately, SRISTI, IISc and FRLHT do seem to do this.

NOTES

1 It is such statements that lead David Downes (1997a) to make the following observations: 'a number of advocates of "farmers' rights" hold that communities in which folk varieties or indigenous knowledge have originated should maintain the exclusive right to control their use in perpetuity, whether they were developed 10 years ago or 1,000'. In spite of this conviction, he notes, these advocates fail to 'explain why such a community should be entitled to a special right not available to others whose inventive predecessors gave the world comparable benefits' (ibid). According to Menon (1997) '[b]y the same token, restrictions can be placed on the use of even old scientific knowledge which is of importance for very ordinary work in the developing countries, as for example chromatography for separating different compounds in plant extracts. The scenario which emerges is a jungle of transactions which would inhibit all creativity and the solution should not be worse than the disease'.

2 Petty patents are also known as utility models, and are included in the *Paris Convention for Protection of Industrial Property*. Inventors' certificates used to be quite common in the former socialist countries.

3 See Dutfield (1999a) for a more detailed treatment of PBRs.

4 U Ghate (IISc) pers. comm. 1999.

10 Conclusions, Unresolved Questions and Recommendations

Conclusions

This study has explored the links between provisions in the CBD relating to IPRs, and international trade-related IPR rules, especially those relevant to seeds, plants and plant varieties. It is true that IPRs are often blamed for problems that have more to do with the inequities inherent to the global economy. Nevertheless, there is some evidence to suggest that because TRIPS is meant to promote free trade and economic liberalization, environmental concerns related to IPRs are accorded less priority than they should. The notion that IPR laws *should* be designed *inter alia* to support conservation, sustainability, equitable benefit-sharing, or transfers of environmentally-sound technologies, is very recent, and is still hard for many policy-makers to accept. Nevertheless, there is no question that IPRs *are* relevant to these issues and that they may sometimes have negative impacts.

Even if the negative impacts are controversial, the relevance of the international IPR regime to the CBD is beyond doubt. When it comes to which treaties should take priority, we must bear in mind that IPRs are meant to serve the public interest as they benefit the rights holders. Since the CBD was opened for signature in 1992, over 170 countries have already ratified it, implying that biodiversity conservation, sustainability and equitable sharing are now public interest issues throughout the world (Tarasofsky 1997). It is essential that the WTO, which is the key institution overseeing and promoting the international trade system, pays much greater attention to MEAs like the CBD. The May 1998 WTO Ministerial Declaration made no mention of the environment, biodiversity or even MEAs. On the contrary, the CBD should be given much greater priority, even by the WTO. Developing countries should be given the time and the opportunity to design national IPR systems in accordance with their interests.

UNRESOLVED QUESTIONS

Policy responses must contend with continuing uncertainties, and the CBD-COP's decisions to investigate linkages between IPRs and the CBD, investigate ways to implement Article 8 (j), and to collaborate with WIPO in part to shed light on these uncertainties, are laudable.

What are the main gaps in our knowledge as identified in this study?

1   It is not certain that increased availability of IPR protection will automatically lead to greater levels of innovation in society. Innovation and creativity flourish in many parts of the world without any (western) IPR laws.[1] On the other hand, allegations are increasingly made that too much IPR protection of basic research is stifling innovation (see Heller and Eisenberg 1998).
2   The role of IPRs in the erosion of agro-biodiversity has been the subject of some polemical debates, yet we still do not know how far biodiversity is affected by IPRs for seeds, plant varieties and/or agrochemicals. But it can be argued that we cannot afford to wait for conclusive proof one way or another before making decisions on the design of environmentally-sound IPRs. It is vital to consider whether and how the precautionary principle may be applied in the IPR context to minimize the risks.
3   Some evidence suggests that most technologies supportive of biodiversity conservation are in the public domain. However, with respect to those which are not, it is unclear whether IPRs hinder or encourage their transfer to developing countries.
4   It is widely accepted that the application of traditional knowledge and technologies can add value to genetic resources. While patents are clearly unsuitable mechanisms to protect the rights of traditional knowledge holders, the use of other IPRs may in some circumstances be feasible.

Consideration of these questions requires us to confront some quite fundamental questions about IPRs, none of which have self-evident answers: Why do IPRs such as patents, copyrights and trademarks exist at all? Is the system we have the best possible system? Can we assume that an IPR system that suits the US is necessarily the most beneficial one for India or Kenya? Is an IPR system that satisfies the needs of Novartis an equally attractive one for, say, a start-up biotech firm in Switzerland? How should we define 'a level playing field' when we speak of access to and availability of legal protection of intellectual property rights? And how might IPR laws be designed *inter alia* to support conservation, sustainability, equitable benefit sharing, or transfers of environmentally-sound technologies?

Like all property rights, intellectual property rights are not God-given but evolve over time and have always depended on governments to legislate for them and to determine their extent. Until recently, one could have argued that while justifications for IPRs may change over time, the nature and extent of these rights have always depended on the state's willingness to define and protect these rights in pursuit of such objectives as economic development or cultural advancement. This assumption is becoming less reliable. Developing countries are now being pressured to enact IPR laws and to invest resources in enforcing these laws not necessarily because such countries have decided these laws are necessary for economic development, but merely because the WTO's rules require them to provide such rights.

A recent communication from the European Union to the WTO General Council (WTO General Council 1999a) stated as follows:

> *It should of course be kept in mind that the TRIPS acquis is a basis from which to seek further improvements in the protection of IPR. There should therefore be no question, in future negotiations, of lowering of standards or granting of further transitional periods.*

In similar vein, a submission from Japan to the General Council (WTO General Council 1999b) stated that:

> *... taking into account the nature of the TRIPS Agreement, that is, a minimum standard of intellectual property protection, we should not discuss the TRIPS Agreement with a view to reducing the current level of protection of intellectual property rights.* To the contrary, the TRIPS Agreement should be improved properly in line with new technological development and social needs. For example, the TRIPS Agreement should deal with higher protection of intellectual property rights which has been achieved in other treaties or conventions in other fora appropriately *[emphasis added]*.

What is especially problematic about these statements is their shared assumption that the only direction the international IPR regime should move towards is ever higher minimum standards. At a time when the logic of a 20-year patent term for all fields of technology and sectors of industry, whether based on economic efficiency or public policy criteria, remains unclear; when the full environment and development impacts of IPRs have not been established; and when many developing countries simply cannot fulfil their highly onerous TRIPS obligations within the transitional periods, there is no justification at all for taking such an aggressive position.

RECOMMENDATIONS

Achieving harmony between the CBD and the IPR-related international trade regime requires enhanced knowledge in the areas considered on page 126. But there is still much that can be done while awaiting definitive answers to the difficult issues involved. Indeed, as we approach the 21st century, there is no better time to examine the impacts and objectives of IPRs more closely in the light of present-day concerns, including the very serious threat of global ecological collapse.[2]

The recommendations that follow concern (a) the development of IPR laws that are CBD-friendly; and (b) ways and means to implement the CBD in harmony with the requirements of the international IPR regime.

TRIPS and UPOV

- The grace periods allowed by TRIPS for developing countries, economies in transition, and the least developed countries to implement their obligations must be taken advantage of so that such countries have enough time to devise appropriate IPR laws conforming to their own interests.
- The right of individual countries to 'police' other countries' implementation of TRIPS should be repudiated by the Council for TRIPS, especially when unilateral sanctions are imposed for the 'failure' of individual countries to effect measures that go beyond their TRIPS obligations.
- Regarding the 2000 review of TRIPS, it is vital that concerned developing country governments act quickly to develop a common strategy concerning issues where their interests converge.

Patents

- Governments need to consider the extent and breadth of patent claims that their laws will permit. Over-broad claims are a particular danger in biotechnology and may stifle innovation and collaboration. Claiming excessive monopoly protection should not be allowed in law or in the practice of examining patents.
- The novelty requirement should be defined carefully so that traditional knowledge or other public domain information cannot be misappropriated.

- Countries should apply an interpretation of prior art that includes public domain knowledge in any part of the world whether published or not.
- Governments should consider applying broad interpretations of the morality and *ordre public* exceptions allowed by TRIPS so that products and technologies whose use may be contrary to social and economic welfare or which might incur severe social and environmental impacts can be denied patent protection on these grounds. However, they should not rely on the patent system alone to decide whether technologies or products should be placed on the market.
- Governments should consider setting up committees within their patent offices to consider the morality/*ordre public* implications of commercially exploiting inventions before such patents can be awarded. There should be a fair representation of interest groups on these committees so that a cross-section of views from different sectors of society can be expressed and a democratic consensus may be reached.
- Patent offices should publish titles and abstracts of each patent application to keep interested members of the public well informed. This would make it possible to challenge patents on the grounds of lack of novelty or inventive step, or excessive breadth, before they are awarded.
- Governments should consider adopting the proposal for certificates of origin in order to encourage benefit sharing. Minimally, declaring the origin of biological raw materials in patent applications should be mandatory wherever this is possible.

Plant variety protection, UPOV and the sui generis *option*

- Regarding the review of TRIPS Article 27 (3b) and subsequent reviews of the Agreement as a whole, it is vital that concerned developing country governments act quickly to develop a common strategy ensuring that the full range of possible options is discussed.
- Whether countries wish to join UPOV in response to Article 27.3 (b) or to develop another *sui generis* system, serious attention should be paid to the *requirements for* and *scope of* plant variety protection. Some of the possibilities referred to earlier for supplementing the system with provisions designed to support certain CBD-related objectives should be considered.

The Convention on Biological Diversity

Conservation and sustainable use of biodiversity

- There is a lack of clarity in our understanding of the links between IPRs and conservation and sustainable use of biodiversity, but minimizing risks makes it vital to consider applying the precautionary principle. It may thus be prudent for developing country governments that have not yet fully implemented TRIPS for the time being to adopt all of the optional exclusions concerning patenting life (as presented in Table 3.1).

Benefit-sharing

- Given that the bargaining position of biodiversity-rich countries holding extensive *in situ* plant genetic resources for agriculture is fairly weak, developing countries might investigate the relative advantages of acting alone, forming genetic resource supply cartels with other countries, or promoting a multilateral system of exchange and benefit-sharing. The latter might be the most constructive strategy.
- The Conference of the Parties to the CBD might wish to consider initiating a process to develop an international code of conduct. Such a code would provide guidelines for best practice concerning access to genetic resources and equitable benefit-sharing. All interested stakeholder groups should be invited to participate in this process.

Technology transfer

- Technology transfers could be facilitated through greater access to patent libraries and databases while bearing in mind that patents may not provide all the information needed to work the inventions. Moreover, it is important to understand that many of these patents may still be in force. Governments should improve public access to patent databases by such means as publishing patent texts on the Internet.
- Developing country governments should explore the possibilities (while being aware of the restrictions) that TRIPS allows for compulsory licensing of patented technologies.
- Users (and prospective users) of indigenous and traditional technologies should develop codes of conduct, ethical guidelines, and practice prior informed consent so that the holders of these technologies are fairly and appropriately compensated and rewarded. These instruments should ideally be developed in close collaboration with the peoples and communities concerned.

Traditional knowledge, innovations and practices

- Users of traditional knowledge, innovations and practices should respect the relevant local customary rules and regulations when negotiating their acquisition and commercialization.
- Research should be conducted in close partnership with local communities and grassroots organizations to adapt existing IPRs

or develop practical, effective and culturally appropriate *sui generis* alternatives.

- Governments should conduct studies to explore the potential of non-patent IPRs such as geographical indications, petty patents and trademarks for protecting traditional knowledge, and make the results of these studies widely available to local communities.
- Governments might consider supporting the development of local knowledge registers (as long as these are bottom-up participatory programmes such as India's Peoples' Biodiversity Registers or SRISTI's innovations databases) that patent examiners could access so as to ensure that traditional knowledge is not pirated. However, they should not claim ownership of these registers, since this would be an infringement of the rights of the knowledge providers.
- Any *sui generis* systems for protecting traditional knowledge should be developed in close collaboration with indigenous peoples and local communities through a broad-based consultative process that reflects a country's cultural diversity.
- Specific principles and objectives might be attached to these *sui generis* alternatives, such as: (i) the promotion of social justice and equity; (ii) the effective protection of traditional knowledge and resources from unauthorized collection, use, documentation and exploitation; and (iii) the recognition and reinforcement of customary laws and practice, and traditional resource management systems, that are effective in conserving biological diversity.

NOTES

1 The knowledge, innovations and practices of indigenous peoples and local communities, for example, are rarely if ever protected by IPRs.

2 See Atkinson and Sherman (1991).

Appendix 1

Neem-related Patents Issued by the United States Patent and Trademark Office, 1985–1998

Title of patent	Year issued	Assignee	Nationality
Stable anti-pest neem seed extract	1985	Vikwood, Ltd (now W R Grace)	USA
Hot-water extracts of neem bark	1985	Terumo Corporation	Japan
Neem bark extracts	1985	Terumo Corporation	Japan
Insecticidal hydrogenated neem extracts	1990	Rohm & Haas Company	USA
Method to prepare an improved storage stable neem seed extract	1990	W R Grace & Co	USA
Azadirachtin-like compounds & insect-destroying agents containing them	1990	Max-Planck-Gesellschaft zur Foederung der Wissenschaften	Germany
Azadirachtin derivative insecticides	1991	Native Plant Institute	USA
Storage stable azadirachtin formulation	1991	W R Grace & Co	USA
Neem oil emulsifier	1992	PPG Industries, Inc	USA
Storage stable azadirachtin formulation	1992	W R Grace & Co	USA
Selective removal of aflatoxin from azadirachtin-containing compositions	1993	AgriDyne Technologies, Inc	USA

Hydrophobic extracted neem oil – a novel fungicide	1994	W R Grace & Co, US Department of Agriculture	USA
Hydrophobic extracted neem oil – a novel fungicide use	1994	W R Grace & Co	USA
Preparation of edible neem oil	1994	Rohm & Haas Company	USA
Storage stable high azadirachtin solution	1994	W R Grace & Co	USA
Neem oil fatty acid distillation residue-based pesticide	1994	Godrej Soaps Limited	India
Insecticidal compositions derived from neem oil & neem wax fractions	1994	W R Grace & Co	USA
Storage stable pesticide compositions comprising azadirachtin & epoxide	1994	AgriDyne Technologies, Inc	USA
Fungicide compositions derived from neem oil & neem wax fractions	1994	W R Grace & Co	USA
Acaricidal combinations of neem seed extract & bifenthrin	1994	FMC Corporation	USA
Preparation of high purity neem seed extracts	1995	Rohm & Haas Company	USA
Fungicidal compositions derived from neem oil & neem wax fractions	1995	W R Grace & Co	USA
Hydrophobic extracted neem oil – a novel insecticide	1995	W R Grace & Co	USA
Preparation of high purity neem seed extracts	1995	Rohm & Haas Company	USA
Preparation of high purity neem seed extracts	1995	Rohm & Haas Company	USA
Stable extracts from neem seeds	1995	Rohm & Haas Company	USA
Hydrophic extracted neem oil-a novel insecticide	1995	W R Grace & Co	USA
Triterpene derivatives of azadirachtin having insect antifeedant & growth inhibitory activity & a process for extracting such compounds from the neem plant	1995	Council of Scientific & Industrial Research	India

Co-extraction of azadirachtin & neem oil	1995	W R Grace & Co	USA
Combinations of neem seed extract & bifenthrin for control of ectoparasites on animals	1995	FMC Corporation	USA
Co-extraction of azadirachtin & neem oil	1996	W R Grace & Co	USA
Neem oil as a male contraceptive	1996	Talwar; Gursaran P, Upadhyay; Shakti N, Dhawan; Suman (inventors)	India
Method for producing azadirachtin concentrates from neem seed materials	1996	Holla; Kadambar S, Sewri (inventors)	India
Method for the production of storage stable azadirachtin from seed kernels of the neem tree	1997	Trifolio-M GmbH	Germany
Triterpene derivatives of azadirachtin having insect antifeedant & growth inhibitory activity & a process for extracting such compounds from the neem plant	1997	Council of Scientific & Industrial Research	India
Reduced-cloud-point clarified neem oil & methods of producing	1997	Thermo Trilogy Corporation	USA
Method for producing azadirachtin by cell culture of *Azadirachta indica*	1997	Rohm & Haas Company	USA
Synergistic use of azadirachtin & pyrethrum	1997	Thermo Trilogy Corporation	USA
Process for preparing purified azadirachtin in powder form from neem seeds & storage stable aqueous composition containing azadirachtin	1998	Dalmia Centre for Biotechnology	India
Process for the isolation of an active principle from *Azadirachta indica* useful for controlling gastric hyperacidity & gastric ulceration	1998	Council of Scientific & Industrial Research	India

Appendix 2

STATEMENT AND RECOMMENDATIONS FROM A WORKSHOP ON BIODIVERSITY CONSERVATION AND INTELLECTUAL PROPERTY RIGHTS, NEW DELHI, 29–31 JANUARY, 1999

Research and Information System on Non-Aligned and Developing Countries (RIS), Kalpavriksh, and IUCN – The World Conservation Union

PREAMBULAR STATEMENT

A Workshop on Biodiversity Conservation and Intellectual Property Rights was organized in New Delhi, on 29–31 January 1999, by the Research and Information System on Non-Aligned and Developing Countries (RIS), Kalpavriksh, and IUCN – The World Conservation Union. More than 60 academics, activists, researchers, NGO representatives, government officials, and representatives of industry from India, together with a number of participants from other South Asian countries, Europe and the US, participated in the Workshop.

The major issue that was deliberated upon in the Workshop was the conflicts and complementarities between the Convention on Biological Diversity (CBD) on the one hand, and the elements of the international intellectual property regime, underlined by the World Trade Organization (WTO) in the Agreement on Trade Related Aspects of Intellectual Property Rights (TRIPS), on the other. The participants identified specific action points that are required to be taken up in the multilateral forums of CBD or WTO, and in the national context within India and other developing countries, that would further the objectives of the CBD through full use of spaces within existing IPR regimes, through further development and adaptation of these using the review process in-built in the Agreement on TRIPS or, where necessary, through creation of new regimes.

The statement and recommended actions below are intended to reflect the range of views expressed at the workshop and to offer a sense of the meeting.

There was strong support for the three objectives of the CBD: conservation of biological diversity, sustainable use of its components, and the fair and equitable sharing of the benefits arising from such use. In addition, participants also recognized the immense contribution of traditional knowledge and practices of local and indigenous communities for conservation, and reaffirmed the need for the effective maintenance of such knowledge systems. In relation to the TRIPS Agreement, participants recognized that the objectives of the Agreement, ie, the protection of IPRs, should provide benefits to both producers and users of technological knowledge in a manner conducive to social and economic welfare in reality. However, concern was expressed that the current IPR regimes, in particular the Agreement on TRIPS, fail to adequately address a number of concerns central to the achievement of the objectives of the CBD. They appear to pose a significant threat to conservation of biodiversity, they do not address a range of equity issues including intergenerational equity, and they render difficult both access to genetic resources and the fair sharing of benefits arising from their use. Perhaps more seriously, they fail to recognize and protect traditional systems of knowledge that are needed to meet the objectives of the CBD fully, especially the local and community knowledge and the knowledge systems of indigenous peoples. There is therefore a need to achieve necessary amendments to existing regimes, and/or develop alternative regimes to address these concerns.

The workshop identified the following actions as steps to address some of these concerns:

RECOMMENDATIONS FOR ACTION

1 Recommendations Relating to International Regimes

Current international regimes which have relevance to IPR and biodiversity issues need to be substantially reviewed, and attempts made both to use the spaces available within them and create new spaces and alternative regimes which can help to conserve biodiversity and protect the rights of indigenous and local communities. In particular, actions are needed in the World Trade Organization (WTO), concerning specifically the Agreement on TRIPS, the Convention on Biological Diversity (CBD), and the other relevant international processes, including those that have been initiated by the World Intellectual Property Organization (WIPO). Besides, the search for alternative international regimes is also important.

A   World Trade Organization (Specifically TRIPS)

At the level of the WTO, and specifically the TRIPS agreement, the following actions should be taken:

1   An open and transparent process, involving civil society, of reviewing article 27.3(b) in 1999 and the review in 2000 of the TRIPS Agreement overall;
2   A full consideration of the relevant provisions of the CBD, the FAO Undertaking on Plant Genetic Resources, the ILO Convention 169, the UNESCO/WIPO Guidelines for Protection of Folklore, the UN Draft

Declaration on the Rights of Indigenous Peoples, international human rights declarations, and other relevant international treaties and processes, while undertaking the above-mentioned reviews;

3   An independent and transparent assessment of the environmental and equity implications of WTO in general and TRIPS in particular, with the involvement of civil society and of relevant international bodies relating to the CBD, the FAO and WIPO, and taking in particular the 'precautionary principle' enshrined in Agenda 21;

4   A review of Article 31 of TRIPS to ensure its conformity with the preamble, and articles 7 and 8 of TRIPS, as well as article 16 of the CBD. The aspects of authorization for commercial and non-commercial activity under Article 31 should be clarified during such review;

5   Expansion of, or at the very least maintenance of, the exceptions in Article 27.3(b) of TRIPS, for patenting of life forms; the expansion should ideally exclude micro-organisms, products and processes thereof, from patentability;

6   The definition of the term 'micro-organism' should not be expanded to cover tissues, cells or cell lines or DNA obtained from higher organisms, including human beings;

7   Expansion or at the very least maintenance of the *sui generis* clause relating to plant variety protection, in order to:
    (i)   ensure implementation of article 8(j) of the CBD relating to indigenous and local communities;
    (ii)   ensure that full consideration of environmental and ethical concerns about IPRs on life forms are addressed; and
    (iii) allow the completion of a biosafety protocol that establishes minimum international standards for the environmental safety of releases of genetically modified organisms.

8   Amending the provisions of Article 27.3(b) by either deleting the term 'effective' in the context of *sui generis* systems of plant variety protection, or defining it such that national priority is paramount in the interpretation of the term, including the following:
    (i)   Conservation and sustainable use of biodiversity;
    (ii)   Promotion of traditional lifestyles;
    (iii) Promotion of food security and health security;
    (iv)   Ensuring equitable benefit sharing;
    (v)   Invoking the precautionary principle;
    (vi)   Respect of the principles of equity and ethics;

9   Exploring ways of interpreting and implementing TRIPS that help achieve the objectives of the CBD;

10 Measures to prevent the unilateral pressure by some members to coerce other members to strengthen IPR regimes beyond the TRIPS requirements;

11 Enhancing the scope of Article 23 of TRIPS to strengthen protection of geographical indications for goods other than wine and spirits, such as Darjeeling tea;

12 The scope of Article 22 of the TRIPS should be expanded to protect denominations relating to geographic origin, and characteristics associated with a specific region;

13 Inclusion of requirements (in Article 29 of TRIPS) for disclosure of the genetic resources and the traditional knowledge used in inventions for

which IPRs are claimed, the country and community of origin of these resources and knowledge, and proof of consent having been sought of the relevant community and equitable benefit-sharing arrangements having been entered into with them, as required by the CBD;

14 Steps to ensure that TRIPS implementation and elaboration fulfils all the objectives stated in Article 7. This should include striking a balance between rights and obligations, a balance that should take into account the objectives of the CBD as well as the principles enunciated at the Earth Summit.

B   Convention on Biological Diversity (CBD)

The CBD process should take the following measures:

1 Assess the relationship of IPRs to access and benefit-sharing provisions, including in the development of guidelines or best practices for achieving equitable benefit-sharing from use of genetic resources. In particular, there should be consideration of mechanisms such as certificates of origin, evidence of prior consent for access to genetic resource, evidence of prior approval of indigenous and local communities for access to traditional knowledge, and disclosure of this evidence in patent applications;

2 Evaluation of the impacts of international processes relating to IPRs, including TRIPS, on the objectives of Article 8(j) of the CBD;

3 Development of a protocol on the protection of indigenous and local community knowledge and resource rights;

4 Providing inputs into the ongoing WIPO processes on 'new beneficiaries' which are assessing issues relating to protection of traditional knowledge; and

5 Development of a code of conduct, or a protocol, on access and benefit-sharing, especially in relation to the resources and knowledge of indigenous and local communities, and of 'developing' countries; these steps could be taken up as concrete points for the inter-sessional process relating to the implementation of Article 8(j), which the CBD COP4 initiated; and of other processes relating to the Biosafety Protocol and the inter-sessional work on access and benefit-sharing.

C   Other Processes

Other international processes relevant to IPRs and biodiversity need to take the following steps:

1 Development of the FAO Undertaking on Plant Genetic Resources, either in itself or as a protocol under the CBD, should incorporate comprehensive protection of indigenous and local community knowledge, along with provisions to conserve biodiversity and sustainably use biological resources;

2 Cooperation at the SAARC[1] level to jointly conserve biodiversity, achieve sustainable use, and promote equitable benefit-sharing, especially through appropriate regional agreements;

3 Ensuring that any agreement on databases (eg the proposed Database Treaty) ensures effective control by communities of their knowledge, mechanisms that ensure effective and equitable sharing of benefits with and within communities, and space for communities to define the terms by which they control access and require benefit-sharing;

4 At all international forums, setting up of 'intercultural panels' to evaluate the terms of 'cross-cultural transactions' by which knowledge relating to biodiversity from one knowledge system is used in another system, including in dispute-resolution processes.

2 *Recommendations Relating to National Regimes*

Many countries of the South Asian region are in the process of, or considering, specific legislation to bring into effect international treaties to which they are a party. In the development of such legislation, and in relevant non-legal measures, several steps need to be taken to ensure conservation, sustainable use, and equitable benefit-sharing.

A *Patent Legislation*

1 Countries should exclude from patentability:
   (i)   All life forms;
   (ii) Existing traditional/indigenous knowledge (in current or translated forms), and essentially derived products and processes from such knowledge; (Use can be made of the European Patent Convention as a precedent for this, of Article 22 of the CBD for arguments relating to adverse impact on biodiversity from other international agreements, and of relevant exemptions provided in the TRIPS agreement).

2 Patent applications should include the following:
   (i)   Disclosure of all places of origin of the material/knowledge used in the application;
   (ii) Disclosure of all communities/persons of origin;
   (iii) Proof of consent having been obtained from the community/persons of origin;
   (iv) Proof of benefit-sharing arrangement having been entered into with the community/persons of origin, in accordance with relevant guidelines developed by national authorities;
   (v)   Disclosure of any previous rejection of application, in the country or other jurisdictions;
   (vi) Prior public notice in all relevant languages in the places and communities of origin. (Grounds for the above can be derived from Article 8(j), Article 15 and the clauses relating to national sovereignty under the CBD).

3 The burden of proof should be on the applicant;

4 Penalties for infringement of any of the above requirements should be severe and should include revocation of patents if already granted, or rejection of application, and appropriate compensation to the aggrieved.

B   Plant Varieties Protection Legislation

1   In view of the objectives of the CBD, UPOV 1978 or UPOV 1991 do not provide adequate models for *sui generis* plant variety protection legislation. Alternative regimes for providing appropriate models should contain the features elaborated below;

2   Applications for plant variety protection should include the following:
   (i)   Disclosure of all places of origin of the material/knowledge used in the application;
   (ii) Disclosure of all communities/persons of origin;
   (iii) Proof of consent having been obtained from the community/persons of origin;
   (iv) Proof of benefit-sharing arrangement having been entered into with the community/persons of origin, in accordance with relevant guidelines developed by national authorities;
   (v)   Disclosure of any previous rejection of application, in the country or other jurisdictions;
   (vi) Prior public notice in all relevant languages in the places and communities of origin;

3   The burden of proof should be on the applicant or plant variety right holder;

4   Farmers' Rights should get full treatment under the Act, and their definition should include: the right to protect farmers' varieties and knowledge, to continue having access to biological and other materials which are important inputs into the farming system, to the cultural and social conditions which make continued innovation and resource use possible, and to save, propagate, use, exchange, share or sell varieties protected under the Act; and the obligation to ensure biodiversity conservation and sustainable use;

5   Farmers' Rights should further include the right to sue breeders if the latters' claims are not realized, with the burden of proving that the product complies with the claims being on the breeder;

6   The Act should contain provision for national and local level gene funds, derived from fees and other levies on plant breeding and the seed industry (other than those covered under agreements with local communities), which can be utilized for the purpose of supporting in-situ farmers' conservation measures and incentives for continued innovation by farmers;

7   The above funds and other sources should be used to provide a range of incentives for farmers to carry on conservation, use, and innovation of agricultural biodiversity, including financial, material, social, and other incentives;

8   The coverage of the Act should expand on a gradual step-by-step basis, applying the precautionary principle, following adequate environmental impact assessments, and assessing their implications for food security;

9   All new varieties being considered for protection should go through an environmental and social impact assessment to ensure that they do not threaten agro-biodiversity and community rights, using fully the precautionary principle in cases of uncertainty; the legislation coverage could expand on a gradual step-by-step basis;

10 Penalties for infringement of any of the above requirements should be severe and should include revocation of plant variety protection if already granted, or rejection of application.

11 All current ex-situ germplasm holdings in the private or public sector should be required to:
   (i)   disclose the places of origin;
   (ii)   disclose the communities/persons of origin;
   (iii) repatriate samples of the material, where relevant, to the communities/persons of origin;
   (iv)   provide full access to farmers to these holdings; and
   (v)   seek permission from the communities/persons of origin for any further use of this material;

12 Extant varieties, as identified by national inventories of biodiversity, will remain outside the purview of protection granted to industrial or formal sector breeders.

C   Biodiversity Legislation

1   Provisions of the CBD should be given complete legal recognition and implemented effectively at a national level;

2   Article 8(j) of the CBD should be implemented under national legislation by:
   (i)   granting ownership of biogenetic material to local communities;
   (ii)   recognizing and protecting the traditional knowledge of these communities, and traditional modes of resource use regulation and dispute resolution under customary law;
   (iii) ensuring the consent and involvement of these communities in the wider use of their knowledge and practices;
   (iv)   mandating a series of equitable benefit-sharing measures;

3   Rules should be enacted under the law laying down broad and inclusive criteria for identifying a 'community'. An essential criterion for such identification of a community should be direct dependence on a natural resource for subsistence;

4   The legislation should require, for both domestic and international access to biodiversity, prior informed consent, mutually agreed terms, and burden of proof on the applicant;

5   The legislation should cover not only biological taxa but also biochemicals and other parts derived from such taxa;

6   The appropriate national biodiversity agencies should scrutinize:
   (i)   market approval for products/ processes coming under the 'mailbox' applications;
   (ii)   patent application for anything derived from biological resources/ knowledge of local community; and
   (iii) other relevant commercial applications from the point of view of:
   (iv)   whether there is any threat to biological diversity, the environment, or human health (the precautionary principles should be applied in case of uncertainty); and
   (v)   whether there are any adverse implications on the rights of local communities;

7   Rules should be formulated under the legislation for equitable benefit sharing;

8   Appropriate institutions should be created or, where already existing, empowered to handle the provisions of the legislation;

9   The legislation should recognize that the appropriate local authority shall have the right of veto over any application referred to the National Authority and/or have the power to specify any special terms and conditions for regulating such access, which should be mandatory on the National Authority to incorporate into the scheme that it may formulate for the specific application;

10 All information relevant to the legislation should be available for public scrutiny;

11 The biodiversity legislation should come into force prior to the plant variety legislation;

12 Benefits derived from IPR-related legislation, and from access regulations, should be ploughed back into conservation of biodiversity, and towards providing incentives for local communities to continue lifestyles and practices relevant to conservation and sustainable use.

D   *Protection of Folklore*

Current laws for copyright protection are unsuitable for protection of folklore. Measures should therefore be taken for the development of a *sui generis* legislation for protection of folklore based on an understanding of 'folklore' as inclusive of the following elements: folk knowledge/practices/expressions of art, craft, music, scientific belief, architecture, agriculture, medicine, and conservation of natural resources.

E   *Geographic Indications/Appellations Act*

Law should be enacted to protect denominations relating to geographic origin, and characteristics associated with a specific region. The provisions of this legislation should provide additional protection as has been provided for in Article 23 of TRIPS.

F   *Other Processes*

1   A database (or registry) of the biodiversity and knowledge wealth of the country should be compiled, consisting of an inventory of all the biological and genetic resources, a documentation and evaluation of the uses of these resources, and clarification of their ownership (local, state/provincial, national);

2   Any effort to develop registers or databases of indigenous or local knowledge should ensure effective control by communities of their knowledge. This should include mechanisms that ensure effective and equitable sharing of benefits with and within communities. Communities should have the right to define the terms by which they control access and require benefit-sharing; these terms should be transparent;

3   The capacity of communities and citizens to deal with biodiversity and IPR issues should be enhanced, through appropriate educational and training programmes which are culturally sensitive;

4   There is a need to revitalize and strengthen local systems of governance to ensure the control of communities over their knowledge and

resources; and in this context there is need for institutional capacity building at the community level (eg *Gram Sabha*) to enable their empowerment;

5 Appropriate authorities should be set up, where biodiversity and IPR issues can be continually discussed among a wide range of actors, including government officials, non-government organisations, local community members, independent scientists and academics, and others. Governments should be required to consider the deliberations of such bodies while developing policies and programmes in these fields. Such bodies could include, amongst others, a parliamentary committee on the subject;

6 Market approval (including in the case of exclusive marketing rights or product patents) should require the following:

(i) Environmental impact assessment of the product/process being applied for, covering impacts on environment and public health (using fully the precautionary principle in the case of uncertainties);

(ii) Assessment of the impacts of the product/process being applied for, on community rights as defined in relevant national legislation; and

(iii) Consultation of the national biodiversity agencies in the case of biological resources and related knowledge.

NOTE

1 South Asian Association for Regional Cooperation.

Appendix 3

THE NAIROBI STATEMENT, FROM AN INTERNATIONAL CONFERENCE ON TRADE-RELATED ASPECTS OF INTELLECTUAL PROPERTY RIGHTS AND THE CONVENTION ON BIOLOGICAL DIVERSITY, NAIROBI, FEBRUARY 6–7, 1999

Organized by the
African Centre for Technology Studies (ACTS)
in conjunction with the
United Nations Environment Programme (UNEP)
(NOT A CONSENSUS DOCUMENT)

INTRODUCTION

The 'International Conference on Trade Related Aspects of Intellectual Property Rights and the Convention on Biological Diversity' was organized by the African Centre for Technology Studies (ACTS) in collaboration with the United Nations Environment Programme (UNEP). It was held at UNEP's headquarters in Nairobi, Kenya (February 6–7, 1999) to explore the interaction between the two international agreements. Its specific objectives were to:

- Raise awareness of the interaction between the TRIPS Agreement of the World Trade Organization (WTO) and the Convention on Biological Diversity (CBD);
- Examine the extent to which the implementation of Article 27(3)(b) of the TRIPS Agreement may undermine goals and principles of the CBD;
- Identify specific ways and means of harmonizing the operations of Article 27(3)(b) of the TRIPS Agreement and the CBD; and
- Generate options for the 1999 review of Article 27(3)(b) of the TRIPS Agreement.

The Conference brought together a diverse group of policy-makers, researchers, private sector members, leading scholars, NGOs, representatives of ministries for the environment, the Secretariat of the Convention on Biological Diversity, representatives of the World Intellectual Property Organization (WIPO), WTO, and a variety of other institutions. The conference was a dialogue among the various stakeholders. It provided, perhaps for the first time, an opportunity for many African government officials and NGOs as well as the private sector to get an understanding of the evolution, nature and complexities of TRIPS and its relationship with the CBD. Given the diversity of views expressed by many participants and the complexity of the issues, this statement does not in any way contain and/or represent consensus.

The Conference deliberated and elaborated on the following issues: the evolution of TRIPS, norm creation under the CBD, the role and perspectives of international institutions, the expansion of intellectual property protection regimes to cover biological resources, the capacity of developing countries to influence policy agendas within the WTO, access to and transfer of new technologies, access to and exchange of genetic resources, and private sector investment in research and development of food technologies, medicines and the relationship of that to sustainable development.

The Conference made a wide range of observations including the following:

- Many developing countries, particularly those of Africa, are going through severe structural adjustment processes and are concerned that not enough has been done under Article 67 of TRIPS to provide them with technical assistance for the implementation of the agreement;
- Members of the WTO may have underestimated the time it takes to build genuine institutional capacities with respect to developing countries fulfilling their obligations under TRIPS;
- That the review of Article 27(3)(b) is taking place only four years after the creation of an entirely new multilateral trade regime;
- That members of the WTO, most of whom are also members of the CBD, should give themselves time to develop national policy, legislative models and codes of best practice under the CBD and TRIPS so that the interaction between Article 27 (3)(b) and the CBD can be more meaningfully evaluated;
- That members of the WTO will have the opportunity to revisit Article 27(3)(b) in future reviews of TRIPS;
- That international norm-creating bodies that have responsibilities for developing policies that affect the control, custody and conservation of biological resources, all have an obligation to allow for an open and deliberate consideration of their policies and norm-creating activities; and
- That states consider ways in which to build constructive linkage and policy dialogue between the WTO, the Food and Agriculture Organization (FAO), the Union for the Protection of Plant Varieties (UPOV), WIPO, UNEP and the Secretariat for the Convention on Biological Diversity.

BACKGROUND

There are growing intense debates about the relationships between TRIPS and the CBD. These debates are part of the wider concerns regarding trade and environment nexus. They are really about the control, custody and conservation of the world's biological resources. This control, custody and conservation has become a matter of pervasive concern amongst peoples of the world.

The debates are being conducted in a number of fora, including the Conference of Parties to the Convention on Biological Diversity (COPs), TRIPS Council, WTO's Trade and Environment Committee, FAO and UPOV. They have recently been stimulated by a wide range of factors including the increasing use of biotechnologies to transform living systems. Some of the decisions made regarding the development and use of these technologies have not paid sufficient attention to their broader social and ethical dimensions. One area of deep concern is the patentability of living organisms. The present review of Article 27(3)(b) of TRIPS touches directly upon this area of concern. In its present form, Article 27(3)(b) amongst other things allows for the patentability of plants, plant varieties and animals. Its terms directly affect the economic, social and cultural aspects of developing states, particularly those of Africa which are custodians of biological stock and associated traditional knowledge.

African countries have now an opportunity to develop common negotiating positions and strategies for this review, future TRIPS reviews, present and future reviews of other WTO agreements (eg the Agreement on Agriculture) as well as negotiating objectives in any round of trade talks. In their efforts at developing and adopting positions for the review of Article 27(3)(b), these countries should give consideration to the following:

1   Potential cross-linkages between this Article and other provisions of TRIPS (eg geographical indications), as well as cross-linkages between TRIPS and other WTO agreements;
2   The need to avoid negotiating bilateral treaties on these matters because such treaties tend to favour states with the most bargaining power and negotiating experience;
3   That the Agreement establishing the WTO recognizes the principle of sustainable development and the need to develop and implement the world's trade regime in a way that gives equal recognition to the needs of all its members;
4   That as Contracting Parties to the CBD they have established a set of obligations and principles to assert their sovereign rights over genetic resources, and to protect and promote the rights of their traditional and local communities; and
5   That they now have the challenge of ensuring that the WTO regime gives more than symbolic regard to the principle of sustainable development and provisions of the CBD and related international instruments such as the International Undertaking on Plant Genetic Resources and UPOV.

NEXT STEPS

In light of the observations made at the Conference, the following steps could be taken to ensure that African countries participate in an informed way in the review of Article 27(3)(b):

1   Informed consultations at the national level should be organized by various groups, bringing together governmental trade, agriculture, intellectual property and CBD negotiators;
2   Existing regional bodies such as the Organization for African Unity (OAU), the UN Economic Commission for Africa (UNECA) and the African Regional Industrial Property Organization (ARIPO), international agencies such UNEP, ACTS, WIPO, IPGRI, FAO, international scholars and a variety of other entities should be quickly mobilized to develop common African negotiating positions and strategies for the review;
3   Efforts to raise awareness of the issues associated with the TRIPS-CBD interface must continue as a matter of priority. In addition, inter-agency mechanisms (eg inter-ministerial working groups) should be established to ensure national policy coherence and consistency in the participation of African states in the CBD Conference of Parties and WTO fora; and
4   Efforts should be made to build an indigenous capability to gather and analyse data on a wide range of public policy issues emerging from the inter-linked complexities of global regulatory regimes. These may allow the countries to respond to and influence quickly and flexibly the changing dynamics of these regimes.

Appendix 4

IUCN RECOMMENDATIONS TO THE CONVENTION ON BIOLOGICAL DIVERSITY, INTERSESSIONAL MEETING ON THE OPERATIONS OF THE CONVENTION, 28–30 JUNE 1999

Agenda Item 4.3. The relationship between Intellectual Property Rights and the Relevant Provisions of the Agreement on Trade-Related Aspects of Intellectual Property Rights and the Convention on Biological Diversity

I INTRODUCTION

In decision IV/8 (on Access and Benefit-Sharing), COP4 requested the intersessional open-ended meeting (called for in decision IV/16) to explore options for access and benefit-sharing mechanisms, to start work on paragraph 10 of decision IV/15, and to make recommendations for further work. In decision IV/15 (on the relationship of the Convention with the Commission on Sustainable Development and biodiversity-related conventions, other international agreements, institutions and processes of relevance), COP4 stressed the need to ensure consistent implementation of the CBD and the World Trade Organization (WTO) agreements, including the Agreement on Trade-Related Aspects of Intellectual Property Rights (TRIPs) '...to promote increased mutual supportiveness and integration of biological diversity concerns and the protection of intellectual property rights [IPRs]...' (paragraph 9). COP also emphasized the need for further work to properly understand the relationship between IPRs, the relevant TRIPs provisions and the CBD (paragraph 10).

The Intersessional Meeting will review the relationship between the CBD and TRIPs. This is a key opportunity for the Parties to the CBD to review an issue with major implications for the achievement of the objectives of the CBD.

Decision IV/8 also established a regionally balanced panel of experts on Access and Benefit Sharing, to meet 4–8 October 1999. This panel will develop a common understanding of basic concepts and explore all the options for access and benefit-sharing on mutually agreed terms. The group will examine relevant case studies submitted to the SCBD, in accordance with decision IV/9, paragraph 15, and decision III/17.

Furthermore, decision IV/6 paragraph 10 requested a report by the Secretariat to the COP on the impact of trade liberalization on the conservation and sustainable use of agricultural biodiversity.

Other relevant provisions include decision III/17 in which COP3 encouraged Governments and relevant international and regional organizations to conduct case studies of the impacts of IPRs on the achievement of the Convention's objectives and to communicate them to the Executive Secretary for dissemination through the Clearing House Mechanism. COP3 also requested the Secretariat to contact the World Intellectual Property Organization (WIPO) and link with the WTO for further cooperation and consultation, as well as to apply for observer status in the Committee on Trade and Environment of the WTO.

In decision II/12, COP2 requested the Executive Secretary to liaise with the WTO to inform it of the goals and ongoing work of the CBD and to invite the WTO Secretariat to assist in the preparation of a paper for COP on synergies and relationship between CBD and TRIPs. The decision also requested the Executive Secretary to consult with all stakeholders, in particular private sector and indigenous and local communities, and to undertake a preliminary study analysing the impact of IPR systems on the conservation and sustainable use of biological diversity and the equitable sharing of the benefits derived from its use.

II THE TRIPS PROCESS

The TRIPs Agreement is now the key international agreement promoting the harmonization of national IPR regimes. TRIPs focuses on four types of intellectual property rights which are relevant to biodiversity: patents, geographical indications, undisclosed information (or trade secrets) and trademarks. Protection and enforcement of IPRs should, according to TRIPs Article 7 (Objectives), promote technological innovation and the transfer and dissemination of technology, 'to the mutual advantage of producers and users of technological knowledge and in a manner conducive to social and economic welfare, and to a balance of rights and obligations.' Article 1 (*Nature and Scope of Obligations*) makes clear that while WTO Members are required to implement the provisions of TRIPs, more extensive protection and enforcement of IPRs is not precluded. Under TRIPs, IPR protection and enforcement must be non-discriminatory as to the nationality of rights holders, and any concession granted by a Member to another Member must be accorded to all other Members 'immediately and unconditionally' (Articles 3 & 4).

Article 27.3(b) of TRIPs, which will be reviewed during 1999, is perhaps the most important in terms of the CBD and its objectives. 27.3(b) provides for exclusion from patentability for 'plants and animals other than microorganisms, and essentially biological processes for the production of plants or animals other than non-biological and microbiological processes'. However, Members shall provide for the protection of plant varieties either by patents or by an effective *sui generis* system or by any combination thereof. The currently dominant interpretation of an 'effective *sui generis* regime' is the International Convention for the Protection of New Varieties of Plants (UPOV Convention). The whole TRIPs Agreement will come up for review by the TRIPs Council in 2000.

III TRIPs AND CBD – BRIDGING THE GAPS

IUCN has examined the relationship between IPRs, TRIPs and the CBD, especially under the IUCN Project on Trade and Biodiversity which is looking at the conflicts and complementarities between the CBD and the international trade regime. The recommendations presented here were derived from work carried out under this project, including the workshop on Biodiversity Conservation and Intellectual Property Rights convened by IUCN in Delhi, India, on 29–31 January, 1999. More than 60 people participated in the workshop, representing academia, government, industry, and NGOs. Further information on this topic can be found in the IUCN Background Paper 'Intellectual Property Rights, Trade and Biodiversity: the Case of Seeds and Plant Varieties', included in this package.

In the CBD, the direct reference to IPRs is in Article 16 on *Access to and Transfer of Technology*. In paragraphs 1 and 2, Parties undertake to provide and/ or facilitate access to and transfer of technologies to other Parties under fair and most favourable terms. Their provision must be on terms which recognize and are consistent with the adequate and effective protection of intellectual property rights. Adoption here of the clause beginning 'adequate and effective protection' was specifically to establish a link with the TRIPs Agreement, which also uses this language. However, paragraph 16.5, which requires the Parties to cooperate to ensure that patents and other IPRs 'are supportive of and do not run counter to' the CBD's objectives, implicitly accepts that conflicts may well arise between certain IPR systems and the CBD. Other articles of the CBD relevant to IPRs are Articles 1 on objectives, 8(j) on *local and indigenous communities*, 10 on *Sustainable Use*, 11 on *Incentive Measures*, 15 on *Access to Genetic Resources* and 17 on *Exchange of Information*.

In addressing the COP's decisions to investigate linkages between IPRs and the CBD, ways to implement Article 8(j), and to collaborate with WIPO, IUCN believes that it is important to recognize that major gaps in knowledge remain, including the following:

- How to strike a balance such that rewards and incentives to right-holders are optimal in terms of the public good.
- How far biodiversity is affected by IPRs for seeds, plant varieties and/or agrochemicals. It is vital to consider whether and how the precautionary principle may be applied in the IPR context to minimize the risks without (a) being construed as an illegal barrier to trade or (b) foreclosing opportunities for developing countries to use IPR law to enhance their life science and technology capacities.
- Whether IPRs hinder or encourage the transfer of private technologies supportive of biodiversity conservation to developing countries.
- How the application of traditional knowledge and technologies can add value to genetic resources. Considered as private rights, it is not clear

how IPRs can act as mechanisms to protect the rights of traditional knowledge holders.

It must be borne in mind that TRIPs does not require national IPR regimes to be identical. Countries have the right to adopt higher standards than TRIPs requires, and they can address CBD-related concerns by imposing certain requirements on the process of applying for IPR protection, such as certification of origin, or creating mechanisms within an IPR law to achieve specific objectives, such as benefit sharing. Current international and national regimes which have relevance to IPR and biodiversity issues need to be thoroughly reviewed and strengthened as appropriate to support the objectives of the CBD. Other processes need to be considered here, including the Food and Agriculture Organization (FAO) Undertaking on Plant Genetic Resources, WIPO and the International Union for the Protection of New Varieties of Plants (UPOV).

IV OPTIONS FOR ACTION

IUCN recommends that the Intersessional Meeting informs the Expert Panel on Access and Benefit Sharing that will meet on 4–8 October 1999 on the need to:

- identify areas that need to be addressed to ensure consistent implementation of the CBD and the WTO and comprehensive consideration of benefit-sharing by COP6 and technology issues by COP7; and
- develop a time-table and modalities to address them, including a possible recommendation to COP5 on the establishment of an *Ad Hoc* Expert Group (in accordance with decision IV/16) to carry out specific work for SBSTTA in preparation for consideration of benefit-sharing by COP6 and technology issues by COP7.

Possible areas of work drawn from the activities carried out by the IUCN Trade and Biodiversity Project that the Panel might want to consider include:

- identifying best practices, developing guidelines and assessing the impacts of international processes relating to IPRs, including TRIPs, on the objectives of the CBD, in particular the implementation of Article 8(j) and 10;
- undertaking the above in relationship with the work of the ad hoc open-ended intersessional working group established in decision IV/9 and in close collaboration with the representatives of peoples and communities concerned;
- considering how trade issues, including IPRs can be addressed in National Biodiversity Strategies and Action Plans, to set priorities for action at the national level and clarifying needs at the international level;
- identifying conflicts and complementarities with other agreements on these issues, such as the FAO Undertaking and exploring points for collaboration;

- exploring the potential of non-patent IPRs such as geographical indications, petty patents and trademarks for protecting traditional knowledge, and making the results of these studies widely available to local communities; and
- developing options for *sui generis* systems for protecting traditional knowledge that consider the promotion of social justice and equity; the effective protection of traditional knowledge and resources from unauthorized collection, use, documentation and exploitation; and the recognition and reinforcement of customary laws and practice, and traditional resource management systems, that are effective in conserving biological diversity.

The *Ad Hoc* Working Group on Article 8(j) to meet in 2000 might consider the following options:

- where possible, designing ways of recognizing and protecting traditional knowledge of these communities, and traditional modes of resource use regulation and dispute resolution under customary law;
- ensuring the prior informed consent and involvement of these communities in the wider use of their knowledge and practices; and
- mandating a series of equitable benefit-sharing measures.

IUCN calls on the Intersessional Meeting to recommend COP5 to:

- Request: SBSTTA6 to address the impacts of IPRs on the implementation of the objectives of the CBD, in preparation for consideration of benefit-sharing by COP6, drawing on the issues and time-table recommended by the Expert Panel on Access, as well as the results of the meeting of the *Ad Hoc* Working Group on Article 8(j); and SBSTTA8 to consider IPR issues relating to transfer of technology and technology cooperation in preparation for COP7, which will deal with this subject.
- Transmit a report to the WTO, in particular the TRIPs Council, identifying areas where further knowledge is required, as those identified above. The report should also include the findings of the Expert Panel on Access and Benefit-Sharing, including a timetable and modalities to address priority issues, and the findings of the meeting of the *Ad Hoc* Working Group on Article 8(j). The application of the precautionary principle should also be emphasized.

Implementation at the national level

IUCN identified, through its Trade and Biodiversity Project and the workshop held on this subject in India, the following options that Parties might want to consider, while implementing the CBD and other international agreements at the national level:

- Application of the precautionary principle by excluding plants and animals from patentability until the environmental and social impacts of allowing such patents can be assessed; and/or adopting an expansive interpretation of *ordre public* and morality.

- Development of legislation covering components of biological diversity as well as biochemicals and other parts and products derived from such components. Such legislation could:
  - require that, for both domestic and international access to biodiversity, prior informed consent, mutually agreed terms, and burden of proof on the applicant be included in any plant variety legislation; and
  - recognize that the appropriate local authority could have the right of veto over any application referred to the National Authority and/or have the power to specify any special terms and conditions for regulating such access. Such terms and conditions could be mandatory on the National Authority to incorporate into the scheme that it may formulate for the specific application.
- The appropriate national biodiversity agencies could scrutinize:
  - market approval for products/ processes coming under the 'mailbox' applications;
  - patent applications for inventions derived from biological resources/local community knowledge; and
  - other relevant commercial applications to determine whether there is any threat to biological diversity, the environment, or human health (the precautionary principle should be applied in case of uncertainty); and whether there are any adverse implications on the rights of local communities.
- Requirement of more exacting standards of novelty or inventive step so that the failure of IPR law adequately to protect traditional knowledge is not compounded by the ability of others to hold patents for inventions closely derived from such knowledge.
- Application of an interpretation of prior art that would take into account relevant public domain knowledge in any part of the world whether published or not. Exclude from patentability existing traditional/indigenous knowledge (in current or translated forms), and essentially derived products and processes from such knowledge.
- Inclusion of the following elements, where available, in applications for patents and plant variety protection:
  - disclosure of all places of origin of the material/knowledge used in the application;
  - disclosure of all communities/persons of origin;
  - proof of consent having been obtained from the community/persons of origin;
  - proof of benefit-sharing arrangements with the community/persons of origin, in accordance with relevant national guidelines;
  - disclosure of any previous rejection of application, in the country or other jurisdictions; and
  - prior public notice in all relevant languages in the places and communities of origin. (Grounds for the above can be derived from Article 8(j), Article 15 and the clauses relating to national sovereignty under the CBD.)
- Protection to Farmers' Rights in plant varieties protection legislation.
- Keeping extant plant varieties, as identified by national inventories of biodiversity, outside the purview of protection granted to industrial or formal sector breeders.

- Development of *sui generis* legislation with WIPO for protection of folklore based on an understanding of 'folklore' as inclusive of folk knowledge/practices/expressions of art, craft, music, scientific belief, religious belief, architecture, agriculture, medicine, and conservation of natural resources.
- Development of legislation to protect denominations of geographic origin (characteristics associated with a specific region). The provisions of this legislation should provide additional protection as provided for in Article 23 of TRIPs.

Further, in the area of information exchange, the Parties could:

- facilitate technology transfers through greater access to patent libraries and databases. Parties could improve public access to patent databases by such means as publishing patent texts on the Internet and using the clearing-house mechanism of the CBD;
- compile a national database (or registry) of biodiversity and traditional knowledge, consisting of a representative inventory of biological and genetic resources, documentation and evaluation of the uses of these resources, and clarification of their ownership (local, state/provincial, national). The agencies responsible for compiling such databases could not claim ownership thereof. Effective control by communities of their knowledge, including mechanisms to ensure effective and equitable sharing of benefits with and within communities, could be ensured; and
- support the development of local knowledge registers for patent examiners to access, thereby helping to avoid traditional knowledge being pirated. However, ownership of these registers could not be claimed, since this would be an infringement of the rights of the knowledge providers.

Concerning institutional development and capacity building, Parties need to:

- enhance the capacity of communities and citizens to deal with biodiversity and IPR issues, through appropriate educational and training programmes which are culturally sensitive; and
- reinvest benefits derived from IPR-related legislation and from access regulations in the conservation of biodiversity, to provide incentives for local communities to conserve and sustainably use biodiversity.

TRIPs negotiations

In response to paragraph 9 of decision II/15, stressing the need to ensure consistency in implementing the CBD and the WTO agreement, the IUCN Project on Trade and Biodiversity, and especially the workshop organized in India, identified the following options for consideration by Parties in the context of WTO negotiations:

- carrying out an independent and transparent assessment of the environmental and equity implications of WTO in general and TRIPs in particular, involving civil society and relevant international bodies such as the CBD, the FAO and WIPO, taking into particular consideration the 'precautionary principle' enshrined in Agenda 21 and CBD;

- developing a common strategy on biodiversity-related issues in the 2000 review of TRIPs where interests converge. The same could be done for the 1999 review of TRIPs Article 27.3(b) to ensure that the *full range* of possible options is discussed;
- adopting an open and transparent process, involving civil society, of reviewing article 27.3(b) in 1999 and the review in 2000 of the TRIPs Agreement overall;
- expanding, or at the very least maintaining, the exceptions in Article 27.3(b) of TRIPs, for patenting of life forms; the expansion could exclude micro-organisms, products and processes thereof, from patentability;
- extending the compliance periods for 27.3(b) for developing and least developed countries;
- amending the provisions of Article 27.3(b) by defining it such that national priority is paramount in the interpretation of the term *sui generis*, including the following:
  - conservation and sustainable use of biodiversity;
  - promotion of sustainable traditional lifestyles;
  - promotion of food security and health security;
  - ensuring equitable benefit sharing;
  - invoking the precautionary principle; and
  - respect of the principles of equity and ethics;
- considering that the definition of the term 'micro-organism' not be expanded to cover tissues, cells or cell lines or DNA obtained from higher organisms, including human beings;
- adopting an expansive interpretation of the *sui generis* clause relating to plant variety protection, in order to:
  - ensure implementation of article 8(j) of the CBD relating to indigenous and local communities;
  - ensure that the full range of environmental and ethical concerns about IPRs on life forms are addressed; and
  - allow the completion of a biosafety protocol that establishes minimum international standards for the environmental safety of releases of genetically modified organisms;
- enhancing the scope of Article 23 of TRIPs to strengthen protection of geographical indications for goods other than wine and spirits and expanding the scope of Article 22 of TRIPs to protect denominations relating to geographic origin, and characteristics associated with a specific region;
- including requirements (in Article 29 of TRIPs) for disclosure of the genetic resources and the traditional knowledge used in inventions for which IPRs are claimed, the country and community of origin of these resources and knowledge, and proof of consent having been sought from the relevant community and equitable benefit-sharing arrangements having been entered into with them, as required by the CBD; and
- reviewing Article 31 of TRIPs to ensure its conformity with the preamble, and Articles 7 and 8 of TRIPs, as well as article 16 of the CBD. The aspects of authorization for commercial and non-commercial activity under Article 31 would need to be clarified during such review.

Other Relevant Fora

Further, IUCN identified possible measures Parties might want to consider in other international processes relevant to IPRs and biodiversity, including:

- ensuring that the development of the FAO Undertaking on Plant Genetic Resources, either in itself or as a protocol under the CBD, incorporates comprehensive protection of indigenous and local community knowledge, along with provisions to conserve biodiversity and sustainably use biological resources;
- providing inputs into the ongoing WIPO processes on 'new beneficiaries' which are assessing issues relating to protection of traditional knowledge; and
- ensuring that any agreement on databases (eg, the proposed Database Treaty) ensures effective control by communities of their knowledge, mechanisms that ensure effective and equitable sharing of benefits with and within communities, and space for communities to define the terms by which they control access and require benefit-sharing.

Appendix 5

ANNOTATED BIBLIOGRAPHY ON INTELLECTUAL PROPERTY RIGHTS, PLANTS, TRADE AND BIODIVERSITY[1]

Author: Achanta, A; Ghosh, P
Reference Type: Book Section
Year: 1994
Title: Technology Transfer and Environment
Editor: Sanchez, V; Juma, C
Book Title: Biodiplomacy
City: Nairobi
Publisher: ACTS
Pages: 157–175
Keywords: CBD, genetic resources, technology transfer, biotechnology, IPRs, patents, trade secrets, breeders rights, TRIPS
Abstract: Analysis of implications for and considerations involved in the technology transfer provisions of the CBD and the Climate Change Convention. The paper critiques the developed world's attitude towards IPRs by discussing the appropriateness of potential technology transferred, the scope of protection offered by IPRs and the aspects that will have to be included in future agreements so as to protect the interests of the developing world.

Author: Acharya, R
Reference Type: Report
Year: 1992
Title: Intellectual Property, Biotechnology and Trade: The Impact of the Uruguay Round on Biodiversity
City: Nairobi and Maastricht
Institution: African Centre for Technology Studies
Type: Biopolicy International
Report Number: 4
Keywords: GATT, IPR, genetic resources, biotechnology, TRIPS, farmers' rights
Abstract: The GATT negotiations have not included breeders' rights or farmers' rights. Their emphasis on patents shows that action to conserve biodiversity must be outside the framework of GATT. However, operating outside GATT might lead to confrontations with the USA. Developing countries should therefore bargain collectively rather than reject GATT.
Author argues that developing countries can gain much biotechnological knowledge that is already in the public domain. These benefits available may be greater

that those from repudiating the common heritage concept of genetic resource access.

Author: Ad-Hoc Group on Biodiversity of Colombia
Reference Type: Conference Proceedings
Year of Conference: 1997
Title: Legal Debate: International Seminar: Development of the Andean Regime Regarding: Access to Genetic Resources Identification of Biodiversity and its Benefits. Elements for National Studies Regarding a Regime for Protecting Traditional Knowledge
Conference Location: Santafe de Bogota
Date: 29 Sept–1 Oct 1997
Keywords: genetic resources, biodiversity, traditional knowledge, IPRs, CBD, Andean Community
Abstract: Synthesis of proposals and debates from a seminar dealing with aspects of the Andean Pact common regime on access to genetic resources.

Author: Adler, R G
Reference Type: Journal Article
Year: 1984
Title: Biotechnology as an Intellectual Property
Journal: Science
Volume: 224
Issue: 4647
Pages: 357–363
Keywords: biotechnology, IPRs
Abstract: Recent advances in biotechnology have created many public policy and legal issues, one of which is the treatment of biotechnological industrial products, particularly under the patent system. In this article biotechnological IPR issues are reviewed in the context of their underlying legal requirements. The implications of other factors, such as international competition, research funding, and gene ownership, are also considered.

Author: Alexander, D
Reference Type: Journal Article
Year: 1993
Title: Some Themes in Intellectual Property and the Environment
Journal: Review of European Community and International Environmental Law
Volume: 2
Issue: 2
Pages: 113–120
Keywords: biotechnology, CBD, IPRs, European Patent Convention, oncomouse, technology transfer, genetic resources, GATT
Abstract: The relationship between intellectual property and environmental protection is a complex one. The author calls on IPR lawyers to cooperate to ensure that IPRs support the objectives of environmental protection.

Author: Alexander, D
Reference Type: Book
Year: 1999
Title: Intellectual Property and the Environment
City: London
Publisher: Cameron May
Keywords: IPRs, biotechnology
Abstract: Intellectual property protection for living organisms and the products of biotechnology has assumed increasing significance in recent years. So too have

mechanisms for granting rights in respect of existing genetic resources. This book explains the law concerning the grant of intellectual property rights over new kinds of living matter and protection for biological resources. It covers the important recent developments in European Union, UK and international law, including the European Patent Convention and the Biodiversity Convention. The book also discusses the policies underlying protection for living matter, the recent legislative initiatives and the Oncomouse and Plant Genetic Systems cases.

Author: Anuradha, R V
Reference Type: Journal Article
Year: 1997
Title: In Search of Knowledge and Resources: Who Sows? Who Reaps?
Journal: Review of European Community and International Environmental Law
Volume: 6
Issue: 3
Pages: 263–273
Keywords: CBD, India, traditional knowledge, genetic resources
Abstract: Explains the significance of traditional knowledge to research into genetic resources, analyses the scope of CBD Articles 8(j) and 15, and examines some of the attempts in India that aim to realize the mandate of the two articles, and some of the questions arising in view of a recent benefit-sharing arrangement between a research institute and a tribal community (TBGRI and the Kanis).

Author: Atkinson, N; Sherman, B
Reference Type: Journal Article
Year: 1991
Title: Intellectual Property and Environmental Protection
Journal: European Intellectual Property Review
Issue: 5
Pages: 165–170
Keywords: IPRs, patents, UK
Abstract: With the enactment of the UK Environmental Protection Act, the themes of IPRs and environmental protection find themselves in a close association. This paper explores the relationship between these hitherto separate spheres and suggests that one should at least begin to question the appropriateness and relevance of the ideas and assumptions of patent law formed a century or more ago to the modern world. The Act may well provide the impetus for a re-examination and ultimate improvement in the ideas and principles which have, on the whole, served so well.

Editors: Balick, M J; Elisabetsky, E; Laird, S A
Reference Type: Edited Book
Year: 1996
Title: Medicinal Resources of the Tropical Forest: Biodiversity and Its Importance to Human Health
City: New York
Publisher: Columbia University Press
Keywords: bioprospecting, medicinal plants, traditional medicine, pharmaceuticals
Abstract: According to WHO estimates, some 80 per cent of people in developing countries rely on harvested wild plants for some part of their primary health care. Covering a wide spectrum of subjects in biodiversity, ethnomedicine, ethnobotany, and pharmacognosy, and including regional work ranging from Africa to Asia to South America, the contributors offer a comprehensive survey of the current literature on the subject of medicinal uses of tropical plants. The authors call attention to the ways in which the natural habitats of these plants can be protected from damage or destruction, provide information on establishing drug discovery efforts, and explore the ethical issue of IPRs pertaining to tropical resources and their diverse

medicinal uses, with an eye towards promoting economic opportunity in developing countries.

Author: Barton, J H; Christensen, E
Reference Type: Book Section
Year: 1988
Title: Diversity Compensation Systems: Ways to Compensate Developing Nations for Providing Genetic Materials
Editor: Kloppenburg, J, Jr
Book Title: Seeds and Sovereignty: The Use and Control of Plant Genetic Resources
City: Durham, USA and London, UK
Publisher: Duke University Press
Pages: 338–355
Keywords: genetic resources, UPOV
Abstract: Argues against theory of compensation based purely on equity. Instead, the collection and conservation of genetic diversity should be rewarded and encouraged by monetary incentives, parallel to those created to encourage plant research and breeding. This could be achieved through the levy of a tax on seed sales, or an approach using a property right.

Author: Barton, J H
Reference Type: Magazine Article
Year: 1991
Title: Patenting Life
Magazine: Scientific American
Volume: 264
Issue Number: 3
Pages: 40–46
Date: March 1991
Keywords: IPRs, biotechnology, patents, genetic resources, agriculture, pharmaceuticals, breeders' rights, oncomouse, GATT
Abstract: Entrepreneurs can now legally protect any novel plant, animal or microorganism they 'invent'. However, the courts have not yet settled many questions about the reach of biotechnology patents.

Author: Barton, J H; Siebeck, W E
Reference Type: Report
Year: 1992
Title: Intellectual Property Issues for the International Agricultural Research Centres: What are the Options?
City: Washington DC
Institution: Consultative Group on International Agricultural Research (CGIAR)
Date: April
Report Number: Issues in Agriculture No 4
Keywords: IPRs, IARCs, UPOV
Abstract: Contains recommendations to the International Agricultural Research Centres in the context of the trend within the agricultural research community to protect intellectual property.

Author: Barton, J H
Reference Type: Book Section
Year: 1994
Title: Ethnobotany and Intellectual Property Rights
Editor: Chadwick, D J; Marsh, J
Book Title: Ethnobotany and the Search for New Drugs
City: Chichester

Publisher: John Wiley & Sons
Pages: 214–221
Keywords: pharmaceuticals, ethnobiology, trade secrets, ILO, IPRs, genetic resources, GATT, TRIPS, CBD, Draft Declaration on the Rights of Indigenous Peoples, WRI, NCI
Abstract: Reviews intellectual property and related legal principles that apply to folk knowledge of a specific medicinal plant and a marketable drug based on that plant. International law recognizes national sovereignty over genetic resources. The combination of trade secrets and patents is the basis of a plausible agreement pattern, but there are gaps. The best approach is to work informally and to explore approaches to protecting indigenous peoples in a model agreement developed by NGOs.

Author: Barton, J H; Siebeck, W E
Reference Type: Report
Year: 1994
Title: Material System for Plant Genetic Resources Exchange: The Case of the International Agricultural Research Centres
City: Rome
Institution: International Plant Genetic Resources Institute
Type: Issues in Genetic Resources
Report Number: 1
Keywords: IARCs, CBD, IPRs, CGIAR, GATT
Abstract: The CBD, which affirms countries' sovereign rights over genetic resources in their territories, has led several countries to develop policies and strategies governing the conservation and use of genetic diversity, including conditions for its release. A system is required to facilitate the unhindered movement of genetic resources and the fair and equitable sharing of benefits derived from their use. This publication, a contribution to the debate on these issues, suggests mechanisms by which these objectives might be achieved including the use of MTAs by the IARCs.

Author: Barton, J H
Reference Type: Journal Article
Year: 1995
Title: Patent Scope in Biotechnology
Journal: International Review of Industrial Property and Copyright Law
Volume: 26
Issue: 5
Pages: 605–18
Keywords: biotechnology, patents
Abstract: Nowadays, very broad patents are being issued in biotechnology. This has given rise to serious conflict and even to legal moves to revoke certain of the patents. This paper reviews the broad patents and the doctrines underlying their breadth; it then evaluates these patents and judges that some do pose barriers to future innovation; finally it suggests legal reforms through which their effective scope might be limited without destroying incentive for innovation.

Author: Baumann, M; Bell, J; Koechlin, F; Pimbert, M
Reference Type: Book
Year: 1996
Title: The Life Industry: Biodiversity, People and Profits
City: London
Publisher: Intermediate Technology Publications, World Wide Fund for Nature, and Swissaid
Keywords: biotechnology, biodiversity, agriculture, pharmaceuticals, HGDP, indigenous peoples, bioprospecting

Abstract: Biodiversity conservation in the face of rapid technological change and the commercialization of biological resources raises fundamental scientific, economic, socio-political and ethical questions. Most of the world's biodiversity is located in the South. The North and its private industry use the countries of the South as reservoirs of genetic resources to develop new products. The diversity of the living world has become the raw material for the new biotechnologies and the object of patent claims. This book presents the views of grassroots NGOs, journalists, industrialists and policy makers who gathered in Switzerland in 1994 to answer a question which was also the title of the conference: 'Are plants and Indians becoming raw materials for the gene industry?' The response of most contributors is very much in the affirmative.

Author: Bell, J
Reference Type: Book Section
Year: 1996
Title: Genetic Engineering and Biotechnology in Industry
Editor: Baumann, M; Bell, J; Koechlin, F; Pimbert, M
Book Title: The Life Industry: Biodiversity, People and Profits
City: London
Publisher: Intermediate Technology Publications
Pages: 31–52
Keywords: biotechnology, biosafety, pharmaceuticals, agriculture
Abstract: Considers the social and environmental impacts of genetic engineering and biotechnology and warns of the danger of 'biotechnological colonialism' caused by the lack of biosafety regulation in Third World countries.

Author: Berard, L; Marchenay, P
Reference Type: Book Section
Year: 1996
Title: Tradition, Regulation and Intellectual Property: Local Agricultural Products and Foodstuffs in France
Editor: Brush, S B; Stabinsky, D
Book Title: Valuing Local Knowledge: Indigenous Peoples and Intellectual Property Rights
City: Covelo, CA
Publisher: Island Press
Pages: 230–243
Keywords: appellations of origin, geographical indications, agriculture, France
Abstract: Discusses agricultural products and foodstuffs that are historically linked to specific places and groups of people. The aim is to develop a method that will permit valuation of these products by designating appellations of origin.

Author: Bhat, M G
Reference Type: Journal Article
Year: 1996
Title: Trade-related Intellectual Property Rights to Biological Resources: Socioeconomic Implications for Developing Countries
Journal: Ecological Economics
Volume: 19
Pages: 205–17
Keywords: IPRs, TRIPS, bioprospecting, agriculture
Abstract: TRIPS has been denounced by developing countries, which have relied heavily on indigenous biotechnology from several decades in the area of high-yielding seeds, bio-pesticides and fertilizers, herbal medicines and household consumables. This study analyses the social, economic and preservation implica-

tions of TRIPS for biological resources. Establishing IPRs to products derived from genetic resources is necessary but not sufficient for bioprospecting and the long-term survival of these resources. Developing countries must also develop suitable institutions and policies governing the use of their resources and enabling local communities to receive benefits of biodiversity conservation and prospecting.

Editor: Biber-Klemm, S
Reference Type: Conference Proceedings
Year of Conference: 1998
Title: Legal Claims to Biogenetic Resources: Proceedings of the International Workshop
Conference Name: Legal Claims to Biogenetic Resources
Conference Location: Berne
Publisher: Swiss National Science Foundation
Volume: National Research Program 42: Foreign Policy
Date: 17 June 1997
Keywords: genetic resources, bioprospecting, IPRs, farmers' rights, CBD, traditional knowledge, Europe, TRIPS, *sui generis*
Abstract: Proceedings of a workshop that sought to contribute to the evolution of the Swiss position vis-à-vis the CBD. In view of the re-negotiation of Article 27.3b of TRIPS, which offers the opportunity to create a new (*sui generis*) system for the protection of plant varieties, the discussions and presentation focused on the question as to whether IPRs are an adequate instrument to secure traditional resource rights. Speakers represented industry, government, NGOs, and academe.

Editor: Bilderbeek, S
Reference Type: Edited Book
Year: 1992
Title: Biodiversity and International Law: the Effectiveness of International Environmental Law
City: Amsterdam, Oxford, Washington DC, Tokyo
Publisher: IOS Press
Keywords: international law, biodiversity, CBD, UNEP, UNDP, UNCTAD, NGOs, common heritage, conservation
Abstract: Deals with various legal issues concerning biodiversity: international environmental law and the preservation of biodiversity; the effectiveness of international environmental law; institutional change and the effectiveness of international law; and the role of NGOs.

Author: BioIndustry Association
Reference Type: Report
Year: 1996
Title: Innovation from Nature: The Protection of Inventions in Biology
City: London
Institution: BioIndustry Association
Keywords: patents, ethics, biotechnology, IPRs, biodiversity
Abstract: This report contains contributions that set out the important issues in the patenting of biotechnological inventions. The publication is intended to contribute to an informed discussion of the ethics and regulation of biotechnology, with particular reference to the forthcoming debate in Europe on the new Directive for the Legal Protection of Biotechological Inventions. The report was prepared by the BioIndustry Association's Intellectual Property Advisory Committee.

Author: Biothai/GRAIN
Reference Type: Report
Year: 1998
Title: Road Maps to a Peoples' Sui Generis Rights Plan of Action
City: Bangkok
Institution: Biothai & GRAIN
Keywords: CBD, farmers' rights, IPRs, UPOV, TRIPS, patents
Abstract: Proceedings of an international NGO seminar that sought to elaborate a coherent response to the TRIPS provision allowing for a *sui generis* alternative to patents for protection of plant varieties. The main outcomes of the seminar were the Thammasat Resolution and a Plan of Action.

Author: Blixt, S
Reference Type: Book Section
Year: 1994
Title: The Role of Genebanks in Plant Genetic Resource Convention under the Convention on Biological Diversity
Editor: Krattiger, A F; McNeely, J A; Lesser, W H; Miller, K R; Hill, Y St; Senanayake, R
Book Title: Widening Perspectives on Biodiversity
City: Gland & Geneva
Publisher: IUCN & IAE
Pages: 255–261
Keywords: CBD, genetic resources, agriculture
Abstract: Explains role of genebanks in plant genetic resource conservation. Urges increased transfers of knowledge and technology to developing countries. Conventional genebanks need additional funds to play a role in implementing the CBD.

Editor: Bodeker, G; Bhat, K K S; Burley, J; Vantomme, P
Reference Type: Edited Book
Year: 1997
Title: Medicinal Plants for Forest Conservation and Health Care
Series Title: FAO Non-Wood Products Series
City: Rome
Publisher: FAO
Volume: 11
Keywords: medicinal plants, conservation, health, traditional medicine, IPRs
Abstract: Collection of papers that clarify the many policy and technical issues associated with the conservation, use, production and trade of medicinal plants. Subjects covered include assessment and management of the medicinal plant resource base; harvesting and processing issues; trade issues; and intellectual property rights regarding traditional medicines of indigenous peoples.

Author: Boyle, J
Reference Type: Book
Year: 1996
Title: Shamans, Software and Spleens: Law and the Social Construction of the Information Economy
City: Cambridge
Publisher: Harvard University Press
Keywords: Moore, IPRs, copyright
Abstract: Author uses his legal background to construct a social theory of the information society. Central to the analysis is a critique of the notion of authorship upon which Western IPRs are founded. This notion is blamed for the restriction of information and stifling of innovation under existing IPR regimes.

Author: Bragdon, S H; Downes, D R
Reference Type: Report
Year: 1998
Title: Recent Policy Trends and Developments Related to the Conservation, Use and Development of Genetic Resources
City: Rome
Institution: International Plant Genetic Resources Institute
Date: June 1998
Type: Issues in Genetic Resources
Report Number: 7
Keywords: *sui generis*, IPRs, UPOV, TRIPS, genetic resources, CBD, farmers' rights
Abstract: The erosion of genetic resources continues at an alarming pace. Simultaneously, technologies which develop and make use of these resources outpace the ability of laws and societies to understand and cope with them. Spurred by technological advances, appreciation of the monetary and non-monetary value of genetic resources has grown, leading to increasing conflict over rights and responsibilities for these resources. Developments in international and national law and policy over the past five years have significantly changed the policy environment relating to the management and control of genetic resources. The task of discerning all the issues of relevance to the conservation and management of genetic resources and then integrating them into consistent policy is extremely complex. This paper analyses developments in the past five years, identifying cross-cutting issues and trends that have emerged including farmers' rights and interests of indigenous and local communities, benefit-sharing, access to genetic resources, patenting and industry trends, and *sui generis* protection of plant varieties.

Author: Bravo, E
Reference Type: Book
Year: 1996
Title: Biodiversidad y Derechos de Los Pueblos
City: Quito
Publisher: Accion Ecologica
Keywords: biodiversity, conservation, IPRs
Abstract: A guide to biodiversity conservation, bioprospecting and IPRs. Chapters are arranged under the following headings: (i) biodiversity: a strategic resource; (ii) Biopiracy; (iii) Biodiversity and food security; and (iv) IPRs or collective rights. The book is rich in case studies which justify concerns of people in South America about biopiracy. (In Spanish.)

Author: Brush, S B
Reference Type: Journal Article
Year: 1993
Title: Indigenous Knowledge of Biological Resources and Intellectual Property Rights: The Role of Anthropology
Journal: American Anthropologist
Volume: 95
Issue: 3
Pages: 653–686
Keywords: genetic resources, traditional knowledge, common heritage, IPRs, agriculture, conservation, NCI, Shaman Pharmaceuticals, anthropology
Abstract: IPRs for ethnobiological knowledge have been proposed as a way to compensate indigenous peoples. Four obstacles are critical: whether general and collective knowledge can be protected; whether certain indigenous groups can claim exclusive control over knowledge and resources; the uncertain status of indigenous peoples; and the lack of a well-developed market for biological resources or traditional knowledge. Anthropologists can play a critical role in the debate by providing analysis and ethnobiological information.

Author: Brush, S B
Reference Type: Report
Year: 1994
Title: Providing Farmers' Rights through *in situ* Conservation of Crop Genetic Resources
City: Rome
Institution: FAO
Type: Commission on Plant Genetic Resources, First Extraordinary Session, 7–11 November 1994
Report Number: Background Study Paper No 3
Keywords: IPRs, farmers' rights, genetic resources, conservation, agriculture, contracts, bioprospecting
Abstract: Explains how the needs for conservation and equity can be joined and resolved through internationally sponsored programmes for *in situ* conservation of crop germplasm. The first major conclusion is that *in situ* conservation is a viable and necessary addition to the existing strategies to preserve plant genetic resources for agriculture. The second is that market financing, whether through IPRs or contracts, is untenable for financing plant genetic resource conservation for agriculture. The author recommends financing farmers' rights and *in situ* conservation through a multilateral trust fund.

Editors: Brush, S B; Stabinsky, D
Reference Type: Edited Book
Year: 1996
Title: Valuing Local Knowledge: Indigenous Peoples and Intellectual Property Rights
City: Covelo, CA
Publisher: Island Press
Keywords: IPRs, indigenous peoples, traditional knowledge, conservation
Abstract: Papers from the 1993 conference on IPR and Indigenous Knowledge, which took place in Lake Tahoe, California. Includes sections on equity and indigenous rights, conservation, knowledge, and policy options and alternatives.

Author: Brush, S B
Reference Type: Book Section
Year: 1996
Title: Is Common Heritage Outmoded?
Editor: Brush, S B; Stabinsky, D
Book Title: Valuing Local Knowledge: Indigenous Peoples and Intellectual Property Rights
City: Covelo, CA
Publisher: Island Press
Keywords: common heritage, traditional knowledge, IPRs, genetic resources, CBD, conservation, agriculture
Abstract: Writer argues that biological resources are and should remain common heritage of mankind. IPRs can be justified on utilitarian grounds but are inappropriate and impracticable for conservation and indigenous knowledge. Instead he advocates public subsidy approach.

Author: Brush, S B
Reference Type: Journal Article
Year: 1998
Title: Bio-cooperation and the Benefits of Crop Genetic Resources: the Case of Mexican Maize
Journal: World Development
Volume: 26
Issue: 5

Pages: 755–766
Keywords: bioprospecting, contracts, genetic resources, agriculture, Mexico, contracts
Abstract: Concern for equity and conservation has prompted the creation of bioprospecting contracts for biological resources from developing countries. One potential type of contract is between farmers who provide crop genetic resources and seed companies or agencies that use these resources. Theoretically bio-contracts will reward peasant farmers for preserving genetic resources and balance equities between farmers and seed companies. Using maize from Mexico as a case study, this paper concludes that contracting is problematic on both efficiency and equity grounds. 'Bio-cooperation' is presented as an alternative. Institutional support and licensing agreements that support human capital development are proposed as alternatives.

Author: Busch, L
Reference Type: Journal Article
Year: 1995
Title: Eight Reasons Why Patents Should Not Be Extended to Plants and Animals
Journal: Biotechnology and Development Monitor
Issue: 24
Pages: 2–4
Keywords: patents, IPRs, biotechnology
Abstract: Biotechnology industry interests normally call for an extension of patents to plants and animals as a requirement to stimulate investments in biotechnological research, and to insure the wide distribution of the benefits from such research. The author, on the other hand, questions whether such an extension will serve this purpose. If IPRs must be extended to living organisms, he argues, another legal form would be needed.

Author: Butler, B; Pistorius, R
Reference Type: Magazine Article
Year: 1996
Title: How Farmers' Rights Can Be Used to Adapt Plant Breeders' Rights
Magazine: Biotechnology and Development Monitor
Issue Number: 28
Pages: 7–11
Keywords: UPOV, farmers' rights, sui generis, IPRs
Abstract: To curb the negative effects of UPOV 1991, the authors propose a remuneration system that would compensate breeders without recognizing intellectual property rights as such.

Author: Buttel, F H; Belsky, J
Reference Type: Journal Article
Year: 1987
Title: Biotechnology, Plant Breeding, and Intellectual Property: Social and Ethical Dimensions
Journal: Science, Technology, & Human Values
Volume: 12
Issue: 1
Pages: 31–49
Keywords: biotechnology, IPRs, UPOV, agriculture, USA
Abstract: Provides an overview of the development of the seed industry in the US, particularly in relation to public plant breeding institutions that have both supported and competed with private sector efforts. Also discusses major types of IPR arrangements pertaining to private plant breeding and identifies several crucial issues in proprietary protection of plant breeding inventions.

Author: Byrne, N
Reference Type: Journal Article
Year: 1993
Title: Plant Breeding and the UPOV
Journal: Review of European Community and International Environmental Law
Volume: 2
Issue: 2
Pages: 136–140
Keywords: UPOV, agriculture, genetic resources
Abstract: Contests view that breeders' rights is a licence to 'pillage' resources of Third World countries and denies that the Union for the Protection of New Varieties of Plants (UPOV) system is to blame for erosion of genetic diversity of crop plants. Furthermore, he argues that if UPOV breeders' rights are not allowed to prevail over farmers' rights, the industrial system will replace UPOV with a stronger system of protection.

Author: Calle, R
Reference Type: Journal Article
Year: 1996
Title: Juridical and Sociocultural Problems on the Definition of a Law Concerning Property, Usage and Access to Genetic Resources in Colombia
Journal: Journal of Ethnopharmacology
Volume: 51
Pages: 127–46
Keywords: Colombia, patents, IPRs, biotechnology, CBD, Andean Pact, UPOV, traditional knowledge
Abstract: The property, usage, and access to genetic resources is today one of the primary topics in international business, as a result of the strategic importance of the resources for the biotechnology industry. This paper describes some of the technical, juridical, and socio-cultural difficulties that Colombia has to confront in order to set appropriate guidelines on patenting living organisms, and on the access and usage of genetic resources.

Author: Cameron, J; Makuch, Z
Reference Type: Report
Year: 1995
Title: The UN Biodiversity Convention and the WTO TRIPS Agreement: Recommendations to Avoid Conflict and Promote Sustainable Development
City: Gland
Institution: World Wide Fund For Nature
Type: Discussion Paper
Keywords: TRIPS, CBD, UPOV, IPRs
Abstract: Negotiation of the CBD took place with little discussion of linkages to GATT-TRIPS. The authors analyse the relationship and potential conflicts between these two agreements and make recommendations to defuse any such conflicts and ensure that the objectives of the CBD are not undermined by TRIPS.

Editors: Chadwick, D J; Marsh, J
Reference Type: Edited Book
Year: 1994
Title: Ethnobotany and the Search for New Drugs
Series Title: Ciba Foundation Symposium (185)
City: Chichester
Publisher: John Wiley & Sons
Keywords: ethnobiology, IPRs, pharmaceuticals, medicinal plants, traditional medicine, NCI, ethnopharmacology

Abstract: Contains papers and discussions from a symposium which presented studies of traditional medicine around the world and debated ways to encourage conservation of natural habitats and cultivation of medicinal plants. IPR are considered, including the application of patent laws and methods of compensation for the local communities.

Author: Challa, J; Kalla, J C
Reference Type: Journal Article
Year: 1995
Title: World Trade Agreement and Trade-Related Aspects of Intellectual Property Rights-Relevance to Indian Agriculture
Journal: Commonwealth Agricultural Digest
Volume: 4
Pages: 1–20
Keywords: WTO, TRIPS, IPRs, India, agriculture
Abstract: Defines 'intellectual property', explains its origin and the development of IPR laws in India. The article also considers the implications of the global IPR regime for Indian agriculture, arguing that the new regime offers both a challenge and an opportunity for the country.

Author: Christie, A
Reference Type: Journal Article
Year: 1988
Title: The Novelty Requirement in Plant Breeders' Rights Law
Journal: International Review of Industrial Property and Copyright Law
Volume: 19
Issue: 5
Pages: 646–657
Keywords: UPOV
Abstract: According to the author's analysis of the (pre-1991) UPOV Convention, the distinctness requirement is considered to be quite different from the novelty requirement of patent law. Consequently, a publicly known but not previously commercialized plant variety is protectable under the system whether or not the applicant was the first to breed the variety.

Author: Christie, A
Reference Type: Journal Article
Year: 1989
Title: Patents for Plant Innovation
Journal: European Intellectual Property Review
Issue: 11
Pages: 394–408
Keywords: patents, UPOV, EU
Abstract: Study of plant patenting that reviews the availability of patent protection for plant innovation, analyses the scope of such protection, and considers the issues from an international perspective, but with particular reference to the European Community.

Author: Cleveland, D A; Murray, S C
Reference Type: Journal Article
Year: 1997
Title: The World's Crop Genetic Resources and the Rights of Indigenous Farmers
Journal: Current Anthropology
Volume: 38
Issue: 4
Pages: 477–514

Keywords: genetic resources, agriculture, indigenous peoples, IPRs, contracts, farmers' rights, human rights, environmental rights

Abstract: Farmer or folk crop varieties developed over many generations by indigenous farmers are an important component of global crop genetic resources for use by both industrial and indigenous agriculture. Currently there is a debate between advocates of indigenous farmers' rights in their folk varieties and the dominant world system, which vests IPRs to crop genetic resources only in users of those resources for industrial agriculture. While indigenous peoples at the individual and group levels do have a broad range of IPRs in their folk varieties, they define and use them differently from the industrial world. Therefore industrial world IPRs are generally inappropriate for protecting the IPRs of indigenous farmers, but some could be used effectively, To meet indigenous farmers' need for protection, new approaches are being developed that embed indigenous farmers' rights in folk varieties in cultural, human, and environmental rights. More research on the cultural, social, and agronomic roles of folk varieties, ongoing negotiation of the meaning of key concepts such as 'crop genetic resources', 'rights', and 'indigenous', and an emphasis on a common goal of sustainability will help to resolve the debate.

Author: The Corner House
Reference Type: Report
Year: 1997
Title: No Patents on Life! A Briefing on the Proposed EU Directive on the Legal Protection of Biotechnological Inventions
City: Sturminster Newton, UK
Institution: The Corner House
Keywords: patents, EU
Abstract: Condemnation of 'patenting life', which rebuts the argument that without patents fewer health care products will become available. Moreover, the paper argues that life patents hinder research, restrict the research agenda, restrict competition, exploit public-funded research, restrict access to treatment, enable companies to capture markets at the expense of jobs, and legalize biopiracy.

Author: Correa, C M
Reference Type: Journal Article
Year: 1992
Title: Biological Resources and Intellectual Property Rights
Journal: European Intellectual Property Review
Volume: 14
Issue: 5
Pages: 154–157
Keywords: genetic resources, IPRs, farmers' rights, patents, UPOV
Abstract: Describes the emerging international IPR regime concerning genetic resources, with particular emphasis on Farmers' Rights, patents and the UPOV Convention. The author considers the implications of these for developing countries and the possible options.

Author: Correa, C M
Reference Type: Report
Year: 1994
Title: Sovereign and Property Rights over Plant Genetic Resources
City: Rome
Institution: Food and Agriculture Organization
Type: Commission on Plant Genetic Resources Background Study Paper No 2
Keywords: genetic resources, FAO, IUPGR, IPRs, patents, UPOV, TRIPS, trade secrets, appellations of origin, folklore, farmers' rights, CBD

Abstract: Deals with the concept of sovereign rights and its application to plant genetic resources, particularly in the context of the IUPGR and the CBD; analyses the applicability and extent of IPRs over plant genetic resources; and discusses the so-called 'informal' innovations and the implementation of farmers' rights at the national and international level.

Author: Correa, C M
Reference Type: Book Section
Year: 1996
Title: Intellectual Property Rights and Agriculture: Strategies and Policies for Developing Countries
Editor: Van Wijk, J; Jaffe, W
Book Title: Intellectual Property Rights and Agriculture in Developing Countries
City: Amsterdam
Publisher: University of Amsterdam
Pages: 100–113
Keywords: IPRs, agriculture, geographical indications
Abstract: The paper deals first with the different IPRs that are relevant to agriculture. Second, it considers the relevance of such rights. It is suggested that the 'technological distance' and varying degrees of 'technical protection' explain to a great extent differences in the relative importance of IPRs in agriculture. Thirdly, the system of plant genetic resources is briefly described. The tension between conservation goals and the diffusion of modern varieties is addressed. Finally, the paper considers the requirements and difficulties in developing special IPRs to protect traditional varieties.

Author: Cosbey, A
Reference Type: Report
Year: 1996
Title: The Sustainable Development Effects of the WTO TRIPS Agreement: A Focus on Developing Countries
City: Winnipeg
Institution: International Institute for Sustainable Development
Keywords: TRIPS, IPRs, patents, UPOV, biodiversity, CBD, pharmaceuticals, agriculture
Abstract: This paper examines the TRIPS Agreement and analyses those areas in which the Agreement will impact on sustainable development in developing countries such as Pakistan. Sustainable development, throughout the paper, embraces the fundamentally interrelated concerns of environment, development and economy. After brief introductions to the Agreement itself, and to the concept of IPRs, the paper examines the possible effects of the Agreement, focusing on agriculture, manufacturing and copyrighted goods. It ends by proposing a number of policy actions which might contribute to sustainable development in the context of the Agreement, and suggesting ways to interpret provisions to developing countries' advantage.

Author: Costa e Silva, E da
Reference Type: Journal Article
Year: 1995
Title: The Protection of Intellectual Property for Local and Indigenous Communities
Journal: European Intellectual Property Review
Volume: 17
Issue: 11
Pages: 546–549
Keywords: indigenous peoples, TRIPS, CBD, IPRs

Abstract: Presents and analyses recent legislative processes in Latin America relevant to the intellectual property rights of indigenous peoples. These processes are concerned with national and regional implementation of GATT-TRIPS in conformity with the requirements of the CBD *vis-à-vis* indigenous peoples.

Author: Costa e Silva, E da
Reference Type: Report
Year: 1996
Title: Biodiversity-Related Aspects of Intellectual Property Rights
City: Tokyo
Institution: United Nations University
Type: UNU/IAS Working Paper
Keywords: Brazil, IPRs, CBD, TRIPS, biodiversity, conservation
Abstract: Reviews legal developments internationally and in Brazil relating to biodiversity conservation and IPRs. One of the greatest challenges the international community faces is to determine a balance between the common interests of biodiversity conservation and the private interest related to the activities of industries which use biodiversity resources as a main source of materials. This balance is hard to achieve. An IPR framework must consider the particular characteristics of access to genetic resources, technology transfer agreements, biotechnology and the protection of traditional knowledge and practices.

Author: Crespi, S
Reference Type: Journal Article
Year: 1995
Title: Biotechnology Patenting: The Wicked Animal Must Defend Itself
Journal: European Intellectual Property Review
Volume: 9
Pages: 431–441
Keywords: IPRs, biotechnology, CBD, neem, Biotics, contracts, farmers' rights
Abstract: Vigorous defence of biotechnology patents. The author dismisses the objections to such patents, such as ethics and morality, and argues that 'patenting life' is a meaningless slogan.

Author: Crucible Group
Reference Type: Book
Year: 1994
Title: People, Plants and Patents: The Impact of Intellectual Property on Trade, Plant Biodiversity, and Rural Society
City: Ottawa
Publisher: International Development Research Centre
Keywords: biodiversity, conservation, agriculture, IPRs, patents, IARCs, farmers' rights, breeders' rights, UPOV, INBio
Abstract: Decisions about IPRs, particularly for plants, have major implications for food security, agriculture, rural development, and the environment for every country in the world. For the developing world in particular, the impact of IPRs on farmers, rural societies, and biodiversity will be profoundly important. In this fast-changing and politicized field, this book identifies and examines the major issues and the range of policy alternatives including consensus positions and the various conflicting viewpoints.

Author: Dawkins, K; Suppan, S
Reference Type: Report
Year: 1996
Title: Sterile Fields: The Impacts of Intellectual Property Rights and Trade on Biodiversity and Food Security. With Case Studies from the Philippines, Zimbabwe and Mexico

City: Minnesota, US
Institution: Institute for Agriculture and Trade Policy
Date: November
Keywords: Philippines, Zimbabwe, Mexico, IPRs, WTO, TRIPS, agriculture, biodiversity
Abstract: Presents the negative impacts of IPRs and free trade on biodiversity and food security, concluding with a series of recommendations to respond to these conflicts. The paper contains reports on the present situation in three developing countries: the Philippines, Zimbabwe and Mexico.

Author: Dawkins, K
Reference Type: Magazine Article
Year: 1997
Title: US Unilateralism: A Threat to Global Sustainability?
Magazine: Bridges
Volume: 1
Issue Number: 4
Pages: 11
Keywords: TRIPS, CBD, IPRs, USA, Thailand, traditional medicine
Abstract: When the Thai government received a letter from the US State Department questioning the TRIPS-compatibility of its draft legislation allowing Thai healers to register traditional medicines, a storm of protest was aroused. This case exemplifies how the US continues to threaten and punish countries for their 'unsatisfactory' IPR laws. The author considers such actions as being threatening also to global environmental sustainability.

Author: de Alencar, G; van der Ree, M
Reference Type: Magazine Article
Year: 1996
Title: 1996: An Important Year for Brazilian Biopolitics?
Magazine: Biotechnology and Development Monitor
Issue Number: 27
Pages: 21–22
Date: June
Keywords: Brazil, genetic resources, CBD, TRIPS, patents
Abstract: In 1996, the Brazilian Congress and the Federal Government concluded an enduring five-year debate on patents by adopting a new patent law. Late in 1995, the 'Access to Genetic Resources Bill' was proposed by the Senate, which will deepen the debate regarding the implementation of the CBD.

Author: de Kathen, A
Reference Type: Journal Article
Year: 1996
Title: The Impact of Transgenic Crop Releases on Biodiversity in Developing Countries
Journal: Biotechnology and Development Monitor
Issue: 28
Pages: 10–14
Keywords: biodiversity, biosafety, GMOs
Abstract: An increasing number of transgenic crops are deliberately released into centres of biodiversity, which are mostly found in developing countries. Since these centres are important for the future of the world's major food crops, there is great concern about the potential ecological impact of these releases. Information and knowledge about the ecological impact are, however, still marginal. This article focuses on hypothetical risks, with the potato serving as an example.

Author: Dhar, B; Chaturvedi, C
Reference Type: Journal Article
Year: 1998
Title: Introducing Plant Breeders' Rights in India: A Critical Evaluation of the Proposed Legislation
Journal: Journal of World Intellectual Property
Volume: 1
Issue: 2
Pages: 245–262
Keywords: India, IPRs, breeders' rights, UPOV, TRIPS
Abstract: The authors analyse critically the key features of proposed Indian legislation on plant variety protection. They reflect upon the manner in which the respective interests of the farmers and commercial breeders have been taken into consideration. The article underscores the importance of looking beyond the narrow confines of the system which recognizes the contribution only of the commercial plant breeders in the progress of agriculture.

Author: Downes, D
Reference Type: Book Section
Year: 1995
Title: The Convention on Biological Diversity and the GATT
Editor: Goldberg, D; Housman, R; Van Dyke, B; Zaelke, D
Book Title: The Use of Trade Measures in Select Multilateral Environmental Agreements
City: Geneva
Publisher: United Nations Environment Programme
Volume: 10
Series Title: Environment and Trade Series
Keywords: CBD, GATT, TRIPS, genetic resources, biotechnology
Abstract: This chapter discusses the relationships between trade-related provisions of the CBD and the GATT/WTO. The Convention is generally consistent with the GATT/WTO and has such a large and growing number of parties that trade challenges appear unlikely. Nevertheless, issues of compatibility with GATT/WTO could arise in interpreting and implementing certain provisions. The likelihood that questions will arise depends upon future developments that are difficult to predict, such as trends in the market value of genetic resources and in national capacities for biotechnology.

Author: Downes, D
Reference Type: Report
Year: 1997
Title: Using Intellectual Property as a Tool to Protect Traditional Knowledge: Recommendations for Next Steps
City: Washington DC
Institution: Center for International Environmental Law
Type: CIEL Discussion Paper prepared for the Convention on Biological Diversity Workshop on Traditional Knowledge. Madrid, November 1997 (discussion draft)
Keywords: geographical indications, patents, IPRs, traditional knowledge, trademarks, CBD
Abstract: Although IPRs currently provide limited incentives to communities, it is argued that some form of IPRs could be a valuable tool for communities to use to control their traditional knowledge and gain greater shares of the benefits. CBD Parties are urged to explore possible modifications to existing IPRs, or the creation of *sui generis* rights, that could accomplish these goals. Various recommendation are proposed, including: exploring the use of geographical indications, trademarks and authors' moral rights; supporting the establishment of national and interna-

tional registries of traditional knowledge; and considering a requirement for patent applicants to disclose traditional knowledge and its origin as well as the origin of genetic resources used in the invention.

Author: Doyle, J
Reference Type: Journal Article
Year: 1985
Title: Biotechnology Research and Agricultural Stability
Journal: Issues in Science and Technology
Volume: 2
Issue: 1
Pages: 111–124
Keywords: biotechnology, agriculture
Abstract: Argues that biotechnology should be applied in ways that lower costs to farmers, reduce chemical dependency, increase production efficiency, broaden genetic diversity, and enhance biological and economic stability. However, many of these goals are unlikely to be achieved without policy changes.

Author: Duessing, J H
Reference Type: Book Section
Year: 1996
Title: The Role of Intellectual Property Rights in the Exploitation of Plant Genetic Resources and for Technology Transfer under the Convention on Biological Diversity
Editor: Brush, S B; Stabinsky, D
Book Title: Valuing Local Knowledge: Indigenous Peoples and Intellectual Property Rights
City: Covelo, CA
Publisher: Island Press
Keywords: genetic resources, IPRs, CBD, CGIAR, FAO, agriculture, breeders' rights, biotechnology, technology transfer
Abstract: Analyses CBD from pro-business perspective. National sovereignty is now a kind of property right, but it does not adequately protect a biological resource once it leaves the legal domain or control of a culture (for example through the CGIAR system). This makes it difficult to implement important parts of the convention. Standardized international IPRs with acceptance of national sovereignty over genetic resources point to a solution.

Author: Dutfield, G
Reference Type: Report
Year: 1997
Title: Can the TRIPS Agreement Protect Biological and Cultural Diversity?
City: Nairobi
Institution: African Centre for Technology Studies
Type: Biopolicy International
Report Number: 19
Keywords: geographical indications, IPRs, TRIPS, CBD, patents, trademarks, geographical indications, biodiversity, WTO
Abstract: Criticism of TRIPS is fully justified. However, creative interpretations of TRIPS that comply with its requirements but also address issues outside the remit of the WTO, such as protecting traditional knowledge and supporting the aims of the CBD, are not precluded. Neither is the development of laws that go beyond the agreement's requirements. While acknowledging that TRIPS contains no panaceas whatsoever for communities whose basic human rights are being abused, this paper seeks to fill a gap in the critical literature by considering options that TRIPS allows for laws that protect traditional knowledge while addressing the 'biodiversity-related aspects of intellectual property rights'.

Author: Dutfield, G
Reference Type: Book Section
Year: 1999
Title: Protecting and Revitalising Traditional Ecological Knowledge: Intellectual Property Rights and Community Knowledge Databases in India
Editor: Blakeney, M
Book Title: Intellectual Property Aspects of Ethnobiology
City: London
Publisher: Sweet and Maxwell
Pages: 101–122
Keywords: traditional knowledge, IPRs, India,
Abstract: While scientific and commercial interest in traditional knowledge and resource management practices have never been greater, human cultural diversity is eroding at an accelerating rate. Concerned scientists are calling for the documentation of such knowledge before it disappears. But some indigenous peoples' organizations worry that documentation initiatives are likely to be top-down and exploitative. This article consists of five sections: (a) the growing interest in and respect for traditional knowledge; (b) the protection of traditional knowledge as an IPR issue;(c) case studies of patents and traditional knowledge; (d) the protection of IPRs and traditional rights in India; and (e) an evaluation of Indian initiatives to document traditional knowledge.

Author: Duvick, D N
Reference Type: Journal Article
Year: 1991
Title: Industry and Its Role in Plant Diversity
Journal: Forum for Applied Research and Public Policy
Issue: Fall
Pages: 90–94
Keywords: agriculture, genetic resources
Abstract: Agribusiness involvement in plant genetic resources is grounded on three essential factors: the availability of germplasm, the willingness of farmers to pay for the value bred into the improved varieties, and the likelihood of maintaining market control of the products derived from investments in R&D. Because all three factors have rarely been in place at the same time, the involvement of seed companies with plant genetic resources has been limited to a relatively small number of species. Also, commercial breeding and sales within crop species often have been restricted to a small number of localities. Nevertheless, in many countries, commercial seed companies play a key role in the use, evaluation, diversity, and conservation of genetic resources.

Author: Duvick, D N
Reference Type: Book Section
Year: 1993
Title: Goals and Expectations of Industry for Intellectual Property Rights for Plant Materials
Editor: Crop Science Society of America
Book Title: Intellectual Property Rights: Protection of Plant Materials
City: Madison, WI
Publisher: CSSA
Pages: 21–27
Keywords: patents, IPRs, agriculture
Abstract: Presents the position of the seed industry with respect to IPR protection for its products. It is argued that for plant genetic supply companies to operate successfully, competitively, and ethically, proprietary rights to germplasm are necessary. Such rights need to be clearly delineated and broadly observed.

Author: Duvick, D N
Reference Type: Book Section
Year: 1993
Title: Possible Effects of Intellectual Property Rights on Erosion and Conservation of Plant Genetic Resources in Centers of Crop Diversity
Editor: Buxton, D R; Shibles, R; Forsberg, R A; Blad, B L; Asay, K H; Paulsen, G M; Wilson, R F
Book Title: International Crop Science I
City: Madison, WI
Publisher: Crop Science Society of America
Keywords: agriculture, genetic resources, farmers' rights, IPRs, conservation
Abstract: Discusses relationship between IPRs and erosion of genetic diversity by comparing the two kinds of plant breeding – by trained scientists and by traditional farmers. The latter make use of in-field genetic diversity while the former depend on global exchange of genetic resources. Professional breeders supply farmers, not with internally variable varieties, but with variable arrays of uniform cultivars. Recently interest has grown in the fate of the small farmers in developing countries, and also in the fate of the banked germplasm collections.

Author: Economic and Political Weekly (editorial)
Reference Type: Magazine Article
Year: 1998
Title: Looking Beyond Basmati
Magazine: Economic and Political Weekly
Pages: 371–372
Date: February 21
Keywords: basmati, India, geographical indications, patents
Abstract: Criticizes the Indian response to RiceTec's basmati rice patent as being too late and out of touch with reality. The failure of the Indian government to enact appropriate legislation such as an act on geographical indications makes it very difficult to take effective action.

Author: Flitner, M; Leskien, D; Myers, D
Reference Type: Report
Year: 1994
Title: Plants and Patents: Some Southern Perspectives
City: Godalming
Institution: World Wide Fund for Nature – UK
Type: Draft Report prepared for WWF UK
Keywords: IPRs, CBD, GATT, TRIPS, farmers' rights, patents, breeders' rights, sui generis, Brazil, Colombia, Kenya, Philippines, India, Peru
Abstract: Presents views of NGOs from several developing countries on IPRs. Generally speaking, they are opposed to GATT-TRIPS, but are aware of the need to respond to the possibility of a *sui generis* system for plant varieties.

Author: Flitner, M; Leskien, D; Myers, D
Reference Type: Report
Year: 1995
Title: Review of National Actions on Access to Genetic Resources and IPRs in Several Developing Countries
City: Gland, Switzerland
Institution: World Wide Fund for Nature
Date: October
Keywords: CBD, TRIPS
Abstract: Reviews recent national laws to implement the CBD and GATT-TRIPS. The authors present the views of local NGOs on new legislation in selected biodiversity-rich countries.

Author: Fowler, C; Mooney, P
Reference Type: Book
Year: 1990
Title: Shattering: Food, Politics and the Loss of Genetic Diversity
Publisher: University of Arizona Press
Keywords: agriculture, genetic resources, UPOV, USDA, CGIAR, RAFI, patents, IRRI, CIMMYT, FAO Commission on Plant Genetic Resources, IBPGR, IARC, International Undertaking on Plant Genetic Resources, Ethiopa
Abstract: Genetic erosion has very serious social effects, including mass starvation. Control over the gene pool is shifting from farmers to scientists and heads of industry, while political considerations determine agricultural policy with increasing frequency. The North is struggling with the South for control over plant genetic resources.

Author: Fowler, C
Reference Type: Book
Year: 1994
Title: Unnatural Science: Technology, Politics and Plant Evolution
Series Title: International Studies in Global Change
City: Yverdon
Publisher: Gordon and Breach
Volume: 6
Keywords: IPRs, agriculture, biotechnology, genetic resources, CGIAR, USA, FAO, USA, UPOV, farmers' rights
Abstract: Seeds and planting materials are central to the agricultural industry that feeds us all. Yet, until recently, there has been little interest in analysing the legal and political processes through which IPRs are constructed for these biological materials. Concentrating on the US experience, this book offers a comprehensive history and sociological analysis of the struggle to own and control biological materials from the 1800s, to the first patent law covering plant varieties, to current international controversies.

Author: Freedman, P
Reference Type: Journal Article
Year: 1994
Title: Boundaries of Good Taste
Journal: Geographical Magazine
Volume: 66
Issue: 4
Pages: 12–14
Keywords: geographical indications, appellations of origin, certification trademarks, IPRs
Abstract: Evaluates the justifications for use of such IPRs as geographical indications, appellations of origin and certification trademarks in the protection and marketing of certain products such as French wines, Stilton cheese and Scotch whisky. Whereas those in favour of such IPRs argue that there is a genuinely inextricable link between the soil, climate, traditional practices of local artisans and the end product, others might say that they are a form of covert protectionism, serving the needs of small producer cartels, inhibiting free trade and keeping prices high.

Author: Friis-Hansen, E; Konin, J; Boesen, J; Knudsen, H
Reference Type: Book Section
Year: 1994
Title: Financial Mechanisms and Biotechnology Transfer
Editor: Sanchez, V; Juma, C

Book Title: Biodiplomacy
City: Nairobi
Publisher: ACTS
Pages: 271–287
Keywords: CBD, biotechnology, CGIAR, IPRs, genetic resources
Abstract: Discusses important issues in the CBD concerning technology transfer and financial mechanisms and points out some of the difficulties ahead.

Author: Frisvold, G B; Condon, P T
Reference Type: Journal Article
Year: 1998
Title: The Convention on Biological Diversity and Agriculture: Implications and Unresolved Debates
Journal: World Development
Volume: 26
Issue: 4
Pages: 551–570
Keywords: CBD, conservation, agriculture, IPRs, technology transfer, genetic resources, biotechnology
Abstract: The CBD addresses two controversies that surround plant genetic resources. One debate has been over property rights governing PGRs and the distribution of benefits from their use. The second has been over the adequacy of measures to maintain crop genetic diversity. This paper examines how these debates are linked and reviews multilateral attempts to address them.

Author: Gadgil, M; Devasia, P
Reference Type: Magazine Article
Year: 1995
Title: Intellectual Property Rights and Biological Resources: Specifying Geographical Origins and Prior Knowledge of Uses
Magazine: Current Science
Volume: 69
Issue Number: 8
Pages: 637–9
Date: 25 October
Keywords: IPRs, patents, CBD, TRIPS
Abstract: Proposes a kind of certificates of origin system so that patent applications must fully disclose geographical origins and any prior use in the case of inventions related to biological material and/or derived from traditional knowledge.

Author: Gaia Foundation; Genetic Resources Action International
Reference Type: Report
Year: 1998
Title: TRIPS versus CBD: Conflicts Between the WTO Regime of Intellectual Property Rights and Sustainable Biodiversity Management
City: London & Barcelona
Institution: Gaia Foundation & GRAIN
Date: April
Report Number: Global Trade and Biodiversity in Conflict, Issue 1
Keywords: TRIPS, CBD, IPRs, biodiversity, traditional knowledge
Abstract: Because TRIPS and the CBD embody and promote conflicting objectives, systems of rights and obligations, many states are questioning which treaty takes precedence over the other. It is argued that CBD has primacy over the WTO in the areas of biodiversity and traditional knowledge, that the review of TRIPS allows states to exclude all life forms and related knowledge from IPR systems, and that the *a priori* collective rights of indigenous peoples and local communities over their biodiversity and related knowledge must be recognized.

Author: Gaia Foundation; Genetic Resources Action International
Reference Type: Report
Year: 1998
Title: Ten Reasons Not To Join UPOV
City: London & Barcelona
Institution: Gaia Foundation & GRAIN
Date: May
Report Number: Global Trade and Biodiversity in Conflict, Issue 2
Keywords: UPOV, IPRs
Abstract: Provides ten reasons why joining UPOV is contrary to the interests of developing countries and traditional communities.

Author: Genetic Resources Action International
Reference Type: Report
Year: 1997
Title: Patenting, Piracy and Perverted Promises: Patenting Life: The Last Assault on the Commons
City: Barcelona
Institution: GRAIN
Keywords: patents, biotechnology
Abstract: Condemnation of 'patenting life' providing a list of example of what the EU Directive on biotechnological inventions would legalize and the European Parliament should stop. These examples include patents related to the Bt gene; the 'soybean' monopoly patent; the quinoa patent; Brazzein; Dolly the cloned sheep; 'Pharma' Tracy; the oncomouse; turmeric; sangre de drago; the John Moore cell line; umbilical cord cells; and HIV strains donated by human carriers.

Author: Glowka, L; Burhenne-Guilmin, F; Synge, H in collaboration with McNeely, J A; Gündling, L
Reference Type: Report
Year: 1994
Title: A Guide to the Convention on Biological Diversity
City: Gland, Switzerland
Institution: IUCN
Report Number: Environmental Policy and Law Paper No 30
Keywords: Biodiversity Conservation, conservation, FAO, IPRs, informed consent, common heritage, biotechnology
Abstract: A comprehensive analysis of the CBD Articles by the IUCN Environmental Law Centre.

Author: Glowka, L
Reference Type: Book Section
Year: 1997
Title: Legal and Institutional Considerations for States Providing Genetic Resources
Editor: Mugabe, J; Barber, C V; Henne, G; Glowka, L; La Viña, A
Book Title: Access to Genetic Resources: Strategies for Sharing Benefits
City: Nairobi
Publisher: ACTS Press
Pages: 33–51
Keywords: genetic resources, benefit sharing, CBD
Abstract: States providing genetic resources face a range of complex legal and institutional considerations as they seek to determine access to genetic resources and ensure benefit sharing. States will need to determine the best way forward, taking into consideration their individual circumstances. A national planning process is crucial to identifying the legal and institutional approach to be adopted by provider states enabling them to capitalize on the new relationship between providers and users of genetic resources created by the CBD.

Author: Glowka, L
Reference Type: Report
Year: 1998
Title: A Guide to Designing Legal Frameworks to Determine Access to Genetic Resources
City: Gland, Cambridge and Bonn
Institution: IUCN Environmental Law Centre
Type: Environmental Policy and Law Paper
Report Number: 34
Keywords: CBD, IPRs, genetic resources, conservation, traditional knowledge, community registers
Abstract: Highlights principles which should be considered by planners, legislative drafters and policymakers as they work to develop legal frameworks on access to genetic resources in their countries. Contextual information on the CBD and examples of how countries have thus far approached the issue are provided.

Author: Gollin, M A
Reference Type: Book Section
Year: 1993
Title: The Convention on Biological Diversity and Intellectual Property Rights
Editor: Reid, W V; Laird, S A; Meyer, C A; Gamez, R; Sittenfeld, A; Janzen, D H; Gollin, M A; Juma, C
Book Title: Biodiversity Prospecting
Publisher: WRI, INBio, Rainforest Alliance, ACTS
Pages: 289–302
Keywords: CBD, technology transfer
Abstract: A textual analysis of the CBD. Concludes that it does not require technology transfer or anything but consensual terms, and overall will promote strengthened, not weakened, IPR protection worldwide. It does not oblige nations to reform their IPR laws so as to recognize rights in indigenous knowledge.

Author: Gollin, M A
Reference Type: Book Section
Year: 1993
Title: An Intellectual Property Rights Framework for Biodiversity Prospecting
Editor: Reid, W V; Laird, S A; Meyer, C A; Gamez, R; Sittenfeld, A; Janzen, D H; Gollin, M A; Juma, C
Book Title: Biodiversity Prospecting
Publisher: WRI, INBio, Rainforest Alliance, ACTS
Pages: 159–197
Keywords: bioprospecting, IPRs, trade secrets, petty patents, patents, copyright, trademarks, CBD, UPOV, informed consent
Abstract: Outlines how IPRs can be applied to the new technologies, commercial practices and ethical standards of bioprospecting and discusses the merits of creating new bioprospecting rights. IPR laws are no panacea without the harmonization of intellectual property, environmental protection, and commercial laws. The various IPR types are explained and analysed.

Author: Gollin, M A; Laird, S A
Reference Type: Journal Article
Year: 1996
Title: Global Policies, Local Actions: The Role of National Legislation in Sustainable Biodiversity Prospecting
Journal: Boston University Journal of Science and Technology Law
Volume: 16
Issue: 2

Pages: 1–104
Keywords: bioprospecting, CBD, TRIPS, IPRs, INBio
Abstract: Review of national legislation regulating bioprospecting covering such areas as conservation, sustainable utilization of genetic resources, benefit sharing and IPRs.

Author: Greengrass, B
Reference Type: Journal Article
Year: 1989
Title: UPOV and the Protection of Plant Breeders – Past Developments, Future Perspectives
Journal: International Review of Industrial Property and Copyright Law
Volume: 20
Issue: 5
Pages: 622–36
Keywords: UPOV
Abstract: Briefly traces the history of the UPOV Convention, describes its main characteristics, and provides suggestions for enabling the patent and breeders' right systems to complement each other.

Author: Greengrass, B
Reference Type: Journal Article
Year: 1991
Title: The 1991 Act of the UPOV Convention
Journal: European Intellectual Property Review
Volume: 13
Issue: 12
Pages: 466–472
Keywords: UPOV, breeders' rights
Abstract: A key UPOV official explains the changes in the 1991 version of the UPOV Convention.

Author: Greengrass, B
Reference Type: Book Section
Year: 1996
Title: UPOV and Farmers' Rights
Editor: Swaminathan, M S
Book Title: Agrobiodiversity and Farmers' Rights
City: Madras
Publisher: M S Swaminathan Research Foundation
Volume: MSSRF Proceedings Number 14
Pages: 50–56
Keywords: UPOV, farmers' rights
Abstract: Overview of the UPOV Convention by the organization's Vice-Secretary General. Affirms that farmers were the foundation of the seed industry in Western Europe and North America and that in developing countries, farmers should also be regarded as the potential growth point of a professional seed industry. It is concluded that to give practical expression to the Farmers' Rights concept, it may be necessary to think in terms of an IPR system.

Author: Grifo, F T; Downes, D; Cragg, G
Reference Type: Book Section
Year: 1996
Title: Intellectual Property Rights Agreements as a Mechanism to Achieve Biodiversity Conservation: The International Biodiversity Group's Program
Editor: Brush, S B; Stabinsky, D

Book Title: Valuing Local Knowledge: Indigenous Peoples and Intellectual Property Rights
City: Covelo, CA
Keywords: ICBG, ICDPs, bioprospecting, IPRs, traditional knowledge, CBD, conservation, contracts, pharmaceuticals
Abstract: Explains the work of the International Cooperative Biodiversity Groups, which are intended to integrate conservation and development through drug discovery based on natural products.

Author: Grifo, F T
Reference Type: Book Section
Year: 1996
Title: Chemical Prospecting: An Overview of the International Cooperative Groups Program
Editor: Pan American Health Organization
Book Title: Biodiversity, Biotechnology, and Sustainable Development in Health and Agriculture: Emerging Connections
City: Washington DC
Publisher: Pan American Health Organization
Volume: Scientific Publication No 560
Pages: 12–26
Keywords: bioprospecting, ICBGs, NIH, NCI, IPRs
Abstract: Presents the goals and activities of the International Biodiversity Cooperative Groups (ICBG) programme, which consists of bioprospecting partnerships involving the public and private sectors, conservation NGOs and academic institutions, and operating in tropical and dryland regions of Central America, South America and West Africa. The programme seeks to implement the objectives of the CBD.

Author: Gupta, A K
Reference Type: Book Section
Year: 1992
Title: Biodiversity, Poverty and Intellectual Property Rights of Third World Peasants: A Case for Renegotiating Global Understanding
Editor: Swaminathan, M S; Jana, S
Book Title: Biodiversity: Implications for Global Food Security
City: Delhi
Publisher: Macmillan, India
Pages: 236–256
Keywords: traditional knowledge, biodiversity, agriculture, genetic resources, ecosystems management
Abstract: Explains importance of biodiversity and traditional knowledge systems. Author discusses possible mechanisms for compensating conservers of biodiversity.

Author: Gupta, A K
Reference Type: Report
Year: 1993
Title: Creativity, Innovation, Entrepreneurship and Networking at Grassroots Level
Keywords: traditional knowledge, biodiversity, IPRs, SRISTI, agriculture, India
Abstract: The key objectives of SRISTI are to strengthen the capacity of grassroots level innovations and inventors engaged in conserving biodiversity to (a) protect their IPRs (b) experiment to add value to their knowledge (c) evolve entrepreneurial ability to generate returns from their knowledge (d) enrich their cultural and institutional basis of dealing with nature.

Author: Gupta, A K
Reference Type: Magazine Article
Year: 1996
Title: Neem-Mania: What Else?
Magazine: Down to Earth
Issue Number: November 30
Pages: 52–53
Keywords: neem, India, patents, IPRs
Abstract: Argues that companies have the right to patent neem-based products. Moreover, commercialization of neem is a good thing for poor people in India because it will lead to a rise in demand for natural products that such people can be paid to supply. Also, the possibility of over-exploitation is minimal.

Author: Hamilton, N D
Reference Type: Journal Article
Year: 1994
Title: Why Own the Farm if You Can Own the Farmer (and the Crop)?: Contract Production and Intellectual Property Protection of Grain Crops
Journal: Nebraska Law Review
Volume: 73
Pages: 48–103
Keywords: agriculture, IPRs, USA
Abstract: US grain production is experiencing two key developments: (1) the trend towards use of contract production for grain; and (2) the connection between this and the protection of IPRs for seeds and plants. This article surveys the emerging legal issues associated with these two developments.

Author: Hardon, J J; Vosman, B; Van Hintum, T J L
Reference Type: Report
Year: 1994
Title: Identifying Genetic Resources and their Origin: The Capabilities and Limitations of Modern Biochemical and Legal Systems
City: Rome
Institution: Food and Agriculture Organization
Type: Commission on Plant Genetic Resources Background Study Paper
Report Number: 4
Keywords: genetic resources, agriculture, IPRs, parents, UPOV, farmers' rights, CBD, FAO, IUPGR
Abstract: To legally enforce sovereign rights over plant genetic resources (PGRs) it is important that their identity and origin can be established. Modern techniques allow for a detailed description of the heritable material of plants and plant populations. Therefore answers to the following questions can assist discussion on the issue of ownership of PGRs: (i) What are the capabilities and limitations of 'genetic fingerprinting' and related techniques for identifying PGRs and their origin; (ii) What are their implications for enforcing sovereign rights; (iii) What is the feasibility of determining the country of origin considering the different types of PGRs; (iv) What legal requirements exist for IPR protection; (v) What types of material can be protected; (vi) To what extent can legal systems be modified to include a wider range of genetic material; and (vii) What is the significance of various modalities of asserting sovereign rights over PGRs for their conservation and utilization. This report reviews existing legal systems concerned with biological materials and explores to what extent identity and origin of PGRs can be established.

Author: Harrop, S
Reference Type: Journal Article
Year: 1995
Title: The GATT 1994, the Biological Diversity Convention and their Relationship with Macro-Biodiversity Management
Journal: Biodiversity and Conservation
Volume: 4
Pages: 1019–1025
Keywords: biodiversity, TRIPS, GATT, CBD
Abstract: Where a country is particularly endowed with rich biodiversity, such as extensive rain forests, which provide a source for the development of an almost endless range of valuable biotechnology, there is only narrow scope for that country to protect its interests (particularly from the activities of foreign developers) and thus reap for itself appropriate benefits from its biodiversity.

Author: Heller, M A; Eisenburg, R S
Reference Type: Journal Article
Year: 1998
Title: Can Patents Deter Innovation? The Anticommons in Biomedical Research
Journal: Science
Volume: 280
Issue: 1 May
Pages: 698–701
Keywords: IPRs, patents
Abstract: The 'tragedy of the commons' metaphor helps explain why people overuse shared resources. However, the recent proliferation of IPRs in biomedical research suggests a different tragedy, an 'anticommons' in which people underuse scarce resources because too many owners can block each other. Privatization of biomedical research must be more carefully deployed to sustain both upstream research and downstream product development. Otherwise, more IPRs may lead paradoxically to fewer useful products for improving human health.

Editors: Hoagland, K E; Rossman, A Y
Reference Type: Edited Book
Year: 1997
Title: Global Genetic Resources: Access, Ownership, and Intellectual Property Rights
City: Washington DC
Publisher: Association of Systematics Collections
Keywords: genetic resources, IPRs, biotechnology, agriculture, pharmaceuticals, CBD, bioprospecting, FAO, ICBGs
Abstract: Collection of papers from a conference that aimed to explore issues related to ownership of and access to genetic resources and biological specimens. The volume examines the current status of the various treaties, national laws, and agreements in effect around the world; presents case studies that demonstrate how research using international resources benefits the global community; explores models of equitable use of genetic resources; and discusses potential solutions to develop a mutually beneficial compromise for the equitable use of genetic resources.

Author: Hodgkin, T; Engels, J; Hawtin, G
Reference Type: Book Section
Year: 1996
Title: An IBPGR Perspective on Plant Genetic Resources, Intellectual Property Rights and Indigenous Knowledge
Editor: Brush, S B; Stabinsky, D
Book Title: Valuing Local Knowledge: Indigenous Peoples and Intellectual Property Rights

City: Covelo, CA
Publisher: Island Press
Keywords: IBPGR/IPGRI, FAO, International Undertaking on Plant Genetic Resources, farmers' rights, traditional knowledge, conservation, IPRs, agriculture
Abstract: Describes global system of plant genetic resources and effects of IPR legislation on conservation and use of germplasm. Indigenous knowledge is to be given greater recognition but without this hindering exchange of information. Communities will be encouraged to cooperate in the conservation of landraces in situ.

Author: Hurlbut, D
Reference Type: Journal Article
Year: 1994
Title: Fixing the Biodiversity Convention: Toward a Special Protocol for Related Intellectual Property
Journal: Natural Resources Journal
Volume: 34
Pages: 379–409
Keywords: IPRs, CBD
Abstract: The CBD is weakened by the fact that its goals of biodiversity conserving and equitable benefit sharing cannot easily be reconciled. The article first discusses cultural, legal and ethical issues affecting IPRs and the economic dynamics of such rights. It then criticizes the way that the CBD deals with IPRs. Finally, the paper suggests an outline of a protocol in which IPRs may be addressed in a way that is relevant to the goal of biodiversity conservation, while balancing the social needs of both developing and industrially advanced countries.

Author: Illescas, M
Reference Type: Book Section
Year: 1994
Title: Intellectual Property Institutions and Technological Co-operation
Editor: Sanchez, V; Juma, C
Book Title: Biodiplomacy
City: Nairobi
Publisher: ACTS
Pages: 195–209
Keywords: IPRs, CBD, patents, technology transfer
Abstract: Argues that IPRs are an instrument of co-operation between developed and developing countries and must be seen as a means of achieving the ultimate aim of the CBD: the conservation of biodiversity as the common heritage of humankind.

Author: Iwu, M M
Reference Type: Magazine Article
Year: 1996
Title: Implementing the Biodiversity Treaty: How to Make International Co-operative Agreements Work
Magazine: Tibtech
Volume: 14
Pages: 78–83
Date: March
Keywords: CBD, IPRs, genetic resources, contracts
Abstract: The CBD provides an international framework and multilateral mechanism for the exchange of genetic resources and biodiversity conservation. It recognizes the sovereignty of states over their natural resources, and the authority to determine access. The research agreements and legal contracts must address the needs of indigenous people, community rights, sustainable methods of sample collection,

compensation and IPR issues. Implementation requires not only the formulation of legal agreements and contracts, but also the establishment of meaningful and just collaborations, and functional partnerships between industrialized nations and source countries.

Author: Jaffe, W; Van Wijk, J
Reference Type: Report
Year: 1996
Title: The Impact of Plant Breeders' Rights in Developing Countries: Debate and Experience in Argentina, Chile, Colombia, Mexico and Uruguay
City: The Hague
Institution: Ministry of Foreign Affairs
Keywords: IPRs, agriculture, UPOV, Argentina, Chile, Colombia, Mexico, Uruguay
Abstract: So far, empirical evidence of the socio-economic impact of IPRs in agriculture is almost non-existent. This study examines the expected impact of breeders' rights on developing countries with respect to: private investment in plant breeding, breeding policies of public institutes, transfer of foreign germplasm, and the diffusion of seed among farmers. Case studies were conducted in five Latin American countries and conclusions of the investigation are presented in this paper.

Author: Johnston, S with; Yamin, F
Reference Type: Book Section
Year: 1997
Title: Intellectual Property Rights and Access to Genetic Resources
Editor: Mugabe, J; Barber, C V; Henne, G; Glowka, L; La Viña, A
Book Title: Access to Genetic Resources: Strategies for Sharing Benefits
City: Nairobi
Publisher: ACTS Press
Pages: 245–269
Keywords: IPRs, genetic resources, UPOV, TRIPS
Abstract: Discussion of IPRs in the context of the CBD. Problems with conventional IPRs are identified and options for a *sui generis* IPR system are considered.

Author: Juma, C
Reference Type: Book
Year: 1989
Title: The Gene Hunters: Biotechnology and the Scramble for Seeds
Series Editor: African Centre for Technology Studies
City: Princeton
Publisher: Princeton University Press
Keywords: biotechnology, IPRs, patents, UPOV
Abstract: The new biotechnologies, unlike earlier technological revolutions, are applicable to small-scale, labour-intensive production and thus offer Africa and other Third World countries a significant opportunity to transform the economy. The historical role of genetic resources in the global economy, current advances in biotechnology, problems of IPRs in new life forms, and the possible consequences of introducing genetically-engineered micro-organisms into the environment are among the matters discussed.

Author: Kadidal, S
Reference Type: Journal Article
Year: 1993
Title: Plants, Poverty, and Pharmaceutical Patents
Journal: Yale Law Journal
Volume: 103
Issue: 1

Pages: 223–258
Keywords: pharmaceuticals, IPRs, patents, genetic resources, agriculture, INBio
Abstract: In-depth commentary on the industrial use of genetic resources, patenting, and the CBD.

Author: Keystone Center
Reference Type: Report
Year: 1988
Title: Final Report of The Keystone International Dialogue on Plant Genetic Resources.
City: Keystone
Institution: The Keystone Center
Keywords: genetic resources, IPRs, patents, breeders' rights, farmers' rights, agriculture, conservation
Abstract: The Keystone International Dialogue Series on Plant Genetic Resources brought together the significant constituencies in a consensus-building process to promote an international commitment to plant genetic resources. The participants agreed upon the need for additional Dialogue sessions to address: further developments on issues relating to definitions, rights and incentives and a global funding mechanism; and the active involvement of local communities in plant genetic resource activities through the integration of *ex situ*, *in situ* and other alternatives to *ex situ* conservation measures.

Author: Keystone Center
Reference Type: Report
Year: 1990
Title: Final Consensus Report of The Keystone International Dialogue Series on Plant Genetic Resources. Madras Plenary Session
City: Washington DC
Institution: Genetic Resources Communications Systems, Inc.
Keywords: genetic resources, GATT, CBD, TRIPS, farmers' rights, IUPGR, conservation, CGIAR
Abstract: The Keystone International Dialogue Series on Plant Genetic Resources brought together the significant constituencies in a consensus-building process to promote an international commitment to plant genetic resources. The discussions covered a whole range of relevant issues, including IPRs and GATT, the IUPGR and farmers' rights, the CBD, the CGIAR and conservation.

Author: Khalil, M H; Reid, W V; Juma, C
Reference Type: Report
Year: 1992
Title: Property Rights, Biotechnology and Genetic Resources
City: Nairobi
Institution: African Centre for Technology Studies
Type: Biopolicy International
Report Number: 7
Keywords: biotechnology, conservation, genetic resources, traditional knowledge, IPRs, common heritage, human rights, technology transfer
Abstract: Discusses the economic and political aspects of the use and conservation of genetic resources. Regarding indigenous knowledge, human rights, just compensation and incentives for innovation and conservation are all important if we wish to consider recognizing and protecting such knowledge.

Author: Khalil, M
Reference Type: Book Section
Year: 1995
Title: Biodiversity and the Conservation of Medicinal Plants: Issues from the Perspective of the Developing World
Editor: Swanson, T
Book Title: Intellectual Property Rights and Biodiversity Conservation: An Interdisciplinary Analysis of the Values of Medicinal Plants
City: Cambridge
Publisher: Cambridge University Press
Pages: 232–253
Keywords: biodiversity, conservation, medicinal plants, traditional medicine, IPRs, patents
Abstract: First, addresses the place of medicinal biodiversity in the folk cultures of some communities in the developing countries and reviews conservation efforts made by some countries that have recognized the significance of medicinal biota. Second, explores the impact of uniform patent protection on biodiversity conservation in developing countries. What is needed by the world is not a uniform IPR system, but a diverse one which respects the rights of traditional cultures. Moreover, developing countries should recognize the rights of indigenous communities before commensurate recognition flows from industrialized countries. One way of doing this is to extend legal cover to domestic knowledge.

Author: King, A B; Eyzaguirre, P B
Reference Type: Journal Article
Year: 1999
Title: Intellectual Property Rights and Agricultural Biodiversity: Literature Addressing the Suitability of IPR for the Protection of Indigenous Resources
Journal: Agriculture and Human Values
Volume: 16
Issue: 1
Pages: 41–49
Keywords: IPRs, biodiversity, agriculture, indigenous peoples, traditional knowledge
Abstract: Intellectual property has been suggested as a means to protect indigenous resources from misappropriation, and to create increased investment in their conservation. This article reviews four books that discuss the problems that arise from the application of IPR for the protection of indigenous resources. All of them highlight a salient issue: that current IPR systems may conflict with and undermine the culture, social structure, and knowledge systems of indigenous societies. The books are by Brush, Swanson, Greaves, and Posey and Dutfield.

Author: Kloppenburg, J, Jr
Reference Type: Book
Year: 1988
Title: First the Seed: The Political Economy of Plant Biotechnology
City: Cambridge
Publisher: Cambridge University Press
Keywords: IPRs, genetic resources, biotechnology, agriculture, USA
Abstract: The emergence of the new biotechnologies and of large corporations that produce both seeds and chemicals for the agriculture industry is a significant recent phenomenon. In spite of their dependence on the plant genetic resources of the South, the economic and political power of these corporations and of Northern governments has ensured that they continue to enjoy free access to these resources.

Editor: Kloppenburg, J, Jr
Reference Type: Edited Book
Year: 1988
Title: Seeds and Sovereignty: The Use and Control of Plant Genetic Resources
City: Durham, NC, USA
Publisher: Duke University Press
Abstract: Contributions deal with the history of plant genetic resource transfer, the politics of ownership, access and control of these resources, and the various measures that could be taken to ensure that benefits from their exploitation are shared fairly.

Author: Kocken, J; Roozendaal, G van
Reference Type: Magazine Article
Year: 1997
Title: The Neem Tree Debate
Magazine: Biotechnology and Development Monitor
Issue Number: 30
Pages: 8–11
Date: March
Keywords: neem, India, patents
Abstract: Private sector efforts in patenting neem tree-related processes and products have raised a major controversy. The focus of the debate is a 1992 US patent on a process for extracting and stabilizing azadirachtin, granted to the US company W R Grace. A coalition of non-governmental organizations is opposing this patent on political and legal grounds.

Author: Kothari, A
Reference Type: Book
Year: 1995
Title: Conserving Life: Implications of the Biodiversity Convention for India
City: New Delhi
Publisher: Kalpavriksh
Edition: 2nd
Keywords: CBD, India, biodiversity, patents, protected areas, agriculture
Abstract: Collection of essays covering a large range of issues arising from the CBD and concerning such issues as biodiversity conservation and protected areas, and IPRs and patenting life forms.

Author: Kothari, A; Anuradha, R V
Reference Type: Magazine Article
Year: 1997
Title: Biodiversity, Intellectual Property Rights, and GATT Agreement: How to Address the Conflicts?
Magazine: Economic and Political Weekly
Volume: 32
Issue Number: 43
Pages: 2814–2820
Date: 25 October 1997
Keywords: CBD, TRIPS, IPRs
Abstract: The article examines the impact of IPRs in biodiversity in general and specifically on the objectives of the CBD. It also addresses the broader issue of the relationship between the WTO Agreement and the CBD. It then reflects on the choices available to ensure that the objectives of the CBD are not undermined. (Also published in Biopolicy Online Journal in 1997.)

Author: Krimsky, S; Wrubel, R
Reference Type: Book
Year: 1996
Title: Agricultural Biotechnology and the Environment: Science, Policy and Social Issues
City: Urbana and Chicago
Publisher: University of Illinois Press
Keywords: agriculture, biotechnology, patents
Abstract: Modern agriculture is being transformed by the genetic alteration of seeds, animals and micro-organisms. This book explores the impact of genetic engineering on agricultural practice and the environment from scientific, social, ethical and ecological perspectives.

Author: Laird, S A
Reference Type: Report
Year: 1995
Title: Access Controls for Genetic Resources: The Assertion of Sovereignty
City: Gland
Institution: World Wide Fund for Nature
Date: October
Type: Discussion Paper
Keywords: CBD, genetic resources, IPRs, bioprospecting
Abstract: The CBD gives governments the right to impose conditions on access to biological resources. Governments are now putting in place national systems of access control, and recent developments in this area are examined. Institutions and communities often deal directly with collectors of biological resources. Existing research and commercial agreements, codes of conduct and declarations are analysed in terms of their compliance with the Convention.

Author: Lehmann, V
Reference Type: Magazine Article
Year: 1998
Title: Patent on Seed Sterility Threatens Seed Saving
Magazine: Biotechnology and Development Monitor
Issue Number: 35
Pages: 6–8
Date: June
Keywords: biotechnology, agriculture, patents, terminator technology
Abstract: A patent recently granted on a technology which produces sterile seeds has revived the discussion on the consequences of in-built biological protection against seed saving. Seed companies see this as an incentive to develop new varieties. But what will be the consequences for farmers in developing countries if they cannot re-use their harvest as seed material?

Author: Leskien, D; Flitner, M
Reference Type: Report
Year: 1997
Title: Intellectual Property Rights and Plant Genetic Resources: Options for a Sui Generis System
City: Rome
Institution: International Plant Genetic Resources Institute
Date: June 1997
Type: Issues in Genetic Resources
Report Number: 6
Keywords: sui generis, IPRs, UPOV, TRIPS, genetic resources, CBD, farmers' rights

Abstract: This study aims at the development and evaluation of elements for inclusion in a *sui generis* system for the protection of plant varieties as permitted by the TRIPS Agreement. The report studies the legal obligations posed by TRIPS in relation to plant genetic resources, and analyses the status of plant genetic resources under the existing international regulatory framework, in particular the CBD. The study gives an overview of and discusses possible elements for recognition of Farmers' Rights, which, if included in a protection system for plant varieties, may reconcile the interests of formal breeders with the rights and interests of informal breeders. There is a broad range of possible TRIPS-compatible *sui generis* systems. These should be explored and discussed before ready-made protection systems currently being used in many industrialized countries are adopted.

Author: Lesser, W
Reference Type: Book
Year: 1998
Title: Sustainable Use of Genetic Resources Under the Convention on Biological Diversity: Exploring Access and Benefit Sharing Issues
City: Wallingford
Publisher: CAB International
Keywords: CBD, IPRs, technology transfer, appellations of origin, patents, UPOV, TRIPS, bioprospecting, biotechnology, agriculture, CGIAR, farmers' rights, FAO, genetic resources, INBio, community registers, trademarks, trade secrets, MTAs
Abstract: While only limited progress has been made in applying the CBD, countries are acting unilaterally on the placement of genetic resources as their sovereign right to exploit. This book focuses on the presentation of legal and economic issues regarding the sustainable use and transfer of genetic resources and associated technologies, identifying steps that can be taken and their expected consequences.

Author: Maskus, K
Reference Type: Journal Article
Year: 1998
Title: The Role of Intellectual Property Rights in Encouraging Foreign Direct Investment and Technology Transfer
Journal: Duke Journal of Comparative and International Law
Volume: 9
Issue: 1
Pages: 109–161
Keywords: IPRs, technology transfer
Abstract: A review of globalization which suggests that emerging countries have strong and growing interests in attracting trade, foreign direct investment, and technological expertise. In this context, IPRs are an important element in a broader policy package that governments in developing economies should design with a view toward maximizing the benefits of expanded market access and promoting dynamic competition in which local firms take part meaningfully. This broad package would include promoting political stability and economic growth, encouraging flexible labour markets and building labour skills, continuing to liberalize markets, and developing forward-looking regulatory regimes in services, investment, IPRs, and competition policy.

Author: Masood, E
Reference Type: Journal Article
Year: 1998
Title: Social Equity versus Private Property: Striking the Right Balance
Journal: Nature
Volume: 392
Pages: 537

Keywords: bioprospecting, CBD, TRIPS, Organization of African Unity
Abstract: Nowhere do the rhetoric and the reality facing bioprospecting come into sharper conflict than in attempts by developing countries to bridge their international commitments to two separate agreements: the CBD and TRIPS. For example, the Organization of African Unity's task force on access to genetic resources argued that TRIPS should comply with the CBD, and not the other way round. The OAU is pushing member countries to adopt its own model legislation before the first review of TRIPS next year.

Author: McNally, R; Wheale, P
Reference Type: Journal Article
Year: 1996
Title: Biopatenting and Biodiversity: Comparative Advantages in the New Global Order
Journal: The Ecologist
Volume: 26
Issue: 5
Pages: 222–228
Keywords: biotechnology, IPRs, biodiversity, patents, Monsanto, CBD, HGDP
Abstract: Over the last two decades, the biotechnology industry has been stretching the interpretation of patent law in order to obtain IPRs over genetically engineered living organisms. Such patent rights, coupled with moves to gain exclusive access to the biodiversity of the South, are leading to a new global order. Opposition to such 'biotechnological imperialism' is gaining in momentum.

Author: Menon, U
Reference Type: Journal Article
Year: 1995
Title: Access to and Transfer of Genetic Resources
Journal: International Journal of Technology Management
Volume: 10
Issue: 2/3
Pages: 311–324
Keywords: genetic resources, benefit sharing, FAO, CGIAR, IPRs, Costa Rica, USA, India, INBio, CBD, breeders' rights, IUPGR
Abstract: Outlines the work of FAO and the CGIAR relating to free access to the world's plant genetic resources. Reports on various meetings held to discuss regulation and attitudes towards IPRs and the free exchange of technology, with a diversity of opinions between the developed and developing countries. Two examples of the problems are discussed in detail: India and US AID, and Costa Rica and Merck. Finally the paper suggests an approach that recognizes both the need for free access to genetic resources and private rights.

Author: Mooney, P R
Reference Type: Magazine Article
Year: 1993
Title: Profiteering from the Wisdom of the South
Magazine: Choices
Issue Number: December
Pages: 10–12
Date: December
Keywords: IPRs, biodiversity
Abstract: Though much of the world's biodiversity is found in the South, control over genes, plants, animals and other living organisms is increasingly in the hands of Northern interests. The author argues that the growing trend towards the patenting of life forms violates the intellectual integrity of indigenous and other Third World communities and is stifling innovation in the South.

Author: Mooney, P R
Reference Type: Journal Article
Year: 1993
Title: Genetic Resources in the International Commons
Journal: Review of European Community and International Environmental Law
Volume: 2
Issue: 2
Pages: 149–151
Keywords: biodiversity, INBio, Costa Rica, bioprospecting
Abstract: Argues that the North's dependence on the South's biodiversity has increased due to genetic erosion. The INBio-Merck agreement is criticized and developing countries are urged not to engage in individual environmental entrepreneurial competition with each other, but to bargain collectively.

Author: Mooney, P R
Reference Type: Report
Year: 1996
Title: The Parts of Life: Agricultural Biodiversity, Indigenous Knowledge, and the Role of the Third System
City: Uppsala
Institution: Dag Hammarskjold Foundation
Report Number: Development Dialogue. Special Issue (1996:1–2)
Keywords: biodiversity, IUPGR, FAO, CBD, CGIAR, IARCs, agriculture, pharmaceuticals, genetic resources, IPRs, Human Genome Diversity Project, farmers' rights, TRIPS
Abstract: Describes the debates at FAO in the early 1980s resulting in the creation of the Commission and the IUPGR, and the discussions of the Keystone Dialogue Series on Plant Genetic Resources. The author comments on the process leading to, and the outcome of, the 1996 Leipzig conference on plant genetic resources, the CBD Conference of the Parties, and the 1996 World Food Summit. He explains the need to reform the CGIAR system, comparing the official view with those who maintain that food security means supporting local farmers in pursuing their practices and technologies within their own development framework. He discusses the commercial prospecting of other genetic resources to develop new products, including human genes. Linked to this is the growing concentration of capital and power among corporations in the area of food security and biodiversity. Finally, he discusses the roles of the different actors and particularly those of civil society organizations (the Third System).

Author: Moran, W
Reference Type: Journal Article
Year: 1993
Title: Rural Space as Intellectual Property
Journal: Political Geography
Volume: 12
Issue: 3
Pages: 263–277
Keywords: geographical indications, GATT, agriculture
Abstract: Under free trade agreements nations are questioning the commercial legislation governing production of their partners. Also, for specific commodities, groups of producers and countries are bringing litigation against other trading partners over the use of place-names by successfully claiming that they are intellectual property. Both processes are part of the globalization of production under capitalism but their effects may be contradictory. Increased similarity in the commercial legislation of countries will enhance the advantage of the most competitive regions and nations, leading to greater regional specialization in rural production.

Editor: Moran, A G
Reference Type: Edited Book
Year: 1994
Title: IPR Sourcebook Philippines: With Special Emphasis on Intellectual Property Rights in Agriculture and Food
City: Los Baños
Publisher: University of the Philippines, Los Baños College of Agriculture & Managemement and Organizational Development for Empowerment
Keywords: IPRs, agriculture, Philippines
Abstract: This collection of conference papers, other papers, and discussion transcripts deals with local applications and implications of IPR, and with ethical and legal dimensions in policy review and advocacy of IPR.

Author: Moufang, R
Reference Type: Book Section
Year: 1998
Title: The Concept of 'Ordre Public' and Morality in Patent Law
Editor: Overwalle, G van
Book Title: Octrooirecht, Ethiek en Biotechnologie/Patent Law, Ethics and Biotechnology/Droit des Brevets, Ethique et Biotechnologie
City: Brussels
Publisher: Bruylant
Pages: 65–77
Keywords: patents, biotechnology, Europe, TRIPS
Abstract: Argues that patent law is not ethically neutral. The moral foundations of patent law largely depend on the values of technical progress and free market economy since the primary task of patent law is to protect technical innovation by exclusive property rights. Considerations based on ethical arguments pervade the entire normative structure of the patent system and play an important role in its further development.

Author: Mugabe, J; Barber, C V; Henne, G; Glowka, L; La Viña, A
Reference Type: Report
Year: 1996
Title: Managing Access to Genetic Resources: Towards Strategies for Benefit-Sharing
City: Nairobi
Institution: African Centre for Technology Studies
Type: Biopolicy International
Report Number: 17
Keywords: genetic resources, prior informed consent, IPRs
Abstract: Reviews provisions in the CBD dealing with access to genetic resources, benefit sharing, national sovereignty and prior informed consent from the position of developing countries. Also briefly analyses exemplary legislation from the Andean Pact and the Philippines. Concludes with recommendations.

Author: Mugabe, J; Clark, N
Reference Type: Journal Article
Year: 1996
Title: Technology Transfer and the Biodiversity Convention: Issues of Conservation and Sustainable Use
Journal: Science, Technology and Development
Volume: 14
Issue: 3
Pages: 1–31
Keywords: technology transfer, CBD, IPRs

Abstract: This paper is concerned with how to facilitate the development and transfer of technology relevant to conservation of biodiversity and sustainable use of its components. It examines the range and nature of technologies relevant to the objectives of the CBD and suggests ways or means to facilitate the development and transfer of such technologies. Developing countries treat IPRs as a barrier to transfer of technology while developed countries argue that to stimulate and promote private investments in technological development, countries should strengthen IPRs. However, neither position is informed by empirical evidence of how IPRs affect the transfer of specific technologies to developing countries. [An earlier version of this paper was published in ACTS' Biopolicy series.]

Editors: Mugabe, J; Barber, C V; Henne, G; Glowka, L; La Viña, A
Reference Type: Edited Book
Year: 1997
Title: Access to Genetic Resources: Strategies for Sharing Benefits
City: Nairobi
Publisher: ACTS Press
Keywords: genetic resources, benefit sharing, CBD, IPRs
Abstract: This collection underscores the importance of informed national approaches to enforce access to genetic resources and benefit-sharing provisions of the CBD. It discusses key issues concerning access to genetic resources and sharing of benefits arising from their use; and examines ongoing efforts to formulate and implement national measures.

Author: Nature (Editorial)
Reference Type: Magazine Article
Year: 1995
Title: Patenting Nature Now
Magazine: Nature
Volume: 377
Pages: 89–90
Date: 14 September
Keywords: patents, neem
Abstract: Discussion of the neem patents controversy which concludes that these patent should be judged by the terms on which they were granted – not on the extent to which they conflict with traditional knowledge systems that have only a marginal role in the modern world.

Author: Nijar, G S
Reference Type: Report
Year: 1996
Title: TRIPS and Biodiversity – The Threat and Responses: A Third World View
City: Penang
Institution: Third World Network
Type: TWN Paper
Report Number: 2
Keywords: TRIPS, CBD, biodiversity, WTO, IPRs, indigenous peoples, traditional knowledge
Abstract: Considers the biodiversity crisis and the implications of TRIPS for biodiversity and the Third World. It is argued that TRIPS undermines the objectives of the CBD. In response, the author proposes various responses in the context of the WTO provisions, the WTO Committee on Trade and Environment, and the CBD.

Author: Nijar, G S
Reference Type: Book Section
Year: 1997
Title: Developing a 'Rights Regime' in Defence of Biodiversity and Indigenous Knowledge
Editors: Mugabe, J; Barber, C V; Henne, G; Glowka, L; La Viña, A
Book Title: Access to Genetic Resources: Strategies for Sharing Benefits
City: Nairobi
Publisher: ACTS Press
Pages: 233–243
Keywords: traditional knowledge
Abstract: There are two options with respect to protection of traditional knowledge. The first is to do nothing on the premise that to provide any kind of protection of rights is to bring indigenous communities and their resources into the fold of the market economy. The second is to formulate a rights regime which reflects the culture and value system of these communities as a device to prevent their knowledge from being usurped, commoditized, privatized and to ward off any threats to the integrity of these societies. It is argued that there is little option but to formulate a rights regime, and the elements of such a regime are identified in this chapter.

Editor: Overwalle, G van
Reference Type: Edited Book
Year: 1998
Title: Octrooirecht, Ethiek en Biotechnologie/Patent Law, Ethics and Biotechnology/Droit des Brevets, Ethique et Biotechnologie
City: Brussels
Publisher: Bruylant
Keywords: IPRs, biotechnology, patents
Abstract: Collection of papers by lawyers, academics and ethicists considering the ethical dimensions of patent law with respect to biotechnological inventions.

Author: Peralta, E C
Reference Type: Book Section
Year: 1994
Title: A Call for Intellectual Property Rights to Recognise Indigenous Peoples' Knowledge of Genetic and Cultural Resources
Editor: Krattiger, A F; McNeely, J A; Lesser, W H; Miller, K R; Hill, Y St; Senanayake, R
Book Title: Widening Perspectives on Biodiversity
City: Gland & Geneva
Publisher: IUCN & IAE
Pages: 287–289
Keywords: IPRs, indigenous peoples, genetic resources
Abstract: International and national laws should recognize indigenous peoples' intellectual contributions to the use of genetic resources and cultural expressions.

Author: Pimbert, M
Reference Type: Journal Article
Year: 1997
Title: Issues Emerging in Implementing the Convention on Biological Diversity
Journal: Journal of International Development
Volume: 9
Issue: 3
Pages: 415–425
Keywords: CBD, biodiversity, conservation

Abstract: Discusses developments emerging as the CBD is implemented, and some of the issues currently under debate in various forums concerning biodiversity. Biodiversity is central to the development and environment discourse, although the complexity of the problem of biodiversity loss and erosion, and the numerous actors and interests involved in its management, make international negotiations and agreements controversial and highly politicized. Key issues are national sovereignty; conservation and sustainable use of biodiversity; access and sharing of benefits of biodiversity.

Author: Plenderleith, K
Reference Type: Journal Article
Year: 1996
Title: Farmers' Rights: Who Owns the Genetic Treasure Chest?
Journal: Appropriate Technology
Volume: 23
Issue: 2
Pages: 23–4
Keywords: agriculture, CBD, FAO, patents
Abstract: For hundreds of years farmers have been developing the crops that we depend on for our food security. Recent changes in international law mean that farmers may lose out just when the value of their work is becoming evident. This article explains some of the systems being proposed to reward agricultural innovation.

Author: Posey, D A
Reference Type: Report
Year: 1996
Title: Provisions and Mechanisms of the Convention on Biological Diversity for Access to Traditional Technologies and Benefit Sharing for Indigenous and Local Communities Embodying Traditional Lifestyles
City: Oxford, UK
Institution: Oxford Centre for the Environment, Ethics and Society
Date: April
Type: OCEES Research Paper
Report Number: 6
Keywords: CBD, IPRs, traditional resource rights, indigenous peoples, *sui generis*
Abstract: Analyses provisions of the CBD that both support and enhance the role of these communities through the recognition of their traditional technologies and call for wider use and application of traditional 'knowledge, innovations, and practices'. IPRs are inadequate to guarantee equity and protection. Instead, alternative (*sui generis*) systems for protection and equitable benefit sharing are necessary, such as Traditional Resource Rights (TRR), that harmonize the CBD with international human rights instruments.

Author: Posey, D A; Dutfield, G
Reference Type: Book
Year: 1996
Title: Beyond Intellectual Property: Toward Traditional Resource Rights for Indigenous Peoples and Local Communities
City: Ottawa
Publisher: International Development Research Centre
Keywords: IPRs, traditional knowledge, indigenous peoples, agriculture, pharmaceuticals, health, traditional resource rights, bioprospecting, CBD, TRIPS, FAO
Abstract: A handbook for indigenous, traditional and local communities providing useful information and case studies on the issues raised by the use and appropriation of traditional intellectual, cultural and scientific resources. It is presented in an

accessible style and format so that it may serve as a practical guide to the key questions, legal tools, and options available for protection of and just compensation for traditional knowledge and biogenetic resources. In this way it is hoped that traditional communities, individuals, and institutions will be in a better position to set the terms of their relationships with researchers, companies, and others, and to determine whether involvement in research and commercial projects is in their best interest.

Author: Posey, D A; Dutfield, G
Reference Type: Book Section
Year: 1998
Title: Plants, Patents and Traditional Knowledge: Ethical Concerns of Indigenous and Traditional Peoples
Editor: Overwalle, G van
Book Title: Octrooirecht, Ethiek en Biotechnologie/Patent Law, Ethics and Biotechnology/Droit des Brevets, Ethique et Biotechnologie
City: Brussels
Publisher: Bruylant
Pages: 109–132
Keywords: patents, indigenous peoples, CBD, traditional knowledge, WTO, TRIPS
Abstract: In developing countries, IPRs are considered as unfairly favourable towards industrialized nations, and a code for unethical and unsustainable exploitation of local communities and their resources. Indeed, from the perspective of indigenous peoples and traditional societies, both patents and plant breeders' rights are immoral. This is not only because monopolies are against the moral order of these societies, but also because these legal instruments can never be applied equitably.

Author: Prescott-Allen, R; Prescott-Allen, C
Reference Type: Book
Year: 1983
Title: Genes from the Wild: Using Wild Genetic Resources for Food and Raw Materials
City: London
Publisher: International Institute for Environment and Development
Keywords: agriculture, genetic resources, conservation
Abstract: Describes the growing contribution of wild genetic resources to the production of food and raw materials, describes their characteristics, explains the benefits and problems of using them and outlines the ways in which they are threatened and the measures taken to conserve them.

Author: Price, S C
Reference Type: Book Section
Year: 1992
Title: The Economic Impact of Novel Genes in Plant Biotechnology: Not without Strong Intellectual Property Rights
Editor: Adams, R P; Adams, J E
Book Title: Conservation of plant genes: DNA banking and *in vitro* biotechnology
City: San Diego & London
Publisher: Academic Press
Keywords: IPRs, biotechnology, agriculture, patents, UPOV, USA
Abstract: The historical basis of patents is reviewed along with the development of IPRs as they pertain to plants and biotechnology. The thesis is advanced that patents and licensing will not inhibit research and development, but actually promote R&D amid the free exchange of information and materials. This is a worldwide concept that applies equally to developed and developing countries.

Author: Quiroz, C
Reference Type: Journal Article
Year: 1994
Title: Biodiversity, Indigenous Knowledge, Gender and Intellectual Property Rights
Journal: Indigenous Knowledge and Development Monitor
Volume: 2
Issue: 3
Pages: 12–15
Keywords: biodiversity, traditional knowledge, IPRs
Abstract: Evidence of the accelerating depletion of natural resources and other environmental and social problems has resulted in a global consensus on the need to see development in terms of long-term sustainability. This interest in sustainable development has been accompanied by an interest in important related issues, such as the conservation of natural resources (eg biodiversity), indigenous knowledge systems (eg cultural diversity), gender and IPRs. This article explores the relationship between those issues and gives some recommendations for further research and action.

Author: Rangnekar, D
Reference Type: Report
Year: 1996
Title: GATT, Intellectual Property Rights, and the Seed Industry: Some Unsolved Problems
City: Kingston upon Thames, Surrey
Institution: Kingston University – Faculty of Human Sciences
Date: June
Type: Economics Discussion Paper 96/5
Keywords: GATT, IPRs, UPOV, agriculture
Abstract: Reflects on recent changes for the international protection of IPRs achieved through GATT. Specific aspects of the global harmonization of domestic regimes of protection are identified. These substantive changes contrast with general presumptions of theoretical economics on IPRs. Through a survey of economic literature on this subject, the paper concludes that the achievements at GATT are not supported by theory. Emphasis is given to the subject of plant variety protection.

Author: Raustiala, K; Victor, D G
Reference Type: Magazine Article
Year: 1996
Title: Biodiversity since Rio: The Future of the Convention on Biological Diversity
Magazine: Environment
Volume: 38
Issue Number: 4
Pages: 17–20, 37–45
Date: May
Keywords: CBD, IPRs, biotechnology, biosafety
Abstract: Describes the problem of biodiversity loss, charts how the biodiversity agenda has expanded to include many other concerns such as access to genetic resources, IPRs, and biotechnology, and reviews the operation of the CBD and its prospects.

Author: Reid, W V
Reference Type: Report
Year: 1992
Title: Genetic Resources and Sustainable Agriculture: Creating Incentives for Local Innovation and Adaptation
City: Nairobi & Maastricht

Institution: African Centre for Technology Studies
Type: Biopolicy International
Report Number: 2
Keywords: agriculture, IPRs, genetic resources
Abstract: Current policy regimes fail to promote local innovation or provide incentives for the upstream exploration of potential values of genetic resources. Changes will require acceptance by all countries of new ownership regimes for genetic resources. It is argued that the only lasting solutions to maintaining the genetic resources base of agriculture are in situ conservation, recognition of local and national ownership of genetic resources, and research and investment aimed at informal innovation.

Editor: Reid, W V; Laird, S A; Meyer, C A; Gamez, R; Sittenfeld, A; Janzen, D H; Gollin, M A; Juma, C
Reference Type: Edited Book
Year: 1993
Title: Biodiversity Prospecting: Using Genetic Resources for Sustainable Development
City: Washington DC
Publisher: World Resources Institute, Instituto Nacional de Biodiversidad, Rainforest Alliance, African Centre for Technology Studies
Keywords: bioprospecting, INBio
Abstract: The proliferation of bioprospecting in the tropics makes it urgent to develop equitable legal arrangements so that the natural environment is enhanced rather than diminished, and developing countries benefit.

Author: Reid, W V
Reference Type: Book Section
Year: 1994
Title: Biodiversity Prospecting: Strategies for Sharing Benefits
Editor: Sanchez, V; Juma, C
Book Title: Biodiplomacy
City: Nairobi
Publisher: ACTS
Pages: 241–268
Keywords: bioprospecting, INBio, Costa Rica, IPRs, genetic resources, conservation
Abstract: Reviews some examples from the rapidly growing number of bioprospecting ventures, and offers suggestions on designing effective and equitable bioprospecting programmes, with a particular focus on the use of biodiversity in the pharmaceutical industry. The premise is that appropriate policies and institutions are needed to ensure that the commercial value obtained from biogenetic resources is a positive force for development and conservation.

Author: Reid, W V
Reference Type: Book Section
Year: 1997
Title: Technology and Access to Genetic Resources
Editor: Mugabe, J; Barber, C V; Henne, G; Glowka, L; La Viña, A
Book Title: Access to Genetic Resources: Strategies for Sharing Benefits
City: Nairobi
Publisher: ACTS Press
Pages: 53–70
Keywords: genetic resources, benefit sharing, CBD, biotechnology
Abstract: Biotechnology is one of the most rapidly evolving fields of science today. In many respects, technological changes are blurring the distinctions between agricultural, industrial and pharmaceutical applications of biodiversity. New

technologies also affect the economic value of biodiversity and genetic resources, and help to determine potentially useful provisions in benefit-sharing arrangements between suppliers and recipients of biodiversity. Policies to regulate access to genetic resources and biochemical samples under the CBD must take into account trends in the biotechnology industry and, in particular, the implications of these trends for effective benefit-sharing arrangements.

Author: Roberts, T
Reference Type: Journal Article
Year: 1996
Title: Patenting Plants Around the World
Journal: European Intellectual Property Review
Issue: 10
Pages: 531–536
Keywords: IPRs, patents, UPOV, TRIPS
Abstract: Reviews plant-related IPR practice in Europe and the United States, with some comments on positions in other countries; notes the requirements of the TRIPS Agreement; and offers some comments.

Author: Rolston, H
Reference Type: Magazine Article
Year: 1993
Title: Whose Woods These Are: Are Genetic Resources Private Property or Global Commons?
Magazine: Earthwatch
Issue Number: March/April
Pages: 17–18
Date: March/April
Keywords: genetic resources, INBio, bioprospecting, CBD, IPRs
Abstract: Discussion of genetic resource politics which concludes that ownership issues and rights to exploit ought to be conceived as a commons that we all have to protect. North and South, governments and industry, are all obliged to save the commons if they are to share it.

Editor: Rothschild, D
Reference Type: Edited Book
Year: 1996
Title: Protecting What's Ours: Indigenous Peoples and Biodiversity
City: Oakland
Publisher: South and Meso American Indian Rights Center
Keywords: genetic resources, indigenous peoples, HGDP, IPRs, bioprospecting
Abstract: A useful guide to genetic resource issues for indigenous peoples. There are informative chapters on bioprospecting, IPRs, the Human Genome Diversity Project, agro-biodiversity, and international law. Case studies reveal the various threats facing indigenous peoples due to corporate interest in their knowledge and resources. The book concludes by outlining various strategies that indigenous peoples could adopt to ensure that they are not exploited.

Author: Rubin, S M; Fish, S C
Reference Type: Journal Article
Year: 1994
Title: Biodiversity Prospecting: Using Innovative Contractual Provisions to Foster Ethnobotanical Knowledge, Technology and Conservation
Journal: Colorado Journal of International Environmental Law and Policy
Volume: 5
Pages: 23–58

Keywords: bioprospecting, CBD, INBio, Shaman Pharmaceuticals, patents, traditional knowledge
Abstract: Biodiversity prospecting has until recently failed to provide conservation incentives. The CBD established certain principles and objectives which bioprospecting contracts might follow. Authors discuss certain contract provisions that might optimize benefits to the host country as well as specific compensation packages, such as those involving technology transfers, royalties, concession fees, etc.

Author: Rural Advancement Foundation International
Reference Type: Report
Year: 1990
Title: Folkseed: a Journalistic Overview of the Battle over Plant Genetic Resources
City: Ottawa
Institution: RAFI
Keywords: genetic resources, UPOV, WIPO, GATT, farmers' rights, traditional knowledge, IBPGR, IPRs, breeders' rights, FAO, agriculture
Abstract: Compares the innovations of traditional farmers with those of the modern plant breeders, and emphasizes the importance of Third World crop germplasm. It is argued that the extension of IPR protection for folk varieties is playing to the rules of a game 'cooked up in Washington' and should not be supported. The overview concludes with a list of traditional farming practices that could be patentable should US proposals on TRIPS be adopted.

Author: Rural Advancement Foundation International
Reference Type: Report
Year: 1994
Title: The Benefits of Biodiversity: 100+ Examples of the Contribution by Indigenous and Rural Communities in the South to Development in the North
City: Ottawa
Institution: RAFI
Date: March
Type: Occasional Paper Series
Report Number: Vol 1, No 1
Keywords: traditional knowledge
Abstract: Compilation of data intended to give an insight into the enormous contribution made by the South to the wellbeing of Northern citizens and the economic benefit of Northern corporations.

Author: Rural Advancement Foundation International
Reference Type: Book
Year: 1994
Title: Conserving Indigenous Knowledge: Integrating Two Systems of Innovation. An Independent Study by the Rural Advancement Foundation International
City: New York
Publisher: United Nations Development Programme
Keywords: IPRs, Human Genome Diversity Project, FAO, CGIAR
Abstract: Identifies issues and trends in IPR systems and argues that the indigenous system of innovation is left unprotected. In view of the inherent unfairness of this situation, the author suggests various alternatives to IPRs.

Author: Salazar, R; Cabrera, J A
Reference Type: Journal Article
Year: 1996
Title: Derechos de Propiedad Intelectual en Costa Rica a la Luz del Convenio sobre Diversidad Biologica
Journal: Journal of Ethnopharmacology

Volume: 51
Pages: 177–93
Keywords: CBD, IPRs, Costa Rica
Abstract: Analyses IPRs and acquisition of biological samples in light of the CBD, with emphasis on Costa Rica. It examines the existing legal framework for the protection of biodiversity in that country, especially evaluating the law regarding protection of biota, which was approved in 1992. This includes information regarding access to genetic resources, and regulation for this law. It examines the CBD, whose objectives and goals, above all, emphasize the subject of distribution of benefits to be derived from the use of biological resources. (In Spanish.)

Author: Scalise, D G; Nugent, D
Reference Type: Journal Article
Year: 1995
Title: International Intellectual Property Protection for Living Matter: Biotechnology, Multinational Conventions and the Exception for Agriculture
Journal: Case Western Reserve Journal of International Law
Volume: 27
Pages: 83–118
Keywords: IPRs, agriculture, WIPO, UPOV, biotechnology, USA, patents, CBD, INBio
Abstract: Argues that TRIPS, the CBD and UPOV are all failed opportunities as far as the US biotech industry is concerned. If the international community desires an equitable sharing of wealth and technology with developing nations, it should not use the mechanism of IPR conventions to achieve that goal. Forcing the financial burden on the biotech industry creates a disincentive to future investment and consequently sacrifices the progress of technology. Proposes a UN-supervised fund to support technology-sharing and the promotion of agreements like the one between INBio and Merck.

Author: Secretariat of the Convention on Biological Diversity
Reference Type: Report
Year: 1996
Title: The Impact of Intellectual Property Rights Systems on the Conservation and Sustainable Use of Biological Diversity and on the Equitable Sharing of Benefits from its Use: A Preliminary Study.
City: Montreal
Institution: CBD Secretariat
Date: 22 September 1996
Type: Note by the Executive Secretary for the Conference of the Parties to the Convention on Biological Diversity, Third Meeting. Buenos Aires, Argentina. 4 to 15 November 1996. Item 14.1 of the provisional agenda.
Report Number: UNEP/CBD/COP/3/22
Keywords: IPRs, CBD, traditional knowledge, breeders' rights, trademarks, appellations of origin, patents, technology transfer
Abstract: Provides a preliminary review of the impact of IPR systems on the conservation and sustainable use of biodiversity and on the equitable sharing of benefits from its use. The paper reviews the range of viewpoints that have been expressed on the issue and provides examples of recent policy proposals.

Author: Secretariat of the Convention on Biological Diversity
Reference Type: Report
Year: 1996
Title: The Convention on Biological Diversity and the Agreement on Trade-Related Intellectual Property Rights: Relationships and Synergies
City: Montreal
Institution: CBD Secretariat

Date: 5 October 1996
Type: For the Conference of the Parties to the Convention on Biological Diversity, Third Meeting. Buenos Aires, Argentina. 4 to 15 November 1996. Item 14 of the provisional agenda.
Report Number: UNEP/CBD/COP/3/23
Keywords: IPRs, CBD, TRIPS, patents, technology transfer
Abstract: Reviews relationships and synergies between the CBD and TRIPS, and concludes with a list of options for future work.

Author: Sehgal, S
Reference Type: Magazine Article
Year: 1996
Title: IPR Driven Restructuring of the Seed Industry
Magazine: Biotechnology and Development Monitor
Issue Number: 29
Pages: 18–21
Date: December
Keywords: IPRs
Abstract: Until recently, success in the seed business could be traced to the strength of a company's classical breeding programme. But with the advent of the first transgenic plants, such breeding, as well as access to germplasm, genes and biotechnologies, has become of considerable strategic importance. Genetic material, biotechnologies and their associated IPRs are leading to a new restructuring of the relations between agrochemical, agro-biotechnology, food processing, and seed industries.

Author: Seiler, A
Reference Type: Journal Article
Year: 1998
Title: Sui Generis Systems: Obligations and Options for Developing Countries
Journal: Biotechnology and Development Monitor
Issue: 34
Pages: 2–5
Keywords: WTO, TRIPs, IPRs, plants, patents, UPOV, sui generis
Abstract: In 1999, the *sui generis* option for the protection of plant varieties will be evaluated by the TRIPS Council. The shape of a TRIPS-compatible *sui generis* system will play a key role in establishing alternatives to patents on plant varieties. Five different *sui generis* approaches are considered: (i) granting community IPRs; (ii) community and collective intellectual rights; (iii) modified plant variety protection (like UPOV but with modifications); (iv) comprehensive biodiversity legislation; and (v) sectoral community rights regime.

Author: Shand, H
Reference Type: Journal Article
Year: 1993
Title: Agbio and Third World Development
Journal: Bio/Technology
Volume: 11
Issue: March
Pages: 13
Keywords: biotechnology, patents, GATT, CBD, agriculture
Abstract: Expresses concern about the social and economic impacts of new agricultural biotechnologies, especially on Third World farmers. International tension over the ownership of genetic resources will intensify with the danger that the exchange of genetic material and information will be severely constricted. At stake is future control of the world's food supply, the sustainability of agriculture, and the hope of economic development for many Third World nations.

Author: Shand, H
Reference Type: Book
Year: 1997
Title: Human Nature: Agricultural Biodiversity and Farm-Based Food Security.
City: Ottawa
Publisher: RAFI
Keywords: FAO, IUPGR, biodiversity, CBD, IPRs
Abstract: An independent study prepared by Rural Advancement Foundation International for the United Nations Food and Agriculture Organization. It assesses the current state of biodiversity for food and agriculture and human diversity, and seeks to contribute a policy agenda to resolve the various interrelated problems caused by worldwide 'biological meltdown'.

Author: Sharma, D
Reference Type: Book
Year: 1995
Title: GATT to WTO: Seeds of Despair
City: Delhi
Publisher: Konark Publishers
Edition: Second
Keywords: India, agriculture, patents, IPRs, WTO, GATT, TRIPS
Abstract: Argues that the terms of the WTO agreements one-sidedly favour the interests of farmers and citizens in the North, and the social and economic impacts on countries like India could be devastating.

Author: Shiva, V
Reference Type: Book
Year: 1995
Title: Captive Minds, Captive Lives: Ethics, Ecology and Patents on Life
City: Dehra Dun, India
Publisher: Research Foundation for Science, Technology and Natural Resource Policy
Keywords: India, IPRs, ethics, agriculture, patents, neem, TRIPS, agriculture, farmers' rights
Abstract: IPRs have emerged as the most significant trade issue in recent years. However, IPRs, especially in the area of life forms, are not a mere trade issue. They primarily raise ethical, ecological, epistemological and economic issues, and these are discussed by the author in this book.

Author: Shiva, V
Reference Type: Magazine Article
Year: 1996
Title: Agricultural Biodiversity, Intellectual Property Rights and Farmers' Rights
Magazine: Economic and Political Weekly
Pages: 1621–1631
Date: June 22
Keywords: CBD, TRIPS, IPRs, farmers' rights, agriculture, UPOV
Abstract: Under pressure from the US and to meet the requirements of TRIPS, new IPR legislation is being introduced in India in the area of plant genetic resources. Against this, people's organizations and others are fighting to protect farmers' rights to their biodiversity and to survival. This paper describes the conflict between farmers and the transnational seed industry, and outlines a people's charter for farmers' rights.

Author: Sperling, L; Loevinsohn, M
Reference Type: Conference Proceedings
Year of Conference: 1996
Title: Using Diversity: Enhancing and Maintaining Genetic Resources On-farm
Editor: 1995
Conference Name: Using Diversity
Conference Location: New Delhi, India
Publisher: International Development Research Centre
Keywords: conservation, agriculture
Abstract: Conservation of threatened farmer-developed varieties and the breeding and selection of new cultivars are often seen as distinct activities and the concerns of different organizations. The 'Using Diversity' workshop explored the common ground between the two approaches. It brought together scientists, farmers and NGO workers from across South Asia who share the conviction that genetic diversity, on-farm, is key to rural people's food security and that farmers must be involved in its maintenance and enhancement.

Author: Starr, J; Hardy, K C
Reference Type: Journal Article
Year: 1993
Title: Not by Seeds Alone: The Biodiversity Treaty and the Role for Native Agriculture
Journal: Stanford Environmental Law Journal
Volume: 12
Pages: 85–123
Keywords: CBD, agriculture, genetic resources, IPRs, biodiversity
Abstract: Discusses the importance of plant biodiversity, the places on earth where it is most prevalent, and the positive benefits that humans derive from genetically diverse plant life. Examines native agricultural practices that maintained diversity for many years, the causes of the disappearance of plant diversity, and the implications of this genetic loss. Highlights some scientific and legal attempts to address the loss of diversity, including the CBD. Finally, the author analyses those aspects of the CBD that focus upon conservation of genetic resources within their native environment, and examines the reasons behind the US failure to sign the CBD.

Author: Stenson, A; Gray, T
Reference Type: Book Section
Year: 1997
Title: Cultural Communities and Intellectual Property Rights in Plant Genetic Resources
Editor: Hayward, T; O'Neill, J
Book Title: Justice, Property and the Environment: Social and Legal Perspectives
City: Aldershot & Brookfield, VT
Publisher: Ashgate Publishing
Pages: 178–193
Keywords: IPRs, indigenous peoples
Abstract: Examines and rejects the view that cultural communities are morally entitled to intellectual property rights to their knowledge related to plant genetic resources. It is argued that neither moral entitlement nor utilitarian theories support the notion that traditional communities should have IPR protection for their knowledge.

Editor: Sterckx, S
Reference Type: Edited Book
Year: 1997
Title: Biotechnology, Morality and Patents
City: Aldershot
Publisher: Ashgate
Keywords: biotechnology, IPRs, patents
Abstract: Documents an international workshop held in January 1996 on the ethical aspects of the patenting of biotechnological inventions. The book includes contributions from Greenpeace and animal welfare societies, geneticists, moral philosophers, patent lawyers and politicians from European countries and the USA. The general public perception of biotechnology is discussed and how these perceptions relate to ethical, social and cultural factors. The legal framework is laid out by several experts in the field of patent law and the situation in the US is also described. Attention is focused on the European Commission's Directive on the legal protection of biotechnological inventions.

Author: Straus, J
Reference Type: Journal Article
Year: 1987
Title: The Relationship between Plant Variety Protection and Patent Protection for Biotechnological Inventions from an International Viewpoint
Journal: International Review of Industrial Property and Copyright Law
Volume: 18
Issue: 6
Pages: 723–37
Keywords: biotechnology, patents, UPOV
Abstract: The relationship between plant variety protection and patent protection for biological inventions has, as a consequence of scientific and technological developments of recent years, crystallized into a highly controversial problem. This article reviews scientific and legal developments at the international level.

Author: Study Committee on Biotechnology and Intellectual Property Rights with Respect to Developing Countries
Reference Type: Report
Year: 1991
Title: The Impact of Intellectual Property Rights in Biotechnology and Plant Breeding in Developing Countries
City: The Hague
Institution: Ministry of Foreign Affairs
Keywords: IPRs, agriculture, breeders' rights, USA, Europe, UPOV, biotechnology
Abstract: The study shows that the desirability of introducing IPR protection for plant material in developing countries must be related to the stage of development. If no or little national breeding activity and/or biotechnological research take place, there is little advantage to the country to establish either breeders' rights or patent protection in these fields. Moreover, absence of IPR protection for plant material will not block the country's access to plant genetic resources or biotechnological inventions protected elsewhere.

Author: Subramanian, A
Reference Type: Journal Article
Year: 1992
Title: Genetic Resources, Biodiversity and Environmental Protection: An Analysis, and Proposals Towards a Solution
Journal: Journal of World Trade
Volume: 26

Pages: 105–109
Keywords: biodiversity, IPRs, copyright, appellations of origin
Abstract: Genetic resources have the property that access to one unit is sufficient for the purpose of propagating millions of copies of them. This leads to market failure with potentially significant consequences for environmental protection. A solution to correcting this market is proposed which consists of the grant of a new property right (genetic resource right) akin to and inspired by IPRs. The solution has the attractions of addressing the problem of forest degradation, of being a market-based solution and of providing a simple means of securing international cooperation which would not necessarily rely on public financial transfers.

Author: Suppan, S
Reference Type: Report
Year: 1998
Title: Biotechnology's Takeover of the Seed Industry
City: Minneapolis
Institution: Institute for Agriculture and Trade Policy
Date: June 4
Report Number: Information About Intellectual Property Rights no 23
Keywords: biotechnology, IPRs, agriculture
Abstract: Describes the growing dominance of the global seed industry by a small number of life-science corporations such as Monsanto. In spite of the optimistic claims of such companies, there is little discussion of how the application of agricultural biotechnology to agricultural trade policy's emphasis on monoculture production will reverse the loss of plant diversity essential for reinvigorating plant breeding programmes.

Editor: Swaminathan, M S
Reference Type: Edited Book
Year: 1995
Title: Farmers' Rights and Plant Genetic Resources. Recognition and Reward: A Dialogue
City: Madras
Publisher: Macmillan India
Keywords: farmers' rights, patents, IPRs, UPOV, breeders' rights
Abstract: Proceedings of workshop held in Madras in January 1994, whose purpose was to develop practical methods of recognizing and rewarding the contributions of tribal and rural people to the conservation and enhancement of plant genetic resources. The book deals with many facets of the problem and suggests a draft legislation containing transparent and implementable procedures for recognizing and rewarding farmers' rights.

Editor: Swaminathan, M S
Reference Type: Edited Book
Year: 1996
Title: Agrobiodiversity and Farmers' Rights
Series Title: MSSRF Proceedings Number 14
City: Madras
Publisher: M S Swaminathan Research Foundation
Keywords: FAO, UPOV, IPGRI, CBD
Abstract: Proceedings of the 1996 Technical Consultation on an Implementation Framework for Farmers' Rights that took place in Madras, India. The volume includes texts of presentations made by representatives of the FAO Commission on Genetic Resources for Food and Agriculture, the WTO, UPOV and IPGRI and transcripts of discussions, and concludes with a series of recommendations from the participants.

Editor: Swanson, T
Reference Type: Edited Book
Year: 1995
Title: Intellectual Property Rights and Biodiversity Conservation: An Interdisciplinary Analysis of the Values of Medicinal Plants
City: Cambridge
Publisher: Cambridge University Press
Keywords: IPRs, biodiversity, conservation, CBD, pharmaceuticals, medicinal plants
Abstract: Provides a detailed analysis of the economic and scientific rationales for biodiversity conservation. It discusses the justification for, and implementation of, IPR regimes as incentive systems to encourage conservation. An interdisciplinary approach is used, encompassing fields of study that include evolutionary biology, chemistry, economics and legal studies. The arguments are presented using the case study of the use of medicinal plants in the pharmaceutical industry.

Author: Swanson, T
Reference Type: Book Section
Year: 1995
Title: The Appropriation of Evolution's Values: An Institutional Analysis of Intellectual Property Regimes and Biodiversity Conservation
Editor: Swanson, T
Book Title: Intellectual Property Rights and Biodiversity Conservation: An Interdisciplinary Analysis of the Values of Medicinal Plants
City: Cambridge
Publisher: Cambridge University Press
Pages: 141–175
Keywords: biodiversity, conservation, IPRs
Abstract: Explains how the decline of biodiversity has been generated by the human development process; categorizes the opportunity costs of such development, ie the values of biodiversity; and demonstrates the nature of the institution required to bring these values into the calculus. It is essential to invest in a diversity of institutions in order to capture the values of biodiversity.

Author: Swanson, T
Reference Type: Journal Article
Year: 1996
Title: The Reliance of Northern Economies on Southern Biodiversity: Biodiversity as Information
Journal: Ecological Economics
Volume: 17
Pages: 1–8
Keywords: biodiversity, agriculture
Abstract: Addresses the issue of how biodiversity is used as an input into important industrial research and development processes. Results are reported from a survey of the agricultural research and development industry, demonstrating how the environment engenders new problems in a systematic fashion and how the industry makes recourse to biodiversity for stocks of information to address these problems. The reliance of this northern-based industry on southern-based biodiversity is found to be substantial and the elimination of biodiversity could be disastrous for these important industries in the near term.

Author: Swanson, T
Reference Type: Book
Year: 1997
Title: Global Action for Biodiversity: An International Framework for Implementing the Convention on Biological Diversity

City: London
Publisher: Earthscan, in association with IUCN
Keywords: biodiversity, CBD, IPRs
Abstract: The book highlights the gaps in the CBD remaining to be filled, offers explanations of the concepts involved, and provides a set of policy prescriptions intended to facilitate the development of institutions and obligations within the international community which will give real effect to the aspirations of the CBD.

Author: Tansey, G
Reference Type: Book
Year: 1999
Title: Trade, Intellectual Property, Food and Biodiversity: Key Issues and Options for the 1999 Review of Article 27.3(b) of the TRIPS Agreement
City: London
Publisher: Quaker Peace and Service
Keywords: IPRs, TRIPS, agriculture, patents, CBD, UPOV
Abstract: This paper draws on various perspectives presented in the literature on IPRs, food, farming, biodiversity, TRIPS and related agreements. It aims to highlight the policy questions for developing countries by TRIPS Article 27.3(b); examine the key ethical, economic, environment and social issues surrounding its provisions; and consider the possible contributions of overseas development assistance.

Author: Tarasofsky, R
Reference Type: Journal Article
Year: 1997
Title: The Relationship Between the TRIPs Agreement and the Convention on Biological Diversity: Towards a Pragmatic Approach
Journal: Review of European Community and International Environmental Law
Volume: 6
Issue: 2
Pages: 148–156
Keywords: CBD, TRIPS, genetic resources, sui generis, UPOV, WTO, traditional knowledge, geographical indications
Abstract: The connection between the CBD and the TRIPS Agreement is the subject of considerable rhetoric and political controversy. This article explores the issues, proposes strategies to harmonizse the objectives of the two agreements, and suggests that the legal regimes governing IPRs may need to be changed.

Author: ten Kate, K; Laird, S A
Reference Type: Book
Year: 1999
Title: The Commercial Use of Biodiversity: Access to Genetic Resources and Benefit-Sharing
City: London
Publisher: Earthscan Publications
Keywords: CBD, genetic resources, bioprospecting, contracts, agriculture, pharmaceuticals
Abstract: The authors explain the provisions of the CBD on access and benefit-sharing, the effect of national laws to implement these, and aspects of typical contracts for the transfer of materials. They provide a sector-by-sector analysis of how genetic resources are used, the scientific, technological and regulatory trends and the different markets in pharmaceuticals, botanical medicines, crop protection and development, horticulture, biotechnology, and personal care and cosmetics.

Author: Thrupp, L A
Reference Type: Journal Article
Year: 1989
Title: Legitimizing Local Knowledge: From Displacement to Empowerment for Third World People
Journal: Agriculture and Human Values
Issue: Summer
Pages: 13–24
Keywords: traditional knowledge, agriculture
Abstract: Increasing attention has been given to 'indigenous' knowledge in Third World rural societies as a potential basis for sustainable agricultural development. The paper reviews the nature of local knowledge and suggests the need to recognize its unique values yet avoid romanticized views of its potential. It is argued that the exploitation of local knowledge by formal institutions should be avoided; instead, people need to establish legitimacy of their knowledge for themselves, as a form of empowerment.

Author: Thrupp, L A
Reference Type: Report
Year: 1996
Title: Linking Biodiversity and Agriculture: Challenges and Opportunities for Sustainable Food Security
City: Washington DC
Institution: World Resources Institute
Keywords: agriculture, biodiversity
Abstract: There is a growing realization that biodiversity is fundamental to agricultural production and food security, as well as a valuable ingredient of environmental conservation. Yet, predominant patterns of agricultural growth have eroded biodiversity in ecosystems. This paper summarizes the main conflicts and complementarities between biodiversity and agriculture, highlighting principles, policies, and practices that enhance diversity in agroecosystems.

Author: Tobin, B
Reference Type: Book Section
Year: 1997
Title: Certificates of Origin: A Role for IPR Regimes in Securing Prior Informed Consent
Editor: Mugabe, J; Barber, C V; Henne, G; Glowka, L; La Viña, A
Book Title: Access to Genetic Resources: Strategies for Sharing Benefits
City: Nairobi
Publisher: ACTS Press
Pages: 329–340
Keywords: patents, IPRs, prior informed consent
Abstract: Proposes multilateral certificates of origin linked to patent rights as a means of securing prior informed consent. Such a system, it is asserted, might be of greater benefit to developing countries and their people than an access/benefit-sharing regime, which might diminish interest in bioprospecting.

Author: Tripp, R; Van der Heide, W
Reference Type: Report
Year: 1996
Title: The Erosion of Crop Genetic Diversity: Challenges, Strategies and Uncertainties
City: London
Institution: Overseas Development Institute

Type: ODI Natural Resource Perspectives
Report Number: 7
Keywords: biodiversity, agriculture
Abstract: Describes the challenges to crop genetic diversity, presents some of the strategies that are being implemented to reverse the erosion of that diversity, outlines several gaps in our knowledge that must be addressed in order to make such strategies more effective, and concludes with some policy implications.

Editor: Tripp, R
Reference Type: Edited Book
Year: 1997
Title: New Seed and Old Laws: Regulatory Reform and the Diversification of National Seed Systems
City: London
Publisher: Intermediate Technology Publications on behalf of the Overseas Development Institute
Keywords: agriculture
Abstract: The development and diversification of national seed systems which are currently taking place require a thorough re-examination of public regulatory responsibilities. Featuring case studies from a wide range of countries, the book presents options for seed regulatory reform that are needed to address failures in government seed provision; innovations in community-level seed activities; the growth of the private seed sector; and the challenge of plant variety protection.

Author: United States Congress – Office of Technology Assessment
Reference Type: Report
Year: 1989
Title: New Developments in Biotechnology: Patenting Life – Special Report
City: Washington DC
Institution: US Government Printing Office
Report Number: OTA-BA–370
Keywords: USA, patents, IPRs, biotechnology, UPOV, agriculture, WIPO, pharmaceuticals
Abstract: This report reviews US patent law as it relates to the patentability of micro-organisms, cells, plants, and animals; as well as specific areas of concern, including deposit requirements and international considerations. The report includes a range of options for congressional action related to the patenting of animals, intellectual property protection for plants, and enablement of patents involving biological material.

Author: van Wijk, J; Cohen, J I; Komen, J
Reference Type: Report
Year: 1993
Title: Intellectual Property Rights for Agricultural Biotechnology: Options and Implications for Developing Countries
City: The Hague
Institution: International Service for National Agricultural Research
Keywords: IPRs, biotechnology
Abstract: Analysis of the complexities, options and implications regarding IPRs in relation to national biotechnology strategies.

Author: van Wijk, J
Reference Type: Journal Article
Year: 1995
Title: Plant Breeders' Rights Create Winners and Losers
Journal: Biotechnology and Development Monitor
Issue: 23
Pages: 15–19
Keywords: breeders' rights, UPOV, Argentina
Abstract: The plant breeders' rights (PBR) system is in use in most OECD countries as well as in some developing countries, but it is controversial. Private seed firms advocate PBR as it would stimulate innovation in plant breeding. Others argue that PBR may hamper the seed supply to farmers and may decrease genetic diversity. A notable problem in the controversy is that empirical evidence on the impact of PBR is lacking. A recent study has attempted to collect some experiences in Latin America, with an emphasis on Argentina.

Author: van Wijk, J; Jaffe, W
Reference Type: Conference Proceedings
Year of Conference: 1996
Title: Intellectual Property Rights and Agriculture in Developing Countries
Editor: 1995
Conference Name: Impact of Plant Breeders' Rights in Developing Countries
Conference Location: Santa Fe de Bogota, Colombia
Publisher: University of Amsterdam
Date: March 7–8, 1995
Keywords: agriculture, IPRs, breeders' rights, Argentina, Chile, Colombia, Mexico, Uruguay, USA, UPOV, TRIPS
Abstract: Proceedings of a seminar which had the following objectives: (i) to present and discuss the results of a project called 'Impact of Plant Breeders' Rights in Developing Countries: Debate and Experience in Argentina, Chile, Colombia, Mexico and Uruguay' with a group of experts; (ii) to provide information, based on the current experience of developing countries, for the design, implementation, management and enforcement of breeders' rights of use for countries introducing this type of IPR protection; and (iii) to assist developing countries in the design of IPR protection policies for agriculture and the international negotiations related to them, through the assessment of the latest trends and events in IPRs related to agriculture and development.

Author: van Wijk, J
Reference Type: Report
Year: 1996
Title: How Does Stronger Protection of Intellectual Property Rights Affect Seed Supply? Early Evidence of Impact
City: London
Institution: Overseas Development Institute
Type: ODI Natural Resource Perspectives
Report Number: 13
Keywords: IPRs, agriculture
Abstract: A study of the relationships between stronger IPR protection in developing countries and seed supply, which finds that stronger plant-related IPR protection has apparently not increased the diversity of plant material available to farmers or enhanced the rate of innovation in plant breeding. Although evidence suggests a strong likelihood that flows of improved genetic material will increase in line with stronger protection, the author predicts that while commercial farmers might benefit from this, middle and lower income farmers will not, because of likely restrictions on seed saving and exchange.

Author: van Wijk, J
Reference Type: Journal Article
Year: 1998
Title: Plant Patenting Provision Reviewed in WTO
Journal: Biotechnology and Development Monitor
Issue: 34
Pages: 6–9
Keywords: WTO, TRIPS, IPRs, plants, UPOV, *sui generis*, patents
Abstract: The WTO is set to re-evaluate the obligation of member states to protect plant materials legally. Patenting life forms has proven to be an internationally contentious issue for cultural and ethical reasons, and due to diverging economic interests. The standpoints of interest groups will basically set the lines for the new WTO negotiations: the biotechnology and seed industry and pressure groups that oppose the patenting of life forms.

Author: Verma, S K
Reference Type: Journal Article
Year: 1995
Title: TRIPS and Plant Variety Protection in Developing Countries
Journal: European Intellectual Property Review
Volume: 17
Issue: 6
Pages: 281–289
Keywords: TRIPS, UPOV
Abstract: The TRIPS Agreement permits an effective *sui generis* system for plant varieties. Such a system for developing countries can be modelled broadly on the UPOV Convention, but considerations of economy, ecology, equity and employment should be emphasized to promote a sustainable job-led economic growth strategy in these countries.

Author: Visser, B
Reference Type: Magazine Article
Year: 1998
Title: Effects of Biotechnology on Agro-Biodiversity
Magazine: Biotechnology and Development Monitor
Issue Number: 35
Pages: 2–7
Date: June
Keywords: biotechnology, agriculture, biodiversity
Abstract: Various biotechnologies have been developed which can have both a positive and negative effect on agro-biodiversity. The socio-economic context in which these technologies are developed and utilized will determine which applications, and thus which effects, will dominate.

Author: Vogel, J H
Reference Type: Magazine Article
Year: 1997
Title: Bioprospecting and the Justification for a Cartel
Magazine: Bulletin of the Working Group on Traditional Resource Rights
Issue Number: 4
Pages: 16–17
Keywords: Ecuador, trade secrets, traditional knowledge, bioprospecting
Abstract: A project based in Ecuador attempts to enable indigenous peoples to benefit from bioprospecting by transforming traditional knowledge into trade secrets. Knowledge from communities wishing to participate in the project will be catalogued and deposited in a restricted access database. If communities with the

same knowledge were to compete rather than collaborate, there would be a price war that would benefit only the corporate end-users. To overcome this danger, the project envisages the creation of a cartel comprising those communities bearing the same trade secret.

Author: Walden, I
Reference Type: Journal Article
Year: 1993
Title: Intellectual Property in Genetic Sequences
Journal: Review of European Community and International Environmental Law
Volume: 2
Issue: 2
Pages: 126–135
Keywords: IPRs, sui generis, biodiversity, genetic resources
Abstract: Discusses the potential and limitations of granting countries IPR over their genetic diversity, which would require these countries to control access to their resources. The author's analysis of legal protection of genetic information through a *sui generis* system indicates that such an approach could be difficult to achieve.

Author: Walden, I
Reference Type: Book Section
Year: 1995
Title: Preserving Biodiversity: The Role of Property Rights
Editor: Swanson, T
Book Title: Intellectual Property Rights and Biodiversity Conservation: An Interdisciplinary Analysis of the Values of Medicinal Plants
City: Cambridge
Publisher: Cambridge University Press
Pages: 176–197
Keywords: biodiversity, conservation, IPRs, sui generis, genetic resources
Abstract: Considers the use of property law to protect the commercial exploitation of genetic material in naturally occurring biota. Attention is then given to the extent to which IPRs are currently being used by the biotechnology industry to protect their research investments. The final section reviews some of the issues underlying the creation of some form of *sui generis* property right in such genetic material.

Author: Wells, A J
Reference Type: Journal Article
Year: 1994
Title: Patenting Life Forms: An Ecological Perspective
Journal: European Intellectual Property Review
Volume: 3
Pages: 111–118
Keywords: patents, GMOs, biotechnology, Australia
Abstract: Far from being an inappropriate place for the consideration of ethical and moral issues, patent regimes have continually been used explicitly to make moral value judgements. The ideology of development and technocentricity embodied in the patent system has allowed patent systems to grant patents for new life forms, despite many calls by the broader community for limits to this extension. The ecological implications of allowing these patents are numerous. The author argues that the patent application mechanism should be opened up to a broad range of community views.

Author: Wood, D; Lenne, J M
Reference Type: Journal Article
Year: 1997
Title: The Conservation of Agrobiodiversity On-farm: Questioning the Emerging Paradigm
Journal: Biodiversity and Conservation
Volume: 6
Pages: 109–129
Keywords: agriculture, biodiversity, genetic resources, conservation, CBD
Abstract: The CBD has given a clear mandate for on-farm conservation. However, lack of scientific knowledge has not prevented an explosion of recommendations on how to conserve agrobiodiversity on farm, and it is possible to identify an emerging paradigm. This article reviews some of the assumptions upon which this paradigm is based, showing that if attempts to conserve biodiversity are based on these misconceptions, they are likely to fail. An alternative research agenda is proposed.

Author: World Trade Organization – Committee on Trade and Environment
Reference Type: Report
Year: 1996
Title: Excerpt from the Report of the Meeting Held on 21–22 June 1995: Record of the Discussion on Item 8 of the Committee on Trade and Environment's Work Programme
City: Geneva
Institution: WTO
Date: 5 March 1996
Report Number: WT/CTE/W/3+Corr 1
Keywords: TRIPS, CBD, trade secrets, sui generis, traditional knowledge
Abstract: Record of discussions on Item 8 of the CTE's work programme, which deals with TRIPS. Among the various issues discussed by the national representatives included: technology transfer, patenting life forms, the applicability of trade secrets to traditional knowledge, and the possibility of adopting a *sui generis* system to implement CBD Article 8(j).

Author: World Trade Organization – Committee on Trade and Environment
Reference Type: Report
Year: 1996
Title: Environment and TRIPS
City: Geneva
Institution: WTO
Date: 8 June 1995
Report Number: WT/CTE/W/8
Keywords: TRIPS, CBD, IPRs, UPOV
Abstract: A background document to assist the CTE in its work dealing with TRIPS. It assesses the links between environmental concerns and IPRs by considering the relevant features of the CBD. The paper then provides a negotiating history of the CBD, especially Article 16. It continues by summarizing relevant ongoing work in other international organizations which, with the CBD, indicate the IPR issues that have been raised as having a link with environment. Relevant TRIPS provisions are presented, GATT exemptions are considered, and the paper ends with a note on the UPOV Convention.

Author: World Trade Organization – Committee on Trade and Environment
Year: 1997
Reference Type: Report
Title: Item 8: The Relationship between the TRIPS Agreement and the Convention on Biodiversity – Communication from India
City: Geneva
Institution: WTO
Date: 29 September 1997
Report Number: WT/CTE/W/65
Keywords: TRIPS, CBD, India
Abstract: Presents the view of the Indian government on the relationship of the CBD's IPR-related provisions with TRIPS. It is argued that there are some important contradictions between TRIPS and the CBD: first, the lack of any conditions on patent application to mention the origin of biogenetic resources and traditional knowledge used in the biotechnological invention; second, the lack of provisions in TRIPS on prior informed consent of the country of origin and the knowledge-holder of the biological raw material meant for usage in a patentable invention. These conflicts need to be addressed, and some measures are proposed to do this.

Author: Yamin, F
Reference Type: Report
Year: 1995
Title: The Biodiversity Convention and Intellectual Property Rights
City: Gland, Switzerland
Institution: World Wide Fund for Nature
Keywords: IPRs, CBD, TRIPS
Abstract: Examines the link between IPRs and the CBD. The author proposes recommendations for the CBD to ensure that such rights are supportive of and do not run counter to the objectives of the Convention.

Author: Yusuf, A
Reference Type: Book Section
Year: 1994
Title: Technology and Genetic Resources: Is Mutually Beneficial Access Still Possible?
Editor: Sanchez, V; Juma, C
Book Title: Biodiplomacy
City: Nairobi
Publisher: ACTS
Pages: 233–240
Keywords: CBD, genetic resources, technology transfer
Abstract: The CBD has not resulted in a trade-off between access to genetic resources and access to technology. However, it has established a clear link between the supply of genetic resources and access to technologies which make use of these resources. This link can be exploited to the benefit of both gene-rich and technology-rich countries. Operational modalities and viable mechanisms are called for in order to render such co-operation effective. One possible mechanism is technology collaboration or knowledge-sharing agreements.

NOTE

1 This is part of a much larger annotated bibliography which was completed by the author thanks to the generous support of World Wide Fund For Nature International.

REFERENCES

Agarwal, A and Narain, S (1996) Pirates in the garden of India. *New Scientist*, 26 October, pp14–15.

Anuradha, R V (1997) In search of knowledge and resources: who sows? who reaps? *Review of European Community and International Environmental Law*, 6(3), pp263–273.

Asebey, E J and Kempenaar, J D (1995) Biodiversity prospecting: fulfilling the mandate of the Biodiversity Convention. *Vanderbilt Journal of Transnational Law*, 28, pp703–754.

ASSINSEL (International Association of Plant Breeders) (1998) Position on access to plant genetic resources for food and agriculture and the equitable sharing of benefits arising from their use (Adopted by the General Assembly in Monte Carlo on 5 June 1998).

Atkinson, N and Sherman, B (1991) Intellectual property and environmental protection. *European Intellectual Property Review*, 5, pp165–170.

Axt, J R, Corn, M L, Lee, M and Ackerman, D M (1993) *Biotechnology, Indigenous Peoples and Intellectual Property Rights*. Congressional Research Service, Washington DC.

Bagla, P (1999) Bioprospecting: model Indian deal generates payments. *Science*, 283(5408), pp1614–1615.

Barton, J H (1993) Adapting the intellectual property system to new technologies. In: Wallerstein, M B, Mogee, M E and Schoen, R A (eds) *Global Dimensions of Intellectual Property Rights in Science and Technology*. National Academy Press, Washington DC, pp256–283.

Bell, J (1996) Genetic engineering and biotechnology in industry. In: Baumann, M, Bell, J, Koechlin, F and Pimbert, M (eds) *The Life Industry: Biodiversity, People and Profits*. Intermediate Technology Publications, London, pp31–52.

Bérard, L and Marchenay, P (1996) Tradition, regulation and intellectual property: local agricultural products and foodstuffs in France. In: Brush, S B and Stabinsky, D (eds) *Valuing Local Knowledge: Indigenous Peoples and Intellectual Property Rights*. Island Press, Washington DC and Covelo. pp230–243.

Bhat, M G (1996) Trade-related intellectual property rights to biological resources: socioeconomic implications for developing countries. *Ecological Economics*, 19, pp205–217.

Biothai and Genetic Resources Action International (1998) *Road Maps to a Peoples' Sui Generis Rights Plan of Action*. Biothai and GRAIN.

Blakeney, M (1996) *Trade Related Aspects of Intellectual Property Rights: A Concise Guide to the TRIPS Agreement*. Sweet and Maxwell, London.

Boyle, J 1996. *Shamans, Software and Spleens: Law and the Construction of the Information Society.* Harvard University Press, Cambridge MA.

Bragdon, S H and Downes, D R (1998) *Recent Policy Trends and Developments Related to the Conservation, Use and Development of Genetic Resources.* Issues in Genetic Resources No. 7. International Plant Genetic Resources Institute, Rome.

Brush, S B (1994) Providing Farmers' Rights through *in situ* conservation of crop genetic resources. Background Study Paper no. 3, First Extraordinary Session of the Commission on Plant Genetic Resources, Rome, 7–11 November 1994.

Brush, S (1996) Is common heritage outmoded? In: Brush, S and Stabinsky, D (eds) *Valuing Local Knowledge: Indigenous People and Intellectual Property Rights.* Island Press, Washington DC and Covelo, pp143–164.

Butler, B and Pistorius, R (1996) How Farmers' Rights can be used to adapt Plant Breeders' Rights. *Biotechnology and Development Monitor*, 28, pp7–11.

Buttel, F H and Belsky, J (1987) Biotechnology, plant breeding, and intellectual property: social and ethical dimensions. *Science, Technology and Human Values*, 12(1), pp31–49.

Cameron, J and Makuch, Z (1995) *The UN Biodiversity Convention and the WTO TRIPS Agreement: Recommendations to Avoid Conflict and Promote Sustainable Development.* World Wide Fund For Nature, Gland.

Centre for Science and Environment (1996). Defining rights. *Notebook*, 5, 7. CSE, New Delhi.

Chrispeels, M J and Sadava, D E (1994) *Plants, Genes, and Agriculture.* Jones and Bartlett, Boston and London.

Cleveland, D A and Murray, S C (1997) The world's crop genetic resources and the rights of indigenous farmers. *Current Anthropology*, 38(4), pp477–496.

COICA (Coordinadora de las Organizaciones Indígenas de la Cuenca Amazònica) (1996) Pueblos indígenas amazònicos rechazan el robo y la privatizaciòn de sus conocimientos. Press release, 24 June.

Colchester, M (1997) Salvaging nature: indigenous peoples and protected areas. In: Ghimre, K B and Pimbert, M P (eds) *Social Change and Conservation.* UNRISD and Earthscan Publications, London. pp97–130.

Coleman, P (1997) U S trade in intangible intellectual property: royalties and licensing fees. *Industry, Trade, and Technology Review* (US International Trade Commission) pp23–37.

Collins, H B (1998) From: 'An open dialogue on technology protection system-Terminator technology'. (Transcript given to author by Mr A Heitz (UPOV).)

Convention on Biological Diversity Secretariat (1996a) *The Impact of Intellectual Property Right Systems on the Conservation and Sustainable Use of Biological Diversity and on the Equitable Sharing of Benefits from its Use. A Preliminary Study. Note by the Executive Secretary.* 22 September 1996. UNEP/CBD/COP/3/22.

Convention on Biological Diversity Secretariat (1996b) *Ways and Means to Promote and Facilitate Access to, and Transfer and Development of Technology, Including biotechnology. Note by the Secretariat.* 12 August 1996. UNEP/CBD/SBSTTA/2/6.

Convention on Biological Diversity Secretariat (1997) *Report of the Workshop on Traditional Knowledge and Biological Diversity*. Madrid, 24–28 November 1997. UNEP/CBD/TKBD/1/3.

Convention on Biological Diversity Secretariat (1998) *Access to genetic resources and means for fair and equitable benefit sharing. Case study submitted by Switzerland*. UNEP/CBD/COP/4/Inf.16.

Convention on Biological Diversity Secretariat (1999) *Consequences of the Use of the New Technology for the Control of Plant Gene Expression for the Conservation and Sustainable Use of Biological Diversity*. UNEP/CBD/SBSTTA/4/9.

Correa, CM (1994) *Sovereignty and Property Rights Over Plant Genetic Resources*. Background Study Paper No. 2 for Commission on Plant Genetic Resources, First Extraordinary Session, Rome, 7–11 November 1994.

Costa e Silva, E da (1995) The protection of intellectual property for local and indigenous communities. *European Intellectual Property Review*, 17(11), pp546–549.

Costa e Silva, E da (1996) *Biodiversity-Related Aspects of Intellectual Property Rights*. United Nations University. United Nations University/IAS Working Paper. UNU, Tokyo.

Crespi, R S (1995) Biotechnology, broad claims and the EPC. *European Intellectual Property Review*, 6, pp 267–268.

Crespi, S and Straus, J (1996) *Intellectual Property, Technology Transfer and Genetic Resources: An OECD Survey of Current Practices and Policies*. Organisation for Economic Co-operation and Development, Paris.

The Crucible Group (1994) *People, Plants and Patents: The Impact of Intellectual Property on Trade, Plant Biodiversity, and Rural Society*. International Development Research Centre, Ottawa.

Dasgupta, S (1996) Ours and theirs. *Down to Earth*, 5 (July 15), pp13–14.

de Kathen, A (1996) The impact of transgenic crop releases on biodiversity in developing countries. *Biotechnology and Development Monitor*, 28, pp10–14.

Dhar, B and Chaturvedi, S (1998) Introducing plant breeders' rights in India – a critical evaluation of the proposed legislation. *Journal of World Intellectual Property*, 1(2), pp245–262.

Doern, G B (1999) *Global Change and Intellectual Property Agencies*. Pinter, New York and London.

Downes, D (1995) The Convention on Biological Diversity and the GATT. In: Goldberg, D, Housman, R, Van Dyke, B and Zaelke, D *The Use of Trade Measures in Select Multilateral Environment Agreements*. Environment and Trade Series No. 10. United Nations Environment Programme, Geneva.

Downes, D (1997a) Comment (on article by Cleveland and Murray). *Current Anthropology*, 38(4), pp498–500.

Downes, D (1997b) Using intellectual property as a tool to protect traditional knowledge: recommendations for next steps. CIEL Discussion Paper prepared for the *Convention on Biological Diversity Workshop on Traditional Knowledge*. Madrid, November 1997.

Downes, D (1998) Integrating implementation of the Convention on Biological Diversity and the rules of the World Trade Organization. IUCN Environmental Law and Policy Paper. IUCN, Gland.

Drahos, P (1995) Global property rights in information: the story of TRIPS at the GATT. *Prometheus*, 13, pp6–19.

Drahos, P (1996) *A Philosophy of Intellectual Property*. Dartmouth, Aldershot and Brookfield.

Drahos, P (1997) Indigenous knowledge and the duties of intellectual property owners. *Intellectual Property Journal*, 11, August, pp179–201.

Dutfield, G (1997a) Between a rock and a hard place: indigenous peoples, multinationals and the nation state. In: Bodeker, G, Bhat, K K S, Burley, J and Vantomme, P (eds) *Medicinal Plants for Forest Conservation and Health Care*. FAO Non-Wood Products Series No.11. FAO, Rome, pp24–33.

Dutfield, G (1997b) *Can the TRIPS Agreement Protect Biological and Cultural Diversity?* Biopolicy International Series No. 19. African Centre for Technology Studies, Nairobi.

Dutfield, G (1997c) Is novelty still required for patents in the United States: the case of turmeric. *Bulletin of the Working Group on Traditional Resource Rights*, 4, pp 9–10.

Dutfield, G (1999a) Protecting and revitalising traditional ecological knowledge: intellectual property rights and community knowledge databases in India. In: Blakeney, M (ed) *Intellectual Property Aspects of Ethnobiology. Perspectives on Intellectual Property, vol 6*. Sweet and Maxwell, London, pp101–122.

Dutfield, G (ed) (1999b) Rights, resources and responses. In: Posey, D A (General Editor) *Cultural and Spiritual Values of Biodiversity*. United Nations Environment Programme, Nairobi (Chapter 11).

The Economic Times (1998) India confronts basmati-pinching French. 4 July. (Internet edition – http://www.economictimes.com/040798/04 econ5.htm).

The Economic Times (1999) LS passes Patents Bill, clears drug, agrochemical EMRs. 11 March. (Internet edition – http://www.economictimes.com/110399).

Evans, G E (1996) The principal of national treatment and the international protection of industrial property. *European Intellectual Property Review*, 3, pp149–160.

Evanson, R E (1996) Economic valuation of biodiversity for agriculture. In: Pan American Health Organization (ed) *Biodiversity, Biotechnology, and Sustainable Development in Health and Agriculture: Emerging Connections*. PAHO, Washington DC, pp153–166.

FIS (International Seed Trade Federation) and ASSINSEL (International Association of Plant Breeders) (1998) Recommendations by the seed industry of developing countries on the revision of the International Undertaking.

Food and Agriculture Organization (1993) *Convention on Biological Diversity and Related Resolutions*. Commission on Plant Genetic Resources, Fifth session, Rome, 19–23 April 1993 (CPGR/93/Inf.3).

Food and Agriculture Organization (1996) *The State of the World's Plant Genetic Resources for Food and Agriculture. Background Documentation Prepared for the International Technical Conference on Plant Genetic Resources. Leipzig, Germany. 17–23 June, 1996*. FAO, Rome.

Foundation for Revitalisation of Local Health Traditions (FRLHT) (1995) *Beyond the Biodiversity Convention – Empowering the Ecosystem People*. FRLHT, Bangalore.

Four Directions Council (1996) *Forests, Indigenous Peoples and Biodiversity*. Contribution of the Four Directions Council to the Secretariat of the Convention on Biological Diversity. FDC, Lethbridge.

Freedman, P (1994) Boundaries of good taste. *Geographical*, 66, pp12–14.

Gadbaw, R M and Richards, T J (1988) *Intellectual Property Rights: Global Consensus, Global Conflict?* Westview Press, Boulder and London.

Gadgil, M (1998) Conserving India's biodiversity: let people speak. *Hindu Survey of the Environment – 1998*.

Gadgil, M, Seshagiri Rao, P R, Utkarsh, G, and Pramod, P (1999, in press) New meanings for old knowledge: the people's biodiversity registers programme. Submitted as an invited paper to *Ecological Applications*.

Gadgil, M and Devasia, P (1995) Intellectual property rights and biological resources: specifying geographical origins and prior knowledge of uses. *Current Science*, 69(8), pp637–639.

Garí, J-A (1997) *The Role of Democracy in the Biodiversity Issue: The Case of Quinoa*. CEDLA (Centre for Latin America Research and Documentation) Papers. CEDLA, Amsterdam.

Gene Campaign (1999) *Convention of Farmers and Breeders (CoFaB): A Draft Alternative Treaty Presented as an Alternative to UPOV*. Gene Campaign, New Delhi.

Gene Campaign and Forum for Biotechnology and Food Security (1997) *Draft Act Providing for the Establishment of Sovereign Rights over Biological Resources*. GC and FBFS, New Delhi.

Gervais, D (1998) *The TRIPS Agreement: Negotiating History and Analysis*. Sweet and Maxwell, London.

Ghate, U (1997) *Village Biodiversity Registers: Promoting Sustainable Use and Equitable Sharing of Benefits in the Context of GATT, UPOV and CBD*. Draft paper.

Gibbs, W W (1994) King cotton. *Scientific American*. March, pp84–85.

Glowka, L (1998) *A Guide to Designing Legal Frameworks to Determine Access to Genetic Resources*. IUCN Environmental Policy and Law Paper No. 34. IUCN, Gland.

Glowka, L, Burhenne-Guilmin, F, Synge, H in collaboration with McNeely, J A and Gündling, L (1994) *A Guide to the Convention on Biological Diversity*. IUCN Environmental Policy and Law Paper No. 30. IUCN, Gland.

Gollin, M (1993) An intellectual property rights framework for biodiversity prospecting. In: Reid, W V *et al* (eds) *Biodiversity Prospecting: Using Genetic Resources for Sustainable Development*. WRI, INBio, Rainforest Alliance, ACTS, Washington DC, pp159–197.

Government of Australia (1996) *Biological Diversity and Intellectual Property Rights: Issues and Considerations*. Submission by the Government of Australia to the third meeting of the Conference of the Parties to the Convention on Biological Diversity. (UNEP/CBD/3/Inf. 20).

Griffiths, T (1993) *Indigenous Knowledge and Intellectual Property: A Preliminary Review of the Anthropological Literature* (Unpublished). Paper commissioned by Working Group on Traditional Resource Rights, Oxford.

Grubb, P (1999) *Patents for Chemicals, Pharmaceuticals and Biotechnology: Fundamentals of Global Law, Practice and Strategy*. Oxford University Press, Oxford.

Gupta, A (Akhil) (1997) *Postcolonial Developments: Agriculture in the Making of Modern India*. Duke University Press, Durham.

Gupta, A K (Anil) (1996a) Technologies, institutions and incentives for conservation of biodiversity in non-OECD countries: assessing needs for technical cooperation. Presented at the OECD *Conference on Biodiversity Conservation Incentive Measures*. Cairns, March 1996.

Gupta, A K (Anil) (1996b) *Getting Creative Individuals and Communities their Due: Framework for Operationalizing Articles 8(j) and Article 10(c)*. Submission to the Secretariat of the Convention on Biological Diversity.

Gupta, A (Anil) (1998) Knowledge network among grassroots innovators: emerging applications of Information Technology. *Honey Bee*, 9(3).

Haas, E B (1980) Why collaborate? issue-linkage and international regimes. *World Politics*, 32, pp357–405.

Håkansta, C (1998) The battle on patents and AIDS treatment. *Biotechnology and Development Monitor*, 34, pp16–19.

Halewood, M (1997) Regulating patent holders: local working requirements and compulsory licences at international law. *Osgoode Hall Law Journal*, 35(2), pp243–287.

Hall, BH and Ham, R M (1999) The determinants of patenting in the US semiconductor industry, 1980–1994. Presented at the NBER Patent System and Innovation conference in Santa Barbara, California, January 1999.

Hamilton, N D (1994) Why own the farm if you can own the farmer (and the crop)? Contract production and intellectual property protection of grain crops. *Nebraska Law Review*, 73, pp48–101.

Heitz, A (1998) Intellectual property rights and plant variety protection in relation to demands of the World Trade Organization and farmers in Sub-Saharan Africa. Paper prepared for the Meeting on Seed Policy and Programmes, organized by FAO in Abidjan (Côte d'Ivoire). November 23–27.

Heller, M A and Eisenberg, R S (1998) Can patents deter innovation? The anticommons in biomedical research. *Science*, 280, pp698–701.

Hettinger, E (1989) Justifying intellectual property. *Philosophy and Public Affairs*, 18, pp31–52.

International Alliance of Indigenous-Tribal Peoples of the Tropical Forests (1996) The Biodiversity Convention: the concerns of indigenous peoples – submission of the International Alliance to the CBD Secretariat, May 1996. In: IATP *Indigenous Peoples, Forests, and Biodiversity*. IWGIA Document 82. IATP and IWGIA, Copenhagen. pp105–129.

Iwu, M M (1996) Biodiversity prospecting in Nigeria: seeking equity and reciprocity in intellectual property rights through partnership arrangements and capacity building. *Journal of Ethnopharmacology*, 51, pp209–19.

Jaffé, W and van Wijk, J (1995) *The Impact of Plant Breeders' Rights in Developing Countries: Debate and Experience in Argentina, Chile, Colombia, Mexico and Uruguay*. Directorate General International Cooperation, Ministry of Foreign Affairs, The Hague.

Jefferson, R A (author-in-chief), Byth, D, Correa, C, Otero, G and Qualset, C (1999) *Genetic Use Restriction Technologies. Technical Assessment of the Set of New Technologies which Sterilize or Reduce the Agronomic Value of Second Generation Seed, as Exemplified by US Patent No. 5,723,765 and WO 94/03619*. (Expert paper annexed to UNEP/CBD/SBSTTA/4/9).

Jenkins, R (1998) Bt in the hot seat. *Seedling*, Sept., pp13–21.

Juma, C, Mugabe, J and Ojwang, J B (1994) *Access to Genetic Resources: Policy and Institutional Issues*. African Centre for Technology Studies, Nairobi.

Kadidal, S (1997) Subject-matter imperialism? Biodiversity, foreign prior art and the neem patent controversy. *Idea: The Journal of Law and Technology*, 37(2), pp371–403.

Kaplinsky, R (1989) Industrial and intellectual property rights in the Uruguay Round and beyond. *The Journal of Development Studies*, 25(3), pp373–400.

Kirim, A S (1985) Reconsidering patents and economic development: a case study of the Turkish pharmaceutical industry. *World Development*, 13(2), pp219–236.

Kondo, E K (1995) The effect of patent protection on foreign direct investment. *Journal of World Trade*, 29(6), pp 97–122.

Kloppenburg, J R (1988) *First the Seed: The Political Economy of Plant Biotechnology, 1492–2000*. Cambridge University Press, Cambridge.

Kocken, J and van Roozendaal, G (1997) The neem tree debate. *Biotechnology and Development Monitor*, 30, pp8–11.

Kothari, A (1995) *Conserving Life: Implications of the Biodiversity Convention for India*. 2nd edition. Kalpavriksh, New Delhi.

Kothari, A and Anuradha, R V (1997) Biodiversity, intellectual property rights, and GATT Agreement: How to Address the Conflicts? *Economic and Political Weekly*, 32, pp2814–2820.

Krattiger, A F and James, C (1993–94) International organization established to transfer proprietary biotechnology to developing countries. *Diversity*, 9/10(4/1), pp36–39.

Krimsky, S and Wrubel, R (1996) *Agricultural Biotechnology and the Environment: Science, Policy, and Social Issues*. University of Illinois Press, Urbana and Chicago.

Lange, P (1997) The non-patentability of plant varieties. The Decision of the Technical Board of Appeal 3.3.4 of February 21, 1995-T 356/93. *Plant Variety Protection*, 83, pp25–33.

Lappé, M and Bailey, B (1999) *Against the Grain: The Genetic Transformation of Global Agriculture*. Earthscan Publications, London.

Lehmann, V (1998) Patent on seed sterility threatens seed saving *Biotechnology and Development Monitor*, 35, pp6–8.

Lerch, A (1998) Property rights and biodiversity. *European Journal of Law and Economics*, 6, pp 285–304.

Lesser, W (1998) *Sustainable Use of Genetic Resources under the Convention on Biological Diversity: Exploring Access and Benefit Sharing Issues*. CAB International, Wallingford and New York.

Leskien, D and Flitner, M (1997) *Intellectual Property Rights and Plant Genetic Resources*. Issues in Genetic Resources No. 6. International Plant Genetic Resources Institute, Rome.

Littman, A (1997) Restoring the balance of our patent system. *Idea: The Journal of Law and Technology*, 37(2), pp545–570.

Llewelyn, M (1995) Article 53 revisited: Greenpeace v Plant Genetic Systems NV. *European Intellectual Property Review*, 10, pp506–11.

Louwaars, N P (1999) *Sui generis* rights: from opposing to complementary approaches. *Biotechnology and Development Monitor*, 36, pp13–16.

Macdonald, S (1998) *Information for Innovation: Managing Change from an Information Perspective*. Oxford University Press, Oxford.

Martin, M (1998) How to sell a wonder herb. *Down to Earth*, 7(12) 15 November, pp29–35.

Magretta, J (1997) Growth through sustainability: an interview with Monsanto's CEO, Robert B Shapiro. *Harvard Business Review*. Jan–Feb, pp79–88.

Maskus, K (1998) The role of intellectual property rights in encouraging foreign direct investment and technology transfer. *Duke Journal of Comparative and International Law*, 9(1), pp109–161.

McFarling, U L (1998) The code war. Biotech firms engage in high-stakes fight over rights to the human blueprint. *San Jose Mercury News*, 17 November.

McGrath, M (1996) The patent provisions in TRIPS: protecting reasonable remuneration for services rendered – or the latest development in Western colonialism? *European Intellectual Property Review*, 7, pp398–403.

McNally, R and Wheale, P (1996) Biopatenting and biodiversity: comparative advantage in the new global order. *The Ecologist*, 26(5), pp 222–228.

Menon, U (1993) The real issue behind neem patents. *AIPSN Bulletin*, 3(3), pp25–26.

Menon, U (1997) Designing a regime of access to genetic resources: beyond the popular logic of Farmers' Rights and Breeders' Rights. In: IPRGI (ed) *Ethics and Equity in Conservation and Use of Genetics Resources for Sustainable Food Security*. Proceedings of a workshop to develop guidelines for the CGIAR 21–25 April 1997, Foz do Iguaçu, Brazil. International Plant Genetic Resources Institute, Rome.

Merges, R P and Nelson, R R (1990) Market structure and technical advance: the role of patent scope decisions. *CCC Working Papers*, 90–100. University of California, Berkeley.

Moran, W (1993) Rural space as intellectual property. *Political Geography*, 12, pp263–277.

Moufang, R (1998) The concept of 'ordre public' and morality in patent law. In: Overwalle, G van (ed) *Octrooirecht, Ethiek en Biotechnologie/Patent Law, Ethics and Biotechnology/Droit des Brevets, Ethique et Biotechnologie*. Bruylant, Brussels, pp65–77.

Mulvany, P (1998) *TRIPS, Biodiversity and Commonwealth Countries: Capacity Building Priorities for the 1999 Review of TRIPS Article 27.3 (b)*. Commonwealth Secretariat and Quaker Peace and Service, Rugby and London.

Myers, N (1989) A major extinction spasm: predictable and inevitable? In: Western, D and Pearl, M C (eds) *Conservation for the Twenty-first Century*. Oxford University Press, Oxford, pp42–49.

National Research Council (1993) *Managing Global Genetic Resources: Agricultural Crop Issues and Policies*. National Academy Press, Washington DC.

NBIAP/ISB (National Biological Impact Assessment Program/Information Systems for Biotechnology) (1994) Transgenic cotton patent under pressure. NBIAP/ISB website (http://www.nbiap.vt.edu).

NBIAP/ISB (1995) Patent office cancels broad patent on transgenic cotton. NBIAP/ISB website (http://www.nbiap.vt.edu).

Nijar, G S (1996a) *TRIPS and Biodiversity: The Threat and Responses: A Third World View*. Third World Network Paper 2. TWN, Penang.

Nijar, G (1996b) *In Defence of Indigenous Knowledge and Biodiversity: A Conceptual Framework and Essential Elements of a Rights Regime*. Third World Network. Third World Network Paper 1. TWN, Penang.

Nordhaus, W D (1969) *Invention, Growth and Welfare: A Theoretic Treatment of Technological Change*. MIT Press, Cambridge.

Nuffield Council on Bioethics (1995) *Human Tissue: Ethical and Legal Issues*. Nuffield Council on Bioethics, London.

Office of Technology Assessment (1989) *New Developments in Biotechnology 5: Patenting Life*. US Congress, OTA, Washington DC.

Patel, P and Pavitt, K (1995) Patterns of technological activity: their measurement and interpretation. In: Stoneman, P (ed) *Handbook of the Economics of Innovation and Technological Change*. Blackwell, Oxford and Cambridge, pp14–51.

Pimbert M P and Pretty, J N (1997) Parks, people and professionals: putting 'participation' into protected area management. In: Ghimre, K B and Pimbert, M P (eds) *Social Change and Conservation*. UNRISD and Earthscan Publications, London, pp297–330.

Plant, A (1934) The economic theory concerning patents for invention. *Economics*, 1, pp167–195.

Posey, D A (assisted by Dutfield, G, Plenderleith, K, Costa e Silva, E da and Argumedo, A) (1996) *Traditional Resource Rights: International Instruments for Protection and Compensation for Indigenous Peoples and Local Communities*. IUCN, Gland.

Posey, D A (1997) Indigenous knowledge, biodiversity, and international rights: learning about the forests from the Kayapó Indians of the Brazilian Amazon. *Commonwealth Forestry Review*, 76(1), pp53–60.

Posey, D A (ed) (1999) *Cultural and Spiritual Values of Biodiversity*. United Nations Environment Programme and Intermediate Technology. Nairobi and London.

Posey, D A and Dutfield, G (1996) *Beyond Intellectual Property: Toward Traditional Resource Rights for Indigenous Peoples and Local Communities*. International Development Research Centre, Ottawa.

Posey, D A and Dutfield, G (1998) Plants, patents and traditional knowledge: ethical concerns of indigenous and traditional peoples. In: Overwalle, G van (ed) *Octrooirecht, Ethiek en Biotechnologie/Patent Law, Ethics and Biotechnology/Droit des Brevets, Ethique et Biotechnologie*. Bruylant, Brussels, pp109–132.

Prakash, S (1998) *Country Study: India*. World Bank/WTO Trade and Development Centre website (http://www.itd.org/issues/india6.htm).

Prescott-Allen, R and Prescott-Allen, C (1996) *Genes from the Wild: Using Wild Genetic Resources for Food and Raw Materials*. Earthscan Publications, London.

Primo Braga, C A and Fink, C (1999, in press) International transactions in intellectual property and developing countries. *International Journal of Technology Management*.

Pushpangadan, P, Rajasekharan, S and George, V (1998) Benefit sharing with Kani tribe: a model experimented by Tropical Botanic Garden and Research Institute (TBGRI). Presented at *Medicinal Plants for Survival: International Conference on Medicinal Plants*. 16–19 February. National Institute of Advanced Studies, Bangalore, India.

Putterman, D M (nd) *Genetic Resources Utilization: Critical Issues in Conservation and Community Development*. Biodiversity Conservation Network website (http://www.bcnet.org/whatsnew/biopros.html).

Rangnekar, D (1996) *GATT, Intellectual Property Rights, and the Seed Industry: Some Unsolved Problems*. Faculty of Human Sciences Economic Discussion Paper 96/5. Kingston University, Kingston upon Thames.

Reid, W V (1992) *Genetic Resources and Sustainable Agriculture: Creating Incentives for Local Innovation and Adaptation*. Biopolicy Series No. 2. African Centre for Technology Studies, Nairobi.

Reid, W V, Laird, S A, Meyer, CA Gamez, R, Sittenfeld, A, Janzen, D H, Gollin, M A and Juma, C (1993) *Biodiversity Prospecting: Using Genetic Resources for Sustainable Development*. World Resources Institute, Instituto Nacional de Biodiversidad, Rainforest Alliance, African Centre for Technology Studies, Washington DC.

Reyes, V (1996) The value of sangre de drago. *Seedling*, 13(1), pp16–21.

Roberts, T (1994) Broad claims for biotechnological patents. *European Intellectual Property Review*, 9, pp373.

Roberts, T (1996) Patenting plants around the world. *European Intellectual Property Review*, 10, pp531–536.

Rural Advancement Foundation International (1994) *Conserving Indigenous Knowledge: Integrating Two Systems of Innovation. An Independent Study by the Rural Advancement Foundation International*. United Nations Development Programme, New York.

Rural Advancement Foundation International (1998a) The Terminator Technology. *RAFI Communique*, Mar–Apr.

Rural Advancement Foundation International (1998b) Aussies 'pirate' others' genius? (Press release, 1 Feb.).

Rural Advancement Foundation International (1998c) Doing well by doing little or nothing? a partial list of varieties under RAFI investigation (RAFI Website – http://www.rafi.ca)

Rural Advancement Foundation International (1998d) The Australian PBR scandal: UPOV meets a scandal 'down under' by burying its head in the sand. *RAFI Communique*, Jan–Feb.

Ryan, M P (1998) *Knowledge Diplomacy: Global Competition and the Politics of Intellectual Property*. Brookings Institution Press, Washington DC.

Santoro, M A and Paine, L S (1995) Pfizer: global protection of intellectual property. Harvard Business School Cases. Harvard Business School, Cambridge.

Schrecker, T, Elliott, C, Hoffmaster, CB, Keyserlingk, E W and Somerville, M A (1994) *Ethical Issues Associated with the Patenting of Higher Life Forms*. Westminster Institute for Ethics and Human Values, McGill Centre for Medicine, Ethics and Law, Montreal.

Schapaugh, W (1989) The seed trade's view on proprietary rights. In: Crop Science Society of America, American Society of Agronomy & Soil Science Society of America, *Intellectual Property Rights Associated with Plants*. American Society of Agronomy Special Publication No 52. CSAA, Madison.

Scherer, F M (1972) Nordhaus' theory of optimal patent life: a geometric interpretation. *American Economic Review*, 62, pp422–427.

Schwab, B (1995) The protection of geographical indications in the European Economic Community. *European Intellectual Property Review*, 5, pp242–246.

Scotchmer, S (1991) Standing on the shoulders of giants: cumulative research and the patent law. *Journal of Economic Perspectives*, 5(1), pp29–41.

Scotchmer, S and Green, J (1990) Novelty and disclosure in patent law. *RAND Journal of Economics*, 21(1), 131–146.

Sehgal, S (1996) IPR driven restructuring of the seed industry. *Biotechnology and Development Monitor*, 29, pp18–21.

Seiler, A (1998) Sui generis systems: obligations and options for developing countries. *Biotechnology and Development Monitor*, 34, pp2–5.

Sell, S (1998) *Power and Ideas: North-South Politics of Intellectual Property and Antitrust*. State University of New York, Albany.

Shelton, D (1995) *Fair Play, Fair Pay: Strengthening Local Livelihood Systems through Compensation for Access to and Use of Traditional Knowledge and Biological Resources*. World Wide Fund for Nature, Gland.

Stenson, A and Gray, T (1997) Cultural communities and intellectual property rights in plant genetic resources. In: Hayward, T and O'Neill, J (eds) *Justice, Property and the Environment: Social and Legal Perspectives*. Ashgate Publishing, Aldershot and Brookfield, pp178–193.

Sterckx, S (ed) (1997) *Biotechnology, Patents and Morality*. Ashgate Publishing, Aldershot and Brookfield.

Straus, J (1998) Biodiversity and intellectual property. *AIPPI Yearbook 1998. XXXVIIth Congress – Rio de Janeiro (May 24–29, 1998) – Workshops I–VII*. International Association for the Protection of Industrial Property, Zurich.

Suppan, S (1998) Biotechnology's takeover of the seed industry. *Information about Intellectual Property Rights, Biotechnology and Biodiversity, No 23*. Institute for Agriculture and Trade Policy, Minneapolis.

Sutherland, J (1997) Global politics, genetic resources and traditional resource rights: 1996 and beyond. In: Elliott L (ed) *Ecopolitics X Conference Proceedings*. Australian National University, Canberra.

Swanson, T (1996) The reliance of northern economies on southern biodiversity: biodiversity as information. *Ecological Economics*, 17, pp1–8.

Swanson, T (1997) *Global Action for Biodiversity: An International Framework for Implementing the Convention on Biological Diversity*. Earthscan, in association with IUCN, London.

Tansey, G (1999) *Trade, Intellectual Property, Food and Biodiversity: Key Issues and Options for the 1999 Review of Article 27.3(b) of the TRIPS Agreement*. Quaker Peace and Service, London.

Tappeser, B and von Weizsäcker, C (1996) Monsanto's genetech-soybeans: safe for consumers? safe for the environment? *Third World Network Biodiversity Convention-COP 3 Briefings, No 4*. TWN, Penang.

Tarasofsky, R (1997) The relationship between the TRIPS Agreement and the Convention on Biological Diversity: towards a pragmatic approach. *Review of European Community and International Environmental Law*, 6(2), pp148–156.

Taylor, C T and Silberman, Z A (1973) *The Economic Impact of the Patent System: The British Experience*. Cambridge University Press, Cambridge.

Thurow, L (1997) Needed: a new system of intellectual property rights. *Harvard Business Review*. Sept–Oct., pp95–103.

Thrupp, L A (1997) *Linking Biodiversity and Agriculture: Challenges and Opportunities for Sustainable Food Security*. World Resources Institute, Washington DC.

Tobin, B (1997a) Know-how licenses: recognising indigenous rights over collective knowledge. *Bulletin of the Working Group on Traditional Resource Rights*, 4, pp17–18.

Tobin, B (1997b) Certificates of origin: a role for IPR regimes in securing prior informed consent. In: Mugabe, J, Barber, C V, Henne, G, Glowka, L and La Viña, A (eds) *Access to Genetic Resources: Strategies for Sharing Benefits*. Nairobi, ACTS Press, pp329–340.

Tobin, B and Ruiz, M (1996) Access to genetic resources, prior informed consent, and conservation of biological diversity: the need for action by recipient nations. Presented at the ERM *Stakeholder Workshop on Implementation of Articles 15 and 16 of the Convention on Biological Diversity by the European Union*. London, February 1996.

Tripp, R (1997) The structure of national seed systems. In: Tripp, R (ed) *New Seed and Old Laws: Regulatory Reform and the Diversification of National Seed Systems*. Intermediate Technology Publications on behalf of the Overseas Development Institute, London, pp14–42.

Tully, J (1993) *An Approach To Political Philosophy: Locke In Contexts*. Cambridge University Press, Cambridge.

United Nations Conference on Trade and Development (1996a) *The TRIPS Agreement and Developing Countries*. United Nations, New York and Geneva.

United Nations Conference on Trade and Development (1996b) *The Biotrade Initiative: A New Approach to Biodiversity Conservation and Sustainable Development*. Study prepared by the UNCTAD Secretariat for the Conference of the Parties to the Convention on Biological Diversity.

United Nations Development Programme (1995) *Statements and Recommendations of Indigenous Representatives on the Conservation and Protection of Indigenous Knowledge*. UNDP, New York.

United Nations Environment Programme (1997) *The Biodiversity Agenda. Decisions from the Third Meeting of the Conference of the Parties to the Convention on Biological Diversity, Buenos Aires, November 1996*. UNEP, Geneva.

United States International Trade Commission (1988) *Foreign Protection of Intellectual Property Rights and the Effect on US Industry and Trade*. Publication No. 2065. USITC, Washington DC.

UPOV (1991) *Seminar on the Nature of and Rationale for the Protection of Plant Varieties under the UPOV Convention*. UPOV, Geneva.

van Overwalle, G (ed) *Octrooirecht, Ethiek en Biotechnologie/Patent Law, Ethics and Biotechnology/Droit des Brevets, Ethique et Biotechnologie*. Bruylant, Brussels.

van Wijk, J (1995a) Broad biotechnology patents hamper innovation. *Biotechnology and Development Monitor*, 25, pp15–17.

van Wijk, J (1995b) Plant breeders' rights create winners and losers. *Biotechnology and Development Monitor*, 23, pp15–19.

van Wijk, J (1996) *How Does Stronger Protection of Intellectual Property Rights Affect Seed Supply? Early Evidence of Impact*. ODI Natural Resource Perspectives No. 13. Overseas Development Institute, London.

van Wijk, J, Cohen, J I and Komen, J (1993) *Intellectual Property Rights for Agricultural Biotechnology: Options and Implications for Developing Countries*. ISNAR Research Report No. 3. International Centre for National Agricultural Research, The Hague.

Vaver, D (1991) Some agnostic observations on intellectual property.

Intellectual Property Journal, 6, pp125–153.

Verma, S K (1995) TRIPS and plant variety protection in developing countries. *European Intellectual Property Review*, 6, pp281–289.

Vogel, J H (1997) Bioprospecting and the justification for a cartel. *Bulletin of the Working Group on Traditional Resource Rights*, 4, pp16–17.

Vogel, J H (1998) An economic analysis of the Convention on Biological Diversity: the rationale for a cartel. Revised paper presented at the UNEP-Mexico IV Foro del Ajusco on Biodiversidad, Globalización y Sustentabilidad en América Latina y el Caribe: de quién es la naturaleza. November 1997.

Wilson, E O (1992) *The Diversity of Life*. Belknap Press, Cambridge, USA.

World Trade Organization – Committee on Trade and Environment (1996a) *Environment and TRIPS*. WTO, Geneva (WT/CTE/W/8).

World Trade Organization – Committee on Trade and Environment (1996b) *Excerpt from the report of the meeting held on 21–22 June 1995: record of the discussion on Item 8 of the Committee on Trade and Environment's work programme*. WTO, Geneva (WT/CTE/M/3+Corr.1).

World Trade Organization – Committee on Trade and Environment (1996c) *Report of the WTO Committee on Trade and Environment*. WTO, Geneva (Press/TE 014)

World Trade Organization – Committee on Trade and Environment (1997) *Item 8: The Relationship between the TRIPS Agreement and the Convention on Biodiversity – Communication from India*. WTO, Geneva (WT/CTE/W/65).

World Trade Organization – Committee on Trade and Environment (1998) *Communication from the Secretariat of the Convention on Biological Diversity*. WTO, Geneva (WT/CTE/W/).

World Trade Organization – General Council (1998) *Preparations for the 1999 Ministerial Conference. General Council Discussion on Mandated Negotiations and the Built-In Agenda, 23 November 1998. Communication from the United States*. WTO, Geneva (WT/GC/W/115).

World Trade Organization – General Council (1999a) *Preparations for the 1999 Ministerial Conference. EC Approach to Trade-Related Aspects of Intellectual Property in the New Round. Communication from the European Communities*. WTO, Geneva. (WT/GC/W/193).

World Trade Organization – General Council (1999b) *Preparations for the 1999 Ministerial Conference. Proposal on Trade-Related Aspects of Intellectual Property. Communication from Japan*. WTO, Geneva (WT/GC/W/242).

INDEX

Page numbers in *italic* indicate tables or boxed text; the letter n following page
numbers indicates material in the notes

IUCN – THE WORLD CONSERVATION UNION

Founded in 1948, The World Conservation Union brings together States, government agencies and a diverse range of non-governmental organizations in a unique world partnership: over 900 members in all, spread across some 139 countries.

As a Union, IUCN seeks to influence, encourage and assist societies throughout the world to conserve the integrity and diversity of nature and to ensure that any use of natural resources is equitable and ecologically sustainable. A central secretariat coordinates the IUCN Programme and serves the Union membership, representing their views on the world stage and providing them with the strategies, services, scientific knowledge and technical support they need to achieve their goals. Through its six Commissions, IUCN draws together over 10,000 expert volunteers in project teams and action groups, focusing in particular on species and biodiversity conservation and the management of habitats and natural resources. The Union has helped many countries to prepare National Conservation Strategies, and demonstrates the application of its knowledge through the field projects it supervises. Operations are increasingly decentralized and are carried forward by an expanding network of regional and country offices, located principally in developing countries.

The World Conservation Union builds on the strengths of its members, networks and partners to enhance their capacity and to support global alliances to safeguard natural resources at local, regional and global levels.

IUCN Publishing Division
Rue Mauverney 28
CH-1196 Gland, Switzerland
Tel: +41 22-999 00 01
Fax: +41 22-999 00 10
Email: mail@iucn.org

IUCN Publications Services Unit
219c Huntingdon Road
Cambridge, CB3 0DL, UK
Tel: +44 (0)1223 277 894
Fax: +44 (0)1223 277 175
Email: info@books.iucn.org